Modern Psychometrics

Comment on first edition:

> An introduction to psychometrics which successfully combines theory and practice.
>
> *Times Higher Education Supplement*

There is no other aspect of psychology that has such an impact on individuals in their daily lives.

Testing and assessment occurs throughout our lives, from schooling and employment to applying for a mortgage or credit. Psychometrics is the science of how to maximize the quality of such assessments.

In Part one of *Modern Psychometrics* Rust and Golombok outline the history of this field and discuss central theoretical issues such as personality and integrity testing and the impact of computer technology. In Part two a practical step-by-step guide to the development of a psychometric test is provided. This will enable anyone wishing to develop their own test to plan, design, construct and validate it to a professional standard.

This text will be useful to students at all levels who are interested in pyschometrics. This second edition has been extensively updated and expanded to take into account recent developments in the field, making it the ideal companion for those studying for the British Psychological Society's Certificates of Competence in Testing.

John Rust is Senior Lecturer in Psychology at Goldsmiths College, University of London, and a well-known test developer.
Susan Golombok is Professor of Psychology and Director of the Family and Child Psychology Research Centre at The City University, London. Together, they have been responsible for the UK standardization of the widely used Wechsler scales.

Modern Psychometrics

- The science of psychological assessment

SECOND EDITION

John Rust and Susan Golombok

London and New York

First edition published 1989
by Routledge
11 New Fetter Lane, London EC4P 4EE
Reprinted 1992, 1995
Second edition published 1999
by Routledge

Simultaneously published in the USA
and Canada
by Routledge
29 West 35th Street, New York, NY 10001

Reprinted 2000

*Routledge is an imprint of the Taylor &
Francis Group*

Typeset in Century Old Style by
RefineCatch Limited, Bungay, Suffolk
Printed and bound in Great Britain by
TJ International Ltd, Padstow, Cornwall

*British Library Cataloguing in Publication
Data*
A catalogue record for this book is
available from the British Library

*Library of Congress Cataloging in
Publication Data*
Rust, John, 1943–
   Modern psychometrics: the science of
   psychological assessment / John Rust and
   Susan Golombok — 2nd ed.
   Includes bibliographical references
   and indexes.
   1. Psychometrics.   I. Golombok,
   Susan.   II. Title.
   BF39.R85   1999
   150′.28′7 – dc21   98–47962

ISBN 0–415–20340–6 (hbk)
ISBN 0–415–20341–4 (pbk)

To
Jamie

Contents

Part two

Figures and tables

Figures

Tables

Preface to the
second edition

It is now more than ten years since *Modern Psychometrics* was first published, and in that time the science has continued to stride ahead. Today, many of the future possibilities tentatively discussed in the first edition are now accepted realities. Furthermore, the main tenet of the book, that psychometrics is so central to modern society that it cannot be ignored, has become the accepted view. Arguments about psychometrics today are no longer about the 'whether' but about the 'how'.

The British Psychological Society has now acted to control the development of the field and introduced its Certificates of Competence in Occupational Testing. The Level A Certificate deals with ability testing, while the Level B certificate covers most aspects of personality testing. The second edition of *Modern Psychometrics* has been rewritten with these competencies in mind. This has mainly involved the introduction of two new chapters on personality and its assessment that address the requirements of Level B. A chapter on integrity testing has also been added. Many of the developments in the forthcoming Certificates of Competence in Educational and Clinical Testing have also been anticipated.

The early chapters continue to consider the role of sociobiology and its precursors on the development of the psychometrics movement. A proper understanding of these issues remains crucial to psychometric practitioners. The major lesson of the troublesome sociobiological disputes of the 1970s was that selection and assessment are important social processes and that the psychometrician cannot stand apart from ideological and political debate. In particular, psychometrics, if it is to fulfil its function of fair assessment and selection, must take a stand on issues of racism and injustice. This is particularly so in view of the overt racism of so many of its historical advocates.

The chapters looking at the practice and application of testing and test construction pay particular attention to current issues such as the use of item response theory, criterion reference testing, narrative reports and the use of computers and artificial intelligence in assessment. Knowledge-based tests of ability, aptitude and achievement are considered, as well as person-based tests of personality, clinical symptoms, mood and attitude. A chapter on integrity testing has been added.

The book is written in two parts. Part one deals with theoretical and more general issues in psychometrics. Part two is a step-by-step guide on how to construct psychometric questionnaires. This progresses through all the stages of test construction, from definition of the original purpose of the test to its eventual validation. The book is intended to provide both a theoretical underpinning to psychometrics and a practical guide.

John Rust
Susan Golombok

Part one

Chapter 1

The development of psychometrics

Definitions and origins

Psychometrics is defined in *Chambers Twentieth Century Dictionary* as the 'branch of psychology dealing with measurable factors', but also as the 'occult power of defining the properties of things by mere contact'. While it is the first of these definitions that we shall be dealing with in this book, there have been times in recent years when the second might have seemed more accurate as a description of current practice, particularly in debates about intelligence. It is impossible to consider the development of modern-day psychometrics without looking at the substantial influence of the intelligence testing movement in the late nineteenth and early twentieth centuries. However, the origins of the subject go back long before then.

Employers have assessed prospective workers since the beginnings of civilization, and in all probability have had consistent and replicable techniques for doing this. The earliest recorded examples of examinations for this purpose are from China at the time of the Chan dynasty around about 1000 years BC. Records show that the officials of the emperor were examined every third year within examination halls specially designed and built for the purpose. There were job sample tests that required the demonstration of proficiency in arithmetic, archery, horsemanship, music, writing, and skills in the performance of rituals and ceremonies. Formal procedures required, then as now, that candidates' names should be concealed, independent assessments by two or more assessors should be made, and that the conditions of examination should be standardized. The pattern set down then – of a 'syllabus' of material which should be learned, and an 'examination' to test the attainment of this knowledge – has not changed in framework for 3,000 years and was in extensive use in Europe, Asia and Africa even before the industrial revolution.

Psychometrics today

Today, we experience assessment in a wide field of our activities, not just the psychological. We are tested at school to monitor our performance. We are tested at the end of school to provide us with our first academic credentials, a process that will continue throughout our learning lives. We have to pass both practical and written tests to obtain our driving licences and to be able to practise our professions. We are tested in order to gain special provision (e.g. for learning difficulties) or to obtain prizes. When we buy on credit or apply for a mortgage we have to fill in forms that are scored in much the same manner. We are tested at work, when we apply for promotion, and when we seek another job. The forms of assessment can also take on many forms – interview, examination, multiple-choice, diagnostic, practical, continuous assessment and so on. But in spite of the wide variety of applications and manifestations, all assessments share a common set of fundamental characteristics – they should be reliable, valid, standardized and free from bias. There are good assessments, and bad assessments, and there is a science of how to maximize the quality of assessment. That science is psychometrics. There is no other aspect of the field of psychology that has such an impact on individuals in their daily lives.

The history of psychometrics

Rapid scientific and social progress in Europe during the nineteenth century led to the development of several assessment techniques, most notably in the medical diagnosis of the mentally ill. However, the most dramatic impact was to come from a branch of pure science – biology. Darwin was the giant figure of the age, and his theory of evolution had considerable implications for the human sciences. In particular, his argument for the evolution of man by natural selection opened the door to human genetics based on evolutionary and biological precepts. In *The Descent of Man*, first published in 1871, Darwin argued that the intellectual and moral senses have been gradually perfected through natural selection, stating as evidence that 'at the present day, civilized nations are everywhere supplanting barbarous nations'.

Darwin's ideas of natural selection involved the intervening stages of 'the savage' and 'the lower races' at an inferior level of evolution to 'the civilized nations'. These ideas were, however, not introduced by Darwin but rather were his natural interpretation of prevailing opinion in England in the nineteenth century. They provided justification for colonialism and the class system, and served to maintain the British Empire.

The evolution of the human intellect was of particular interest to Sir Francis Galton, who in 1869 published *Hereditary Genius: An Inquiry into its Laws and Consequences*. Galton carried out a study of the genealogy of the famous scientific families of the time, and argued that genius, genetic in origin, was to be found in these families (which included his own). Thus we had at the end of the nineteenth century a popular scientific view, in accord with the philosophy and politics of England at that time, that evolutionary theory could be applied to man, and that the white, English, middle-class men of letters were at the peak of the human evolutionary tree. The hierarchical theory gave inferior genetic status to apes, 'savages', the races of the colonies, the Irish, and the English working class, and served as a justification for the social position of the dominant group.

Galton and the origins of psychometrics

Galton is generally credited with being the founder of psychometrics. He established an anthropometric laboratory at the South Kensington Exhibition in 1883, where persons attending the exhibition could have their faculties tested for threepence, and the data generated from this and other studies provided the raw material for the development of the tools of the trade. He also developed the twin study as a technique for looking at heredity, and together with his colleague, Karl Pearson, developed the Pearson Product-Moment Correlation Coefficient for analysing these data.

In fact, the attempts to measure intellect by these early tests were a failure, as very few of Galton's measures – visual, auditory and weight discrimination, threshold levels and other psychophysical variables – were particularly related to each other. Cattell in 1890 and Gilbert in 1894 both carried out large-scale correlational studies using university students as respondents, examining the relationship between academic grades, psycho-sensory tests and anthropometric measures such as size of brain and shape of head. While grades correlated highly with each other they showed no meaningful relationship with the physical or sensory measures (Wissler 1901). However, the techniques and models of analysis still form the basis of present-day psychometrics. Galton also explored the idea of using the normal curve as a model for the distribution of test scores.

Pearson continued to develop the mathematics of correlation, adding partial and multiple correlation coefficients and the chi-square test to the repertoire of available techniques. Charles Spearman (1904), a former army officer turned psychologist, further developed procedures for the analysis of more complex correlation matrices and laid down the foundations of factor analysis. Thus by the first decade of the twentieth century the fundamentals of test theory were in place, and used almost entirely in the development of what had come to be called 'intelligence tests'.

What is intelligence?

The earliest pioneers in the area were generally unclear about what they meant by the concept of intelligence, and the question 'What is intelligence?' is still with us today. Galton (1869) believed that the key element was sensory discrimination but effectively defined intelligence as that faculty which the genius has and the idiot has not.

> The discriminative facility of idiots is curiously low; they hardly distinguish between heat and cold, and their sense of pain is so obtuse that some of the more idiotic seem hardly to know what it is. In their dull lives such pain as can be excited in them may literally be accepted with a welcome surprise.

Herbert Spencer considered it to be 'the mental adjustment of internal relations to external relations'. Charles Spearman emphasized school achievement in subjects such as Greek. It seems clear that these definitions have not arisen out of a scientific psychology but are extensions of the folk psychology of, if not the common man, the common schoolteacher. This psychology recognizes an important distinction between the educated person and the intelligent person. The former is someone who has benefited from a sound education. The latter is someone whose disposition is such that, were they to receive such an education, they would perform very well indeed. Whether a person receives such an education or not is very much a matter of social circumstance, so that a particular educated person is not necessarily intelligent, nor a particular intelligent person educated. Rather, the intelligent person was someone who could make the most of their education, and this was seen as part of the person's 'disposition'.

This view of intelligence was very familiar to scientists in the nineteenth century almost all would have studied Latin and Greek at school and university, including the works of Aristotle and Plato. Thus in Plato's *Republic* Book V, Socrates asks Glaucon

> When you spoke of a nature gifted or not gifted in any respect, did you mean to say that one man will acquire a thing hastily, another with difficulty; a little learning will lead the one to discover a great deal; whereas the other, after much study and application, no sooner learns than he forgets; or again, did you mean that the one has a body that is a good servant of his mind, while the body of the

other is a hindrance to him? – Would not these be the sort of differences which distinguish the man gifted by nature from the one who is ungifted?

Thus, intelligence was not education but educability. It was perceived as being part of a person's make-up, rather than socially determined, and by implication their genetic make-up. Intelligence when defined in this way is necessarily genetic in origin. Further underpinning for this approach came from psychiatry, where elementary tests were being developed to distinguish the insane from the imbecile, and as some of the various forms of mental defect were found to be due to genetic anomaly, so evidence was piled on presupposition.

Intelligence testing and education

Much of the early work on the measurement of the intellect was theoretical; however, applications were obvious and needs were pressing. In any society where opportunities for work or educational facilities are less than the demand, some form of selection is inevitable. If the job or educational programme is demanding in terms of the amount the applicant will need to learn before competency is reached, then there is an inclination to accept those who are seen as easier to teach, a task that could be simplified by testing for educability, or intelligence.

Alfred Binet was the first to provide an intelligence test specifically for educational selection. The main impetus came when the Minister of Public Instruction in Paris in 1904 appointed a committee to find a method that could separate mentally retarded from normal children in schools. It was urged 'that children who failed to respond to normal schooling be examined before dismissal and, if considered educable, be assigned to special classes'. Drawing from item types already developed, Binet put together a set of thirty scales which were standard, which were easy and quick to administer, and which effectively discriminated between children who were seen by teachers to be bright and children who were seen as dull, as well as between mentally retarded children in an institution and children in ordinary schools.

Following Galton and Cattell, psychophysical and sensory tests were known to be poorly related to educability, so Binet emphasized in his tests what he called the higher mental processes: the execution of simple commands, co-ordination, recognition, verbal knowledge, definitions, picture recognition, suggestibility and the completion of sentences. He believed that good judgement was the key to intelligence.

> judgement, otherwise called good sense, practical sense, initiative, the faculty of adapting one's self to circumstances. To judge well, to comprehend well, to reason well, these are the essential activities of intelligence. A person may be a moron or an imbecile if he is lacking in judgement; but with good judgement he can never be either. Indeed the rest of the intellectual faculties seem of little importance in comparison with judgement.

The first scale was published in 1905, but an improved version came out in 1908 in which the tests were sorted into age levels, and in 1911 other improvements were made. Tests that might measure academic knowledge rather than intelligence – reading, writing, or tests of knowledge that had been incidentally acquired – were eliminated. The Binet tests and their derivatives (the Stanford–Binet in the USA and the Burt tests in the United Kingdom) were widely used throughout the world for the next sixty years for diagnosing mental retardation in children.

IQ tests and racism

Modern books on testing often contain an ambiguity of purpose concerning the use of intelligence tests with children. On the one hand they seem to be required in order to identify brighter children who may be allowed to explore their potential unencumbered by the presence of slower learners within the learning environment. On the other hand, the intelligence tests enable us to identify children with learning difficulties in order that special resources can be made available to them. Both of these issues are particularly important to debates over streaming and separate schooling. There is an apparent confusion, not without political overtones, between the idea that the bright children should not be held back by the dull, and the idea that the dull children should be given extra facilities to compensate for their disadvantage.

However, older books are often more straightforward. The originators of psychometrics did not share the current sensitivity on these issues. Terman (1919) states in his introduction to the manual for the first Stanford–Binet:

> It is safe to predict that in the near future intelligence tests will bring tens of thousands of . . . high-grade defectives under the surveillance and protection of society. This will ultimately result in the curtailing of the reproduction of feeblemindedness and in the elimination of enormous amounts of crime, pauperism and industrial inefficiency. It is hardly necessary to emphasise that the high-grade cases, of the type now so frequently overlooked, are precisely the ones whose guardianship it is most important for the state to assume.

This view illustrates the close relationship between the development of academic and social interest in intelligence testing and concerns about human breeding before the Second World War. The eugenics movement in particular was concerned about the dangers of the working classes reproducing more quickly than the middle classes, thereby lowering the average intelligence of the country. Eugenicists believed that we should improve the 'quality' of the human population by selective breeding. However, this interest in social engineering did not stop there: it also expressed itself in definitions of model humanity, the 'superman' in whom intellectual and moral superiority are combined. Thus Terman tells us, about children with high intelligence, that 'really serious faults are not common among them, they are nearly always socially adaptable, are sought after as playmates and companions, they are leaders far oftener than other children, and notwithstanding their many really superior qualities they are seldom vain or spoiled'. Compare this with Darwin in *The Descent of Man* (p. 126): 'The moral sense perhaps affords the best and highest distinction between man and the lower animals.' The intelligence testing movement at the beginning of the twentieth century was not simply like Nazism in its racist aspects – it was its ideological progenitor.

Group tests of intelligence entered widespread use following the First World War, during which the army alpha and beta tests had been introduced and were subsequently applied to millions within the US as a part of the conscription process. A committee under the chairmanship of Robert Yerkes, president of the American Psychological Association, and including Terman devised these tests to the following criteria: adaptability to group use, correlation with the Binet scales, measurement of a wide range of ability, objectivity and rapidity of scoring, unfavourableness to malingering and cheating, independence of school training, minimum of writing and economy of time. In seven working days they constructed ten sub-tests with enough items for ten different forms. These were piloted on 500 subjects from a broad sampling of backgrounds, including schools for the retarded, a psychopathic hospital, recruits, officer trainees and high-school students. The entire process was complete in less than six months. Before 1940, these tests and others based on them were widely used as part of eugenicist programmes in both the USA and Europe, leading to the sterilization of people with low IQ scores and restrictions on their movements between states and countries. Not all proponents of IQ testing were so extreme. Cyril Burt, who applied intelligence testing to school selection in England, was particularly concerned that the examination system was unfair to working-class children, and successfully argued for the introduction of intelligence tests in place of essays for the selection of children for grammar schools, on the grounds that the former would have less class bias. It has frequently been commented that when IQ tests were abolished for the eleven-plus, the number of working-class children in grammar schools again decreased.

The eugenics movement went out of favour following the Second World War, although by this time the ideas of intelligence that had been associated with the movement were fully ingrained in folk psychology. By drawing on a reinterpretation of popular ideas about mental defect, a common interest in breeding and genealogy, and a widespread usage for selection in education and in the army, the various strands of belief had become mutually supporting to such an extent that many considered them to be self-evident.

The use of the Binet scales continued, and the underlying ideological issues were resurrected by the sociobiologists in the 1960s, first Jensen, and then Eysenck, following an analysis of the performance of American black children in the Head Start programme. Sociobiologists believe that, even today, the evolutionary aspects of human intelligence are manifest in the migration and breeding characteristics of different human groups. The aim of Head Start had been to counteract the adverse environmental conditions of black Americans by giving them an educational boost in their early years. When the early analysis of Head Start produced negative results, Jensen argued that the lower average IQ of American black people was not due to environmental factors but to a genetic difference between the black and white races. Eysenck, in his book *Race and IQ*, supported Jensen's contention, and also extended the argument to the inheritance of intelligence in people of Irish extraction.

A heated controversy followed in which Kamin (1974) and many others attacked both the results of Jensen and Eysenck's experiments, and the ideological position of the intelligence-testing movement that had led to this research. Kamin carried out a study-by-study critique of all the evidence for the inheritance of IQ scores and found it wanting. He did the same for studies that had purported to show differences in mean IQ score between racial groups. Following court cases in the USA, the use of overt intelligence tests in education was outlawed in many states, and testing generally came under increased scrutiny by the courts on the issue of cultural bias. While attempts were made to develop statistical models of alternative strategies to remedy any unfairness, such as positive discrimination (where selection processes explicitly favour members of a group which has been disadvantaged) and affirmative action programmes (where direct action is taken against the causes and cycles of disadvantage), the general disfavour into which psychometrics had fallen was widespread to such an extent that its teaching was down-graded or even eliminated in psychology and education courses throughout the world. However, the issue refuses to be buried. Today, Herrnstein and Murray (1994) in *The Bell Curve* argue that poor inner-city communities are a 'cognitive underclass' formed by the interbreeding of people with low IQ. The dearth of people with training in the science of psychometrics now hinders, rather than helps, any serious attempt to counter these arguments.

Issues in intelligence testing

Twin studies of intelligence

Paradoxically, however, by the mid-1980s, testing had become even more common than before. To understand why this happened we need to grasp the nettle that was evaded in the debates of the 1970s. The amount of data available now is so large that we can say confidently as a matter of fact that 50 per cent of the variation in intelligence test scores is inherited. It is also a matter of fact that the mean scores of different racial groups on intelligence tests differ. However, neither of these results are as they seem and both need to be put into a proper perspective.

If we consider initially the genetic argument, the first issue of note is that in looking at twin studies we are dealing not with Mendelian genetics but with biometrical genetics. This difference is important because genetic results are generally interpreted by the man in the street in Mendelian terms, as taught in schools (for example, the inheritance of eye colour). The biometrical genetic technique has arisen more recently largely from agricultural engineering, where it is applied to the breeding of more pro-ductive species of plants and animals. One important difference between the Mendelian and the biometrical approach is that biometrical genetics deals not in absolutes (such as eye colour) but in the amount of variation in a particular trait. To see why this is important consider the theoretical effects of developing a perfectly equitable education within which every person received an identical education. If this were the case there would be no environmental variance at all in educational level, which by default would become 100 per cent genetic. Thus the more fair the educational system becomes, the more that variation between people will be determined by their birth. The fact that this perfectly straightforward aspect of biometrical genetics seems odd to us reflects the extent to which we are prone to misinterpret the results of this approach.

The form of surprise we feel with this failure of interpretation is demonstrated again when we look at the broader set of results in human twin studies. As more and more aspects of personality, ability and performance are investigated under the twin model it is found that almost all psychological characteristics that we can reliably measure on human beings turn out to have both a genetic component and an environ-mental component, each accounting for about half of the variance. Now at once this raises an immediate exclamation: 'How interesting!', 'How amazing!', 'How remarkable that it should be about 50 per cent!' Yet is it remarkable? Surely we have always known that much of our human identity is determined by our parents? Had the genes been different we could be apes, or fruit flies, or oak trees. It is common knowledge that many of our characteristics resemble those of our close relations, and observations of family resemblance are made in primitive societies as well as in the modern world. The human personality exists in an exceptionally complex network, which draws not only on social and psychological factors but also on biology. All these aspects interact with each other and no aspects are independent. It seems as if a scientific confidence trick has been pulled. Common-sense knowledge has been quantified, translated into scientific jargon and served back to us as a justification for racism. But in spite of its technical format there is little new knowledge there – that is, unless we wish to follow up the technology of biometrical genetics and breed people in the manner we breed farmyard animals.

Recent advances in biotechnology have enabled us to look again at many of these issues within a more sophisticated framework. This has led to a heated controversy, not just in psychometrics, but in medicine and even more widely in society. For example, evidence is mounting that susceptibility to an addiction to alcohol is related to a particular gene or genes. If this proves to be true, can it be long before the eugenicist argument is put forward that people who are found to be carrying this gene should be discouraged from reproducing? Two points are worth making here. First, the new techniques have a much wider application than was the case when the notion of IQ was so central to the evolving eugenics movement. In the new debate the psychometrically stigmatized share common interest with many other genetically handicapped groups in society, such as people with diabetes. After all, genetic perfection is an ideal that is never likely to be realized in a single individual (theological debates apart). Second, geneticists today recognize that the important question about gene operation is not the 'that' but the 'how'. The finding that a gene is more common in a particular population is only the beginning. One of the genes responsible for skin cancer, for example, is clearly more common in European white-skinned populations, being that which determines skin pigmentation. Perhaps such a gene became widespread in the past, in spite of its risks, because it enabled their cave-dwelling ancestors to creep up on their enemies undetected in snowy conditions. Whatever its origins, there has been no suggestion that people carrying this gene should be discouraged from breeding. Rather, we seek to use any knowledge of its operation to counter its effects and to understand other ways of dealing with skin cancer.

Thus, the importance of the genome project does not arise from its having confirmed any previous prejudices we may have. It has been known for at least half a century that criminal fathers tended to have criminal sons. What is different today is that we now have the possibility of knowing the biochemical and genetic mechanisms involved and how these interact with the environment during development. Psychometricians who work in the field, such as Robert Plomin (Plomin *et. al.* 1994), while believing like their predecessors that many learning difficulties are related to genes, are more interested in finding ways of identifying the specific learning and environment needs of everyone in order that their potential may be realized. In particular, they recognize that genes can only act in interaction with the environment. Modern debates show that the ethical issues are far more sophisticated than the simplistic notions of the eugenics movement.

Societal differences in intelligence

In looking at the differences in mean IQ scores between different groups Jensen claimed that differences remained even when socio-economic factors were taken into account. However, the adjustment for cultural differences is no simple matter, and it seems implausible that these complex interaction effects can be adjusted for by any simple covariance analysis. Where different sub-groups within society hold differing relations to the power structure, it is the dominant group that defines the parameters by which things are to be judged, including the school curriculum. Generally speaking, members of a group which defines the standards perform higher on those standards, as was found, for example, in French Canada when the major language of instruction was changed from English to French. While previously the English-speaking Canadians had generally performed better than French-speaking Canadians in examinations, following the change this position was reversed.

The social movement of immigrants and other sub-groups in society is a matter for sociology rather than psychology, but clearly relates to the class and power structure in terms of the availability of resources, motivating factors for achievement, expect- ations of success and the perceived role of education. When one social group migrates to be within another, there is never a straightforward mixing of social equals. Many emigrant groups are driven out of their own countries by famine or persecution and arrive in the new society with nothing, and sometimes tend to be treated as nothing. Some groups emigrate to look for work, and will often find themselves at the bottom of the social structure in the new society, doing the jobs that natives refuse to do them- selves. Other groups may have been driven out because of jealousy or political persecu- tion, and may find a place for themselves in the new society providing skills for which there was a need. In all of these cases the tendency is often not towards absorption but to the development of subcultures. Members of these subcultures may, with luck, be free to compete for any advantages available to members of the society in which they find themselves. But it is unlikely that they will be quickly accepted into the groups of people who hold real power, that is, the power to say what counts as an advantage and to define the rules by which that society is controlled. It is those who hold this power within a society who also define what it means to behave 'intelligently' within it.

Test bias and test validity

In cross-cultural terms, differences in intelligence test scores have also been found between nations, with the Japanese apparently obtaining the highest scores. These types of result can often lead to some confusion among sociobiologists in Europe and the USA, but have been rationalized by suggesting that, although the Japanese may be better at simple problem solving, they are probably not so creative. This type of rationalization has also been used in the past whenever women have been found to have higher IQ scores than men on particular tests. Thus, according to Terman, while girls have higher scores overall than boys, the boys 'are decidedly better in arithmetical reasoning, giving differences between a president and a king, solving the form board, making change, reversing the hands of a clock, finding similarities, and solving the "induction test"'.

The girls were 'superior in drawing designs from memory, aesthetic comparison, comparing objects from memory, answering the comprehension questions, repeating digits and sentences, tying a bow knot, and finding rhymes'. It is fairly easy to see here that all of the characteristics for which boys are claimed to be better provide justifications for patriarchy, while the tasks at which girls excel are the ones more suitable for housework or secretarial work!

Wherever a difference between groups is found there is a choice of treating this either as evidence of bias or, alternatively, as evidence of validity, showing that the test is successful in measuring whatever it is supposed to measure. If we take social status as a case in point, there are well demonstrated differences between socio-economic groups in mean IQ scores, with the professional class having the highest score and the unskilled manual class the lowest score. Now there is no a priori reason why this should not mean that IQ scores suffer from class bias. However, these results are never treated in this way. Rather there are aspects of the trait of intelligence, as it is popularly understood, that means that most people expect social class to be related to IQ. Thus, when it turns out to be so related, the result is treated as showing that the IQ test is valid. Whatever the IQ test is measuring, it is something that behaves as expected with respect to social class. But remember, statistics say nothing whatsoever about whether this is a case of validity as opposed to bias. Thus the distinction between these two concepts cannot be a statistical one.

If sex differences are now considered in the same light, we find that as attitudes to sexism have changed over the decades, so have attitudes to sex bias and validity in IQ tests. Thus, when Terman standardized his IQ scale and discovered that at certain ages girls were better than boys at certain sub-tests, he could have treated this as a scientific finding (girls actually are better than boys at these sub-tests), or as validity (girls were expected to be better than boys at these sub-tests; they are; therefore the test is valid), or as evidence of bias (this sub-test is biased against boys). In fact he chose the latter interpretation, and consequently changed the items until the scores for the two sexes were the same, a perfectly reasonable approach given the interpretation he chose to make. This all demonstrates the importance of social values in psychometrics, and that often the social positions which are taken for granted are the very ones we need to question in evaluating a test.

Intelligence and moral worth

The major rebuff for the sociobiologists on this issue must come from their definitions of intelligence. For sociobiologists, intelligence test scores reflect more than the mere ability to solve problems: they are related to Darwin's conception of 'survival of the fittest'. And fitness tends to be perceived in terms of images of human perfection. Generally speaking, if it was found that a particular intelligence test gave low scores to eminent scientists and artists this would not be seen as making a scientific discovery but as being overwhelming evidence that the test was invalid as a measure of intelligence. Furthermore, natural selection and survival of the fittest are seen as operating on groups as well as on individuals. The more successful ethnic groups are presumed to be the more 'intelligent' groups, and also the most evolved in terms of morality. Thus, intelligence as viewed from this perspective appears to be a general quality reflecting the person's moral and human worth, and has been unashamedly related to ethnic differences.

This perceived relationship between moral qualities, intelligence and ethnicity is quite clear in the early biological literature, from Darwin and Galton to Terman and Burt. An important article in this respect was that of W.R. Greg in *Fraser's Magazine* (1868), which inspired a considerable debate. Part of Greg's paper should be repeated, although offensive, because its use of language epitomizes the confusion between political nationalism and intellectual views that was common in this period, and also because it proved to be so influential in the subsequent development of the eugenics movement. Greg claimed that:

> The careless, squalid, unaspiring Irishman, fed on potatoes, living in a pig-sty, doting on a superstition, multiplies like rabbits or ephemera: – the frugal, foreseeing, self-respecting, ambitious Scot, stern in his morality, spiritual in his faith, sagacious and disciplined in his intelligence, passes his best years in struggle and in celibacy, marries late, and leaves few behind him.

This grossly insensitive work was written less than twenty years after the great potato famine in Ireland in which over a million people had starved to death! Afterwards, the British bureaucrat entrusted with overseeing every significant item of famine relief spending during the period stated his 'humble but sincere conviction that the appointed time for Ireland's regeneration has now come. . . . and this has been laid bare by a direct stroke of an all-wise and all-merciful Providence' (Trevelyan 1848). While these divisions between peoples of British and Irish origin also existed in the USA prior to 1850, they were rapidly overtaken there by more pressing concerns arising from the continuing enslavement of the large African population in their midst. Greg's ideas entered into evolutionary theory and were used to dress up dubious political beliefs in an attempt to give them a pseudo-scientific respectability. Both Darwin and Galton quote from Greg, although tastefully leaving out the reference to potatoes. Eugenicist ideas, both implicit and explicit, continued to appear quite frequently in the Western world until the Second World War when they reached their nadir. In 1940 Konrad Lorenz in Nazi Germany wrote:

> If it should turn out that the mere removal of natural selection causes the increase in the number of existing mutants and the imbalance of the race, then race-care must consider an even more stringent elimination of the ethnically less valuable than is done today, because it would, in this case, literally have to replace all selection factors that operate in the natural environment.

The 'success' of ethnic cleansing programmes in the twentieth century does, if anything, imply that genetic survival in the modern world is more likely to be associated with a decline rather than an increase in any moral component to intelligence. A review of the history of the species over the last few thousand years also suggests that this has been the norm rather than the exception as far as human biological evolution is concerned. Certainly, if we believe that humanity today is more morally evolved than in the past we would be well advised to look for explanations in places other than the nature of our genes.

The peculiar ethical ideas of eugenics also manifested themselves as psychological theory. Spearman's 'g' or general factor of intelligence appears in his writings to have an almost spiritual quality (Spearman 1904). He speaks of a 'psychophysiological energy', which he compares to the basic theoretical concepts of physics (force, gravity, etc.). Here Spearman is not creating a new concept, but is making use of a very old and time-honoured metaphor. It is not entirely facetious to suggest that it is this same 'psychophysiological energy' which is thought of as providing the halo around the heads of religious saints or heroes. By using the metaphor in this way, Spearman generates an image of intelligence that not only represents the ability to answer simple arithmetical questions but also implies high moral standing.

The search for this single quality or essence of intelligence received much attention in the first half of the twentieth century, although it was challenged by Thurstone and Guilford. Indeed we owe the origins of factor analysis as a statistical technique to this search. It became clear that whatever these tests were measuring did have some aspect in common, but the extent to which this was likely to be dependent on a common educational system was often overlooked. Once a person receives an education and learns to read and to carry out arithmetic then all other sorts of learning become possible, so it would be very odd if, for example, ability at reading was not correlated with ability at languages or geography. But for the sociobiologist the existence of biological intelligence seems so self-evident that it takes precedence over common educational sense in providing an interpretation for experimental results.

The neuropsychological view of intelligence

Another implicit assumption within traditional approaches to intelligence is the idea that the ability to solve a problem is based on the person possessing efficient basic information-processing components within the brain. Thus, to be good at mental arithmetic a person needs an ability to hold the results of previous calculations in their memory for a short period of time until they are needed for the next step in the procedure. Tests of digit span are designed to measure this component of short-term memory. The respondent is given lists of randomly ordered digits of lengths between four and thirteen, and after an interval of a few seconds asked to repeat them back. Most people can repeat lists of about seven such digits quite easily but find difficulty with ten digits or more. This test is easy to administer both forwards and backwards (with backwards digit span a person would have to repeat the digits in reverse order to that in which they were presented), and we would probably expect people who use numbers frequently to have longer digit spans of this type. But the interpretation of the test has often gone further than this. It is not seen as merely a measure of a skill but as a manner of gaining direct access to the brain component that carries out numerical memory. It has been assumed that unless this brain component is working properly a person cannot expect to be a mathematician. There is the further implication that the component, being within the brain, is part of our biology, and therefore of our genes. Other item clusters within intelligence tests attempted to measure other such components, such as the ability to recognize objects from different angles, to rearrange images of objects in the mind, or to recognize the basic logical relationships defined within symbolic logic. All this carried the implication that basic skill associated with particular brain mechanisms must exist before a person can possibly proceed to any higher or more complex level of knowledge, such as reading or arithmetic. However, the ordering of the hierarchy in this way is not self-evident but a product of a particular rather mechanical view of how the brain functions. Why, for example, should a particular digit span be a prerequisite for being good at arithmetic? Is it not equally plausible that good mathematicians develop longer digit spans through practice?

Eysenck and his colleagues at the Institute of Psychiatry in London perhaps provide one of the best illustrations of the thinking of sociobiologists about the nature of intelligence. They have carried out experiments to attempt to relate scores on IQ tests directly to brain functioning. Thus, for example, Hendrickson (1982b) found that more intelligent individuals tended to have shorter latency for certain components within the EEG evoked-potential response. This response is a very small change in voltage at the surface of the brain measured by an electroencephalograph (EEG), the same type of machine used to measure the better known brain alpha rhythm. Unlike alpha, the evoked potential occurs specifically after the respondent has received a sensory stimulus, such as an auditory 'beep'. The response only lasts for about half a second, and is an oscillation with several peaks and troughs. It is, however, very easy to measure because the responses to a large number of stimuli can be averaged. This eliminates any background effects (such as the alpha rhythm) and, if measured over about a hundred stimuli, produces a characteristic response that varies from situation to situation as well as from respondent to respondent. Using neural imaging apparatus, Haier *et al.* (1992) found that the brains of people with higher IQ metabolize less glucose while thinking than their lower-IQ cohorts. Thinking consisted of learning to play the computer game 'Tetris', during which their brain was imaged with a brain scan. They argued that the slower rate at which the brains of higher-IQ subjects metabolized glucose represented a more efficient use of mental energy.

The interest of the Eysenck school in the results of these experiments is based on the belief in the possibility of a direct relationship between a person's intellectual ability and the speed at which the neurones within the brain actually transmit nerve signals. This would be questioned by those who view intelligence as only having meaning within social, linguistic or ontological settings. Another supporter of the Eysenck approach, Alan Hendrickson, has also suggested that more intelligent people have faster synapses and more efficient RNA. In fact many of these results have been subsequently discredited (Rust 1975b). However, they are of particular interest in that they demonstrate a particular way of thinking about intelligence. All of these results exist within a purportedly scientific framework, that of theory production, operationalization and empirical testing. Very few of the individuals involved question the presupposition that the only real explanation of intelligence is a biological one, so that their aim is not so much to prove such a link as to find out the why and the how. The biology in this sociobiology is of the extreme reductionist variety – to such an extent that the eventual explanation of all human activity in terms of neurone activity is not seen as an empirical matter but as an a priori truth.

Intelligence and cognitive science

The general picture of the great, good and intelligent man, being, as if by right, at the pinnacle of evolution, has recently been dealt a considerable blow by the development of cognitive science. The skills at which such men excel are mental arithmetic and logical reasoning, yet today these cognitive skills have lost much of their gloss. As cognitive science grew in the 1950s, several models of human performance were put forward based on computer models, and generally these emphasized the single-channel information-processing aspect of both the computer and human cognition. Information was shifted about and sorted by short- and long-term memory buffers and by various sorts of filter until it activated behaviour. However, these early models soon proved to be inadequate. First because they faded to take heed of the enormous amount of representational activity that takes place in the computer software, and second because they implied that the limits on human performance are set by the extreme difficulty of carrying out advanced operations like remembering and filtering. Yet ability to remember soon became an easy task for computers, and it was hard to see, given the complexity of the nervous system, why the brain should find it difficult. Seen from the cognitive science perspective it becomes much more difficult to explain why people forget, rather than why people remember. Desktop computers now have the ability to remember entire libraries and yet are far simpler in structure than the brain. Computer programs that utilize parallel processing or multiple machines on a network show that there is no physical reason for a cognitive process to be restricted to a single channel. Evidence from neuroscience suggests that the brain itself, to the extent that it can be treated as a computational machine, is far more complex and more massively parallel than any existing man-made computer (Rumelhart and McClelland 1986). Consequently, any limitations on brain performance are not very likely to be due to lack of information-processing power.

At the same time experiments on human cognition were beginning to show that people generally are rather bad at carrying out intelligent operations. The work of Johnson-Laird, and Tversky and Kahneman, has shown that on the whole people get many simple logical and probability exercises wrong, while even simple computers are able to get them right. By the 1980s the 'complex' activity of arithmetic, seen as higher-order reasoning within intelligence tests, became available to children on calculators for less than five pounds. Increasingly, the development of expert knowledge-based systems demonstrated that many of the skills of intelligent experts were fairly easily modelled on small personal computers. Paradoxically, it was the lower-order activities of perception and motor control that proved much more difficult to model. A comparison of the complexity of existing computers with the very much more complex structure of the brain does suggest that mechanical limitations of this sort are not the apparently self-evident source of human intellectual incapacity that they once were.

In the ancient world, it was movement that differentiated between the animate and the inanimate. Animals and birds moved. The heavenly bodies, wind and sea moved and were thus alive and controlled by intelligent deities. Now we know about gravity and have aeroplanes, so do not need a mystical life force to explain these phenomena. Today, the computer has provided a similar debunking to the myth that higher-order cognitive functioning requires a greater concentration of soul. This debunking of the traditional notion of the superior man with the superior intellect is an ongoing process, and its eventual impact is yet to be determined. However, one side-effect must be to elevate the worth of every human individual and to discredit any justification of wealth and power based on the abilities of some humans to simulate rather simple computers. The knowledge now available within information science is enough to render absurd the notion that the quality of mind arises from our ability to do simple logic, arithmetic and other basic operations of the type measured in IQ tests.

Alternative models of intelligence

Alternative models of intelligence are exemplified by the work of Howard Gardner (1983) and Robert Sternberg (1990). Gardner argues that there are multiple intelligences, each linked with an independent and separate system within the human brain. These are linguistic intelligence, logical-mathematical intelligence, spatial intelligence, musical intelligence, bodily-kinaesthetic intelligence, interpersonal intelligence and intrapersonal intelligence. Many of these correspond with traditional notions that are tested within IQ tests. However, Gardner emphasizes the distinctive nature of some of these intelligences and their ability to operate independently of each other. He associates linguistic intelligence, for example, with skills in the use of oral language. The importance of such skills is increasingly recognized in education today, and tests such as the Wechsler Objective Language Dimensions (Rust 1996b) have been designed to assess this 'oracy'. Bodily-kinaesthetic intelligence, representing excellence in sporting activities, is also a new concept within the field. Interpersonal and intrapersonal intelligence represent the ability to understand other people and the ability to have insight into one's own feelings respectively. These traits had previously been associated with theories of personality rather than ability, although quite clearly a person can be more or less skilled in these areas and it does make good sense to treat them in this way.

Sternberg, in his triarchic model, suggests three major forms of intelligence – analytic, creative and practical. While analytic intelligence, measured by classical IQ tests, is important it is not always the most relevant. He gives an apocryphal example of a brilliant mathematician who appeared to have no insight at all into human relationships, to such an extent that when his wife left him unexpectedly he was completely unable to come up with any meaningful explanation. Doubts about the sufficiency of classical notions of intelligence have also been expressed in the business world. High IQ is associated with the ability to solve problems set by others, such as in a test or examination. A successful business entrepreneur, however, needs to ask good questions rather than supply good answers. It is the ability to come up with good questions that characterizes the creative form of intelligence. People with practical intelligence are 'street wise', and they are often the most successful in life. They know the right people, avoid making powerful enemies, and are able to work out the unspoken rules of the game.

Thus, those with analytic intelligence do well on IQ tests, appear 'clever', are able to solve preset problems, learn quickly, appear knowledgeable, are able to automate their expertise, and normally pass exams easily. Those with creative intelligence are able to identify new questions, are able to see new possibilities in a situation, can generate new ideas and can 'achieve the impossible'. Those with practical intelligence appear to be 'wise', they want to understand and can stand back and deconstruct a proposal or idea, they will question the reasons for wanting to know, and can integrate their knowledge to a deeper purpose.

Although these new ideas of intelligence have received a great deal of popular attention, particularly since the publication of *Emotional Intelligence* (Goleman 1996), their impact on psychometrics has been rather limited. All of these new forms of intelligence can be measured psychometrically. However, when this is done the resultant tests often prove to be rather similar to other personality or ability tests that are already in existence. The ideas are not really new, Aristotle himself having emphasized the importance of distinguishing between wisdom and intelligence. Creativity tests have been around for about fifty years, and while it is always good to have a new slant on an idea, there is nothing intrinsic to the new models that suggests any better way of measuring this elusive quality. Similarly, tests of emotional intelligence resemble personality tests or tests of social skill. However, the new approaches have had an important role in deconstructing the idea that academic success is the sole form of intellectual merit.

The ethics of IQ testing

Intelligence tests certainly measure something, and this something is highly correlated with academic achievement. But the question 'What is intelligence?' may have been approached from the wrong direction. It is necessary to look more seriously at an alternative explanation: that educational achievement may be determining intelligence rather than the other way round. Within this alternative context it may be that, rather than a child being good at reading and good at arithmetic because of a high IQ, it is because the child is good at reading that he does better at arithmetic, and vice versa, the two learning processes being mutually supportive. Thus the core items of intelligence tests may be derivative rather than determining. When intelligence is viewed through the perspective of education, a natural relationship falls into place between the learning process and the achievement of intellectual skills. It seems natural to propose that the higher the educational achievement, the better one becomes through practice at simple intellectual tasks. Modern artificial intelligence systems using inductive logic programming or neural networks also build up their ability to act intelligently as a result of training and instruction.

However, this is not a satisfactory place to leave the matter. It would be improper to suggest that the only reason for attempting to eliminate racism within psychometrics was its factual inaccuracy. Many people would overlook the racism of Darwin and his followers on the grounds that most white people of those times knew no better. While we should not let the matter detract from Darwin's other achievements, these arguments cannot be accepted in their entirety as a number of white men of the period took an entirely different view. In the USA in 1859, John Brown fought and ultimately lost his life in his struggle for the recognition of the intellectual and moral equality of black and white. In the UK, the evolutionary biologist Alfred Wallace (1865) took issue with the eugenicist arguments that he believed to be fundamentally flawed. His observations in South East Asia, America and elsewhere told him that primitive peoples all exhibited a high moral sense, and that if all our ancestors had been similar, on eugenicist arguments, intelligence would never have evolved at all! He also drew attention to the ability of children from primitive tribes to learn advanced mathematics, even though no evolutionary pressure could possibly ever have been exerted on their ancestors in this direction by the natural environment. In his view the evolutionary factors that had led to the development of intelligence and morality in humanity had happened in the distant past and were aspects of our common ancestry.

However, it would be a mistake to suppose that these matters are ones for science alone. Even if the biological theory of eugenics were true and mankind was still evolving in the manner they suggest, it surely could not provide any justification for the policies some of them recommend. Many of the arguments have by now been well covered within the courts. At a more general level, the almost universal recognition of the inherent rightness of campaigns for equality in countries other than one's own demonstrates that the matters of principle that arise within psychometrics cannot simply be treated as questions of empirical verification within science. The fight against the abuses of intelligence testing forms an integral part of the movement for more social responsibility in science, and also demonstrates that science is but a part of human life and cannot stand outside it. While science can develop our understanding, and can help us to predict and control the world, it cannot interpret our findings for us, or tell us how the world should be.

Some people may believe that the worth of human beings is an empirical point; that the study of human genetics and the related disciplines is the job of an impartial scientist who must never be held back in his task for any reason, carrying out for us that special human endeavour: the search for truth. But this absolutist view does not generally hold, and much of what is true scientifically may have more to do with the discipline of engineering than pure science. There is, after all, a difference between the search for the true nature of the atom, and the search for the ideal design for an atomic bomb. Biometrical genetics is an engineering process, designed for the breeding of improved species, and does not necessarily have any relevance to psychology. On the other hand the belief in the equality of all human beings in terms of moral worth is an old one, enshrined in many world religions, and for most people it comes first. No approach which attempts to challenge this basic human belief can expect to be above criticism, and it is quite apparent that the concept of intelligence used by some psychometricians represents more than the straightforward ability to solve problems: judgements of human worth are also implicit.

The limitations of IQ tests

IQ tests have had their day in psychology and in society in general. They have had their uses, particularly in selection, but this has unfortunately been accompanied by gross unfairness. While the employer or the selection board that has used IQ tests may well have obtained good candidates, they will also have had a biased set of candidates, and the bias will reflect the patterns of injustice which already exist within the society. Consequently, any differences will be exacerbated, and unfairness will increase. Exceptions do exist, as for example when Burt introduced the IQ test as an alternative to written tests for English school selection. But this is a particularly interesting case in point, which very well illustrates the major dilemma of IQ testing. The previous written examinations were certainly more biased against working-class children than were the IQ tests, yet in spite of this eventually proved to be more socially acceptable. Why? Because a written examination doesn't basically claim any more than the ability to identify the child's learning. If the child does badly then there is always another chance to make good any learning that had been incomplete. The IQ test on the other hand is specifically designed to get at that part of the child's ability which is least affected by the child's learning – the child's innate potential. To obtain a low score on such a test is damning, and IQ tests exist not within a purely scientific realm of operational definitions but within a world where the term 'intelligence' is already heavily loaded with meaning. Society generally is unlikely to accept a system that condemns children at an early age to a life of low expectations, by both themselves and others.

Once these problems with the way the concept of intelligence was being used were recognized, several strategies were developed to overcome them. First, the word 'ability' was generally substituted for 'intelligence' in existing tests. This is more than just a semantic quibble. Ability is an accurate word for the description of the trait that IQ tests measure, is less far-reaching in its implications, and does not carry with it the automatic connotations of 'intelligence' as moral worth. Second, attention focused increasingly on what a person with high ability was actually able to do – the term was used transitively rather than intransitively.

One consequence of this was that interest developed in abilities that were specific to particular skills, rather than general. Thus the Differential Aptitude Test (1992) consists of sub-tests of verbal reasoning, numerical reasoning, abstract reasoning, perceptual speed and accuracy, mechanical reasoning, space relations, spelling and language usage. One advantage of this separation of abilities is that it enables an employer to match specific abilities onto specific duties of the job for which recruitment is taking place. Thus, accountancy staff may be required to show ability in perceptual speed and accuracy, while technical staff need to have ability in mechanical reasoning. This is much more acceptable practice than simply choosing applicants with 'high intelligence'.

When ability rather than intelligence is considered, it seems much more apparent that the environment, in particular school and university, must have an impact on what a person is able to do. Thus, a person's ability is necessarily influenced by environmental factors. A good education system will increase the ability levels of its students in a very straightforward way. To say that this education has increased the intelligence of these students is to say a rather different and more controversial thing. This said, there are those who advocate the use of IQ tests rather than school examinations for job selection. If this were the case we could simply test all children for IQ at age 11 and abolish the secondary school and university system altogether!

Learning is affected by factors other than schooling, and these can also influence scores on ability tests. Family background is important, acting through such factors as the number of books in the household, the enthusiasm of parents for education and the need to get work at an early age. Physical and mental health can also have an impact, as can social effects such as racism or civil strife. Additionally, ability scores can be influenced by personality factors, attitude and self-esteem. We can talk easily about a person's ability being influenced like this, in a way that would not be possible if we used the word 'intelligence'. Note, however, that all of this is in a word. The actual content of ability and intelligence tests are more or less identical.

Summary

Psychometrics itself has suffered considerable damage from the whole controversy about intelligence testing, but it is now time for urgent remedial action. The use of other forms of psychometric test is increasing in society, and it is important that all issues associated with this phenomenon are properly and objectively evaluated if we wish procedures to be efficient and fair. Many, of course, believe that there should be no testing at all, but this is based on a misunderstanding that has arisen from attempting to separate the process and instrumentation of testing from its function. It is the function of testing that is determining its use, and this function derives from the need in any society to select and assess individuals within it. Given that selection and assessment exist, it is important that that be carried out as properly as possible, and that they be studied and understood. Psychometrics can be defined as the science of this selection and evaluation process in human beings. But in this day and age we must realize that the ethics, ideology and politics of this selection and assessment are as much an integral part of psychometrics as are statistics and psychology. This arises in particular because any science dealing with selection is also by default dealing with rejection, and is therefore intrinsically political.

It is essential that psychometrics be understood in this way if we wish to apply proper standards and control to the current expansion in test use, and if we wish to develop a more equitable society. It is one matter to eliminate IQ tests, it is quite another to question the psychometric concepts of reliability and validity on the grounds that these were developed by eugenicists. It would be just as irrational to dismiss the theory of evolution and consequently most of modern biology! The techniques developed by Darwin, Galton, Spearman and their followers have in fact made a major contribution to our understanding of the principles of psychometrics, and it is to these matters that we now turn.

Chapter 2

The objectives of testing and assessment

Psychometrics and sociobiology

Arguments about the ideological nature of psychometrics have traditionally been seen as one of a kind with arguments about sociobiology. Modern-day sociobiology has developed from social Darwinism, and has been most clearly described by E.O. Wilson (1975). Wilson's arguments span a wide area, and cover most aspects of contemporary society. The essential thesis, however, states that most of the social and political activity of modern man is but a reformulation of the activities of our ancestors. Collecting money on the stockmarket, for example, is seen as nothing more than the modern version of the berry-collecting activity of our cave-dwelling ancestors. The fact that women do not receive equal treatment in society is seen as being due to their natural disposition, as with their animal ancestors, to look after the home and children. Further, the thesis states that these continued social habits are not merely the result of tradition but a direct projection of human genetic make-up. There follows the implication that these traditional social practices are natural and unavoidable. Men should not be expected to do housework, but rather should be out and about ensuring that their family is properly provided for; the genes so decree! Now clearly there is a relationship between this sociobiology and politics, and of course, as we could expect, those political elements that support cultural traditions of racism and sexism have found an ally in sociobiology. The frequent use of sociobiological arguments by the far political right has led more radical scientists and politicians to condemn them out of hand as being politically motivated. However, most of the scientific proponents of sociobiology argue that they are not right wing at all, that they have merely, as scientists, stood back to look at the facts and these (sociobiological) facts are what they have found to be true. They will often turn the argument on their accusers at this point, equating them with those in Nazi Germany and the Soviet Union who burnt books and locked up scientists rather than face up to the cold light of scientific truth.

The political and polemical public controversies on sociobiology and its pop psychological offspring, including the supposed natural inferiority of women and racial differences in IQ, do need to be looked at from a more disinterested viewpoint. First of all it should be obvious that a trap has been set, which has some similarities with that found when attempting to deal with the activities of the fringe religions. The steps are these: sociobiology is a science with profound implications for society; the arguments in its favour are complicated and involve a sophisticated understanding of mathematical genetics; only those with career aspirations within the area are likely to have time to develop the skills necessary to understand these arguments, and to do the necessary research; there is no point in doing any of this unless you already believe in sociobiology. It might be useful to make a comparison here with some of the wilder fringe ideas, such as 'God was a spaceman', or 'the originators of Christianity were members of a hallucinogenic mushroom cult'. In all these cases the sceptic is confronted by a very impressive amount of evidence prepared by a believer or believers. Yet does the scientific method decree that he or she is obliged to go through all of this evidence and disprove the thesis? Such an exercise would probably take years, and by post hoc selection of evidence, very plausible cases can often be made for any queer idea. This is of course a 'no win' situation: unless you believe the hypothesis there is no point in wasting any time on it, yet unless such time is spent by a non-believer the counter evidence may never be gathered and put forward. Now both of these examples don't really matter, as there are (usually) not that many consequences that follow from various people believing that God was a spaceman; but the consequences that follow from encouraging people to believe that some races are genetically inferior are immense.

Even though it is not very scientifically rewarding to spend one's scientific life criticizing the theories of others rather than building one's own, there are those, such as Kamin (1974), who have taken the plunge. However, this straightforward critical approach has two major flaws. First, there is the tendency to be over-critical to such an extent that some credibility is lost, as for example in the perhaps over-strenuous efforts to do down the results of twin studies, particularly when we know that for genetic variation in physical characteristics they are so self-evidently appropriate. Second, such an approach is in the end doomed to failure: the supporters of the approach can always produce new data, or selectively report old data, and as long as there are those who want to believe, a superficially convincing argument can always be made. Most people after all are not scientists, and when two scientists disagree, people tend to choose the side they like best. With so many people finding that their interests are served by supporting national traditions, sociobiology is assured of an indefinite market.

In fact, attacks on sociobiology by philosophers (e.g. Kitcher 1985) have been much more effective. The arguments here are several, but perhaps can be epitomized by the dogmas of the anti-flight lobby at the beginning of the twentieth century. 'If God had meant people to fly he would have given them wings.' Well, in a sense he did – the deity or destiny gave people sufficient intellect to invent the aeroplane, not to mention the space shuttle! If human beings can fly why should they not be able to plan other aspects of their lives as they like? There are presumably no genes that predispose us to build and use flying machines. Certainly no genetic natural selection has taken place, with those people who have flown successfully being more likely to survive than those who have not. The major difference between human beings and all other animals (and birds) is that there is the possibility of transcending genetic limitations. We could, if we wished, choose only to travel by foot, on the grounds that this was the only form of transport that our genes had allowed, or we could choose to keep our diseased appendix as our genes must have had a reason to put it there. Some societies may choose a historical justification for racism or the subjugation of women; other societies can and do choose to do otherwise.

Is psychometrics a science?

Much of the controversy surrounding sociobiology concerns psychology, and in particular psychometrics. One approach to psychometrics, that of trait measurement, discussed later in this chapter, has been very much quoted by sociobiologists. The investigation of the genetic properties of the measured trait of intelligence, IQ, is one of their major interests. This area has been particularly prone to the use of the defence, 'We are but honest scientists doing our job.' If this were genuine science then they would have a strong case, but some may doubt whether pure science is the appropriate description for this type of work. Perhaps theories of psychogenetic engineering should, like theories in nuclear engineering, be more socially accountable. Certainly a stronger social view has been taken on human embryo cloning, where claims of 'pure' science can perhaps be made more strongly than for psychometrics.

Is psychometrics pure science, or is it applied science? Within the physical sciences it is relatively easy to distinguish the pure from the applied aspects of a subject. Thus, for example, in nuclear physics the research that concentrates on the nature of elementary particles is justifiable on the grounds that it extends human understanding, while research on the appropriate grade of plutonium for giving the best nuclear explosion is either unjustified or justified on grounds of national defence. To put it bluntly, the first is science, the second engineering. With psychology there are also those who study the subject academically, and those who are more interested in applications. However, we cannot necessarily define all academic psychology as pure science. Unlike, for example, the physical or chemical sciences, there is not consensus on the fundamental unit of psychology. Behaviour (or more particularly the stimulus and the response) have traditionally been put forward, and more latterly 'information' has become a candidate. With the hard sciences the underlying concepts, although often complex, can be precisely specified and the appropriate experimental methods then follow. In *Philosophical Investigations* (1958) Wittgenstein summed the matter up: 'The confusion and barrenness of psychology is not to be explained by calling it a "young science"; its state is not comparable with that of physics, for instance, in its beginnings. . . . For in psychology there are experimental methods and *conceptual confusion*.' This observation still holds true today. For psychology, the invention of new techniques of analysis leads to new theories that make use of them. It is not so much that no psychology is scientific but rather that the scientific approaches of the different psychological schools are often inconsistent, with the advocates of each putting forward their own as the solitary genuine example. The classical trait approach to psychometrics is one such school and shares this characteristic. Thus while psychologists of a sociobiological persuasion may assume that they are the true and only proponents of real scientific method in psychology, this is still a matter of opinion. Their view of psychometrics is only axiomatically true if the presuppositions of sociobiology are axiomatically true, and this is widely disputed. Further, this argument can be extended to all other measured psychological traits as well. To put it at its most basic: are IQ, neuroticism or attitudes entities worthy of understanding in their own right, or are they measured merely because of the need to make decisions about individuals, and thus simply artefacts of social policy.

Within (and outside) psychometrics there are proponents of both of these views. Most trait psychometricians argue that the psychological traits their tests measure are very real, and are subjects of interest in their own right, while functional psychometricians argue that psychometrics can only be judged in terms of the success or failure of its applications. Both approaches have had their successes and failures. However, as with many such apparently clear-cut dichotomies in science, neither the theory nor the practice of psychometrics is this simple. To have a proper understanding of psychometrics as it is today we need to draw on different aspects of each approach.

What does psychometrics measure?

Psychological and educational tests carry out a form of measurement but, unlike physical measures such as length or weight, there is considerable confusion over what they measure and how they are able to do so. One particular problem is that what is measured is not a physical object but is an intervening construct or a hypothetical entity. In assessing whether a test of creativity, for example, is actually measuring 'creativity' we cannot compare a person's score on the test directly with his or her actual creativity. We are restricted to seeing how the test scores differentiate between creative and non-creative individuals according to some other ideas about how creative people should behave. The measurement of concepts like creativity or intelligence is limited by the clarity with which we are able to define the meaning of these constructs, and this has been a problem for intelligence tests in particular. Within the intelligence testing debate the facetious definition of intelligence as being merely that which is measured by intelligence tests has been widely quoted. However, intelligence tests must be measuring more than this, as otherwise they would not of necessity correlate with anything. But what more are they measuring? In attempting to answer this question it must be recognized that the problems encountered here are conceptual rather than scientific in nature.

Two models of psychometrics: trait and function

The way in which the subject matter of psychometrics is defined divides the two psychometric schools: the trait and the functional. Both these schools are further divided by their underlying philosophies. For the functionalist school the source of the discipline is seen as lying within occupational and educational testing, particularly the examination system. Within the strict functionalist approach, the design of a test is completely determined by its use, and 'what it measures' has no meaning other than this application. In occupational psychology this is referred to as 'local criterion-based validity'. A good test is one that is able to discriminate between people who perform well and people who perform less well on a job, and so long as this is achieved any traits that may be associated with the process are irrelevant. The simple paradigm for test construction provided by the functional psychometric model gives a definition of purpose, a breakdown of the areas relevant to the purpose in terms of, for example, a job specification or educational curriculum or psychiatric diagnostic procedure, and the design of a test specification based on this task specification. The test specification, or test blueprint as it is often called, is normally two-dimensional with a content axis and a manifestation axis, and provides a regulated framework for the choice of test items. This simple paradigm can be applied to almost all assessment and evaluation situations, whether they involve interview or objective test, continuous or final assessment, single test scores or profiles, or personality, achievement or competency testing. It is the one used in the second part of this book.

Functional test design

The major contribution of the functional model to recent psychometrics has been the increased emphasis on test design. Planning frameworks formerly used within educational curriculum design are now generally applied across a whole spectrum of testing situations. The basic model has been the traditional two-dimensional structure of the curriculum, with one axis for content areas of instruction and the other axis representing different manifestations of the content areas. As an example consider the possible design of a test following the completion of a school geography syllabus. This might include a number of content areas such as map reading, political geography, geology and trade, while manifestations may include skills such as having a knowledge of the terms used, understanding the subject, being able to generalize the knowledge, and the application of the knowledge within novel situations. These skills, and variations on them, are based on systems for devising objectives in educational settings (Bloom 1956). The two category systems (that is, content area and manifestation) can provide a two-dimensional grid with the four content areas representing the x-axis and the four manifestations the y-axis. The purpose of this grid is to enable us to find a predetermined number of items for each of the 16 cells that exist within this 4×4 matrix. Thus, as long as the original test specification reflected the balance in the curriculum, so the test items should reflect this same balance. In most tests both axes generally include between four and seven categories. However, this has not come about because all tests have by nature a two-by-two design with from four to seven categories in each. On the contrary there is no implicit a priori rule that says we cannot have, say, five dimensions or thirty-seven categories. Rather, use of this type of test specification has arisen by convention because it has been found to be effective. Humans do not work comfortably with more than three dimensions, and two can be more easily represented. Also, given the desired length of the average test and the time constraints on its administration, more than seven categories on either the horizontal or the vertical axis would generate too many items. On the other hand with only one dimension, or with fewer than three categories, not enough spread would be generated to cover adequately the purpose of the test. There have been and will continue to be many tests where one or three dimensions are appropriate, or where a considerable number of cells will not be filled within a particular two-by-two structure, but these are exceptions that exist within the framework provided by the conventional two-dimensional, four- to seven-category model.

Trait test design

Trait psychometrics arose originally from attempts to be more scientific about common-sense notions of different types of human intellect and personality. An important idea was that of the personality spectrum, suggesting that types of personality were not 'all or none' but had many possibilities between the extremes. Thus, for example, people were not entirely good or entirely bad but their goodness or badness could be represented along a continuum. Personality was all a matter of degree. The first person to use this approach in a scientific way was probably Sir Francis Galton (1869) in his attempt to define the essence of genius. Within the classical trait approach, the basis of individual differences in intelligence is assumed to be related to individual differences in the biology – whether biochemical, physiological, anatomical or neurological – of the human organism. Psychometric tests were thus devised to measure traits that were seen as representing biological variation in personality or aptitude.

The two key sets of philosophical assumptions for this approach are reductionism and determinism. While both of these assumptions are complex and are prone to over-simplification, they do need to be considered, as otherwise there is the danger that what is basically a difference of approach will be seen as an empirical difference requiring experimental evidence to prove the matter one way or the other. In fact neither reductionism nor determinism is open to empirical proof: they are a priori philosophical positions. Consider, for example, the a priori position involved in the following dialogue. Person A: 'Only matters that can be proved by evidence are scientific'; Person B: 'Can you prove that?' (In a *Punch* cartoon this would be followed by the line 'collapse of stout party'.) In the same way the proponent of sociobiology does not require evidence to be sure that there is no such thing as 'free will', or that all social and psychological science will eventually in principle be explicable by biology. These seem to be self-evidently true. Many trait psychometricians today continue to be reductionist in outlook and to believe in the strong version of biological determinism. However, we shall see later that there is no necessary connection between the trait model and these philosophical approaches. Superficially the functionalist and the trait model seem very different. However, they do have common aspects, their method of construction is similar, and in particular they are linked by a fundamental theorem of psychometrics: the theory of true scores, which is described below.

The theory of true scores

The theory of true scores states simply that any score on an item or a test by a respondent can be represented by two component parts: the respondent's true score on whatever the item measures, and some error of measurement. This is traditionally stated as:

$$X = T + E$$

where X symbolizes the observed score, T symbolizes the true score, and E is the error. From this it is clear that if all one knows about a subject and a test is that a particular person obtained a score of X on a test, then one knows nothing at all. In these circumstances the error and true score are inextricably mixed. For example X may be 5, yet this could be the case if $T = 3$ and $E = 2$, but equally so if $T = 110$ and $E = -105$. Thus an observed score (X) on its own is of no use whatsoever. It is the true score (T) we are interested in, and we need additional data to estimate this; primarily we need some idea of the expected size of the error term (E). To put this another way, we cannot know how accurate a score is unless we have some idea of how inaccurate it is likely to be. The theory of true scores takes us through various techniques for obtaining an idea of the size of the error (E). This is done by the process of replication, both by taking more measurements on the same respondents, and by measuring observed scores on different respondents. In deriving the theory of true scores from these data, several additional assumptions have to be made, and these are known as the 'assumptions of the theory of true scores'.

The first is the assumption that all errors are random and normally distributed. This is not particularly controversial as error, by definition, is random and, so long as the scaling factors are appropriate, error will be distributed normally. The normal curve is itself derived from the theory of error. The second assumption is that the true scores (Ts) are uncorrelated with the errors (Es). This can be rather more problematic. There are circumstances under which the assumption fails, particularly where larger errors are associated with low, high or generally extreme scores, but these deviations are all adjustable (in principle at least) by various algebraic transformations of the raw data. The third assumption is that different measures of X on the same respondent are statistically independent of each other. This is rarely true in the strict sense as the estimation of error is not usually very accurate, and the concept of error itself is open to interpretation (see the later discussion of reliability in Chapter 5). The net effects of breeches of this assumption blur the distinctive nature of the true score itself. Thus there will be some variation in the size of the measured true score depending on the particular way in which the error is estimated.

If the three assumptions of true-score theory are made, then a series of very simple equations falls into our lap. These equations produce an assessment of error such that when a particular characteristic of a test is known – its reliability – we can estimate the error and thus the true score. (For a simple description of the mathematical derivation of the classical psychometric statistics from the theory of true scores, see Ferguson's (1981) *Statistical Analysis in Psychology and Education*. For a complete and rigorous statistical treatment of all the assumptions and derivations of the theory of true scores, see Lord and Novick's (1968) *Statistical Theories of Mental Test Scores*.) Although the theory has been widely criticized and many attempts have been made to improve it, the alternatives are generally complicated and usually turn out to have flaws of their own. After more than a century, the theory of true scores continues to provide the backbone of psychometrics.

Criticisms of the theory of true scores

The major criticisms have been directed against the concept of the true score itself. It has been argued that there can be no such thing as a true score, as this is merely a hypothetical entity generated by the theory (Loevinger 1957). This is the essence of the 'intelligence is merely what intelligence tests measure' standpoint. It is argued that we cannot deduce from a score on a test that anything whatsoever 'exists' in the brain, as intelligence is a construct arising from the use of the test. The true score as such is seen as being an abstraction and therefore of no theoretical importance. The response to this criticism has been to differentiate two definitions of true score: the Platonic (Sutcliffe 1965) and the statistical (Carnap 1962). While each of these will be seen to have its respective strengths and weaknesses, it is possible to support the theory of true scores by the statistical definition alone, so we will consider this first.

The statistical true score

The statistical definition defines a true score as being that score which we would obtain if we were to take an infinite number of measures of the observed score on the same person and average them. As the number of observations approaches infinity, then the errors, being random by definition, cancel each other out and leave us with a pure measure of the true score. Of course it is not possible to take an infinite number of measures of X on the same person, or indeed even more than a few such measures, without changing the measuring process itself because of the respondent's perceptions of the situation, practice effects, and so on. But this is unimportant from the point of view of the statistical definition, which states that the true score is the score that we would obtain *were* this possible. There is no need to actually do it.

The Platonic true score

The Platonic concept of a true score is based on Plato's theory of truth. He believed that if anything can be thought about, and the unicorn is often given as an example here, then even if it does not exist in the world, it must exist somewhere if such a thought is to be possible. Non-existence is reserved for objects about which we cannot even think. The Platonic idea of the true score is generally held to be a mistake (Thorndike 1964), with the implication that psychometricians who argue for the existence of a construct from the existence of reliable test scores make a category error. Just as behaviourists argue that there is no 'mind' only behaviour, so, it is said, there is no 'true score', only a series of observed scores and deductions. However, this is an oversimplification. There are many abstract nouns in use which, although not attached directly to objects, certainly exist: for example 'justice'. Certainly, in one sense, we might agree that justice does not physically exist, but we would probably not see this as being equivalent to agreeing with the statement 'There is no justice in the world' or 'There is no such thing as justice'. Just because an abstract object has no physical existence it does not mean that it cannot be of any use or indeed that it is not an object, unless we wish to indulge in semantic quibbling.

The true psychometrics: trait or function?

A particular importance of the statistical definition of the theory of true scores is that it enables the theory to support functional as well as trait-based psychometrics. For example, if we have a selection task of 'getting the best person for a job', then we can define the true scores on the selection test as 'those the use of which would select the best person for the job'. Trait psychometrics, while supported by both the statistical and the Platonic definitions, does tend to be more Platonic in its demands, and for many trait-related tests used in psychology a statistical definition of a true score on its own is probably inadequate. A scale that sets out to measure the level of someone's depression presumes that misery exists in some sense other than the merely statistical.

The best example of the pure form of a functional test is perhaps given in the job-selection situation. In the construction of such a test the first task is to define the personality and skill requirements of a person carrying out the job in question, and this involves the drawing up of a carefully considered job description. Once this is done, the selection test uses an extension of this job description as its blueprint. If this process is properly conducted then the test score should give an estimate of a person's match to the job. In theoretical terms, if the test is purely functional then there is no need to build any psychological constructs into the situation. The test items can be specifically about the tasks the person will need to perform to carry out the job effectively.

Another area in which functional tests have been particularly useful is in educational assessment. Here the specification for the test can be based directly on the curriculum taught.

The 1970s in particular saw a shift away from trait-based and towards functional psychometrics, largely under the influence of decisions made in the American courts on issues of test fairness. An example was the case of *Griggs* v. *Duke Power Co.* (1971), where a challenge to the use of a particular test for promotion purposes led to the court judgement that in employee selection, if racial discrimination is found as a result of using a specific test, then it is necessary for the user of the test to demonstrate its local criterion-based validity within the intended application. These matters will be considered in more detail in Chapter 6.

The functions of a test can be diverse. We may wish to select high-performing managers for an organization, or we may wish to select students for university. We may not wish to select at all, but instead may be interested in identifying areas of strength and weakness in a person's performance in order to remedy defects in training. We may wish to test in order to evaluate teachers, or schools, or the curriculum itself. We may be interested in testing to feed back to a student information about his or her approach to learning, or we may wish to give a final score for the student at the end of a course to give some indication of what he or she has learned. This final score may be intended as a measure of the achievement of competency on particular skills, or of ability to develop further skills, or of both. We may wish to identify individuals with a particular disposition or motivation for a job, or for a course of treatment. We may work in a clinical setting and wish to determine which areas of the brain have been damaged by a stroke, different brain areas being known to be associated with particular skills.

The functional approach is able to produce tests for all of these circumstances and many more, but it has one weakness: we cannot assume that a test developed with one particular purpose in mind will necessarily be of any use for another. In many areas of application, however, this has been seen as a strength of the model rather than a weakness. In education, for example, the separation of the function of formative assessment, where tests are used to identify areas of the curriculum that need to be developed by both teacher and student during the remainder of the educational session, and summative assessment, where a final indication of the student's attainment is given, has been generally well-received. The way in which summative examinations control the curriculum has been widely criticized, and the formative assessment process welcomed as an approach which not only limits this control but also introduces feedback at a time when something can be done about it, rather than when it is too late. However, it should be recognized that the actual content of both types of examination will be broadly similar, and in practice there will be considerable overlap between the content of each.

The functional model insists, almost as a point of principle, that no psychological intervening variables or traits can be relevant. As with behaviourism, the only interesting aspects of traits are the behaviour to which they lead, and as this is measured and defined directly and functionally, the traits are redundant. Within functionalism there is no such thing as, for example, ability in mathematics. There is only the performance of individuals on various mathematics items. The pursuit of such an approach is, however, somewhat idealistic and certainly does not reflect existing practice in the real world. People do tend to use concepts such as 'ability in mathematics' and frequently apply them. Indeed, it is normally on the basis of such concepts that generalization from a test score to an actual decision is made, whether justified or not. How else could a GCSE in mathematics, for example, be used by an employer in selecting a person for a job? Certainly it is unlikely that the mathematics syllabus was constructed with any knowledge of this employer's particular job in mind. Neither is it likely that solving simultaneous equations will actually be a skill called for in the job in question. Indeed how many people who have a GCSE in mathematics have ever 'found x' since leaving school? No, the criteria used in practice here are not functional ones but involve the use of common-sense notions. The everyday use of such notions by ordinary people is called 'folk psychology'. Many universities require successful applicants to be qualified in Latin for similar reasons. These examinations are seen as measuring folk psychological traits.

Thus we see that, in spite of the superficial advantages and objectives of the functionalist approach, trait psychology still cannot be eliminated while it so closely represents the way in which people actually make decisions in the real world. While it could be argued that all such trait-related processes are wrong, and must be replaced by functionalism, this is probably an unreasonable and unwarranted idealism. It is really no good trying to prescribe human thought processes. To an extent much of psychometrics is no more than an attempt to be objective and consistent in predicting how people behave. If this can be achieved by assuming the existence of traits then so be it. Examples of the success of the approach abound, particularly in clinical psychology. A test of depression such as the Beck Depression Inventory (BDI) (Beck *et al.* 1961), although originally constructed around a framework defined by the functional model which identifies a blueprint of depressive behaviours and thoughts, would be of little use if it had to be reconstructed with each application of the concept of 'depression' in different circumstances. Functional tests on their own can only be specific to a particular situation, they cannot be generalized. If we wish to generalize then we need a concept, a trait of depression, to provide justification for saying that the depression scale might be applicable in changed situations, for example with children, or with reactive as well as endogenous depression. To function in this way the BDI needs to have construct validity, and this cannot exist without presupposing the construct and trait of depression itself. The process of construct validation will be considered in Chapter 5. The BDI relates to a wide range of mood changes, behaviours, thought and bodily symptoms which psychologists, psychiatrists and therapists consider to be part of depression. Paradoxically, in spite of the increasing criticism that trait psychometrics has received within the social science curriculum in universities, the use of trait-based tests is on the increase. Even intelligence tests, such as the Wechsler scales, are finding an increased application today, although such tests are now generally referred to as ability or diagnostic tests and the use of the word 'intelligence' is no longer recommended.

These apparent paradoxes can be resolved if it is recognized that the application of psychometrics is itself a social process, and it is not so much a question of right and wrong as what is appropriate or inappropriate. What is appropriate for some circumstances can be inappropriate for others. Within this context the question of which of the two models, the functional or the trait, is scientifically correct becomes meaningless. Both are alternative techniques for dealing with the same underlying phenomena. Perhaps it would be illuminating here to consider parallels with the ways in which the medical model is used in psychiatry. Within this field there are many sets of symptoms that could be interpreted in different ways. For example, is bad spelling due to laziness or due to dyslexia? Or, is a particular instance of crime due to wickedness or to personality disorder? These types of question are disingenuous as they give apparent alternative explanations with the implication that one must be correct and the other incorrect. However, the data are the same whichever model we take. The major distinction between the alternatives is not their correctness but the implications of accepting each. Thus if bad spelling is due to dyslexia, then an examination board may well consider that special exemptions are appropriate, which they would certainly not consider for laziness. Similarly, whether someone has been wicked or is ill determines whether they will be punished or receive help. Here we can decide which of these two solutions is of most benefit to society. So with psychometrics, there is little point in arguing over which of functional or trait theory is correct, rather we need to consider the consequences of applying each.

What is particularly attractive about the functional model is its ability to map directly on to any selection or assessment process, so that justification for the use of a test is shifted to questions about the justification of the selection or the assessment itself. This makes sense, as it is here that the genuine ethical, ideological and political problems exist. Psychometrics has a duty to consider these issues and first to justify the need for a test and its consequences before proceeding to deal objectively with the achievement of the task in hand. It is the responsibility of the psychometrician to consider all aspects of any selection or assessment process, rather than simply the statistical or quantitative aspects of testing technology. This expansion in the scope of psychometrics that has taken place under the functional model has enabled psychometric test results to be seen within the same framework as other forms of functional assessment, such as the structured interview, the unstructured interview, and the general psychology of decision making. All lead to functional decisions and can be evaluated on the same objective functional criteria.

Traits, functions and psychometric debates

The functional approach is also able to throw a fresh light on some of the traditional debates within psychometrics – for example, the argument about whether one factor or many are required to measure the construct of intelligence. Within functionalism, the deciding criterion is simply the use to which the test is to be put. Thus a test for selection must necessarily end with a mapping onto two categories, pass or fail. If 100 items were to be used within the test, then we would only want those items that contributed to the pass or fail decision. As there is only one way in which a scale with two effective final categories, that is our 'pass' or 'fail', can be divided, then by definition there is only one dimension appropriate for our test construction. This usually applies even where the results of several sub-tests are being used in arriving at a decision. Here, weightings of the importance of each sub-test are often derived and weighted scores then summed to generate a score on the one scale necessary for making the pass or fail decision. Even if a manager simply makes a snap decision on the selection of an employee by judgement alone, a decision about what is relevant must have been made, a strategy must have been worked out for weighting these factors, and these must have been combined to produce the decision on a single two-point scale, accept or reject. In these circumstances the existence of only one scale, as opposed to several, turns out to be merely an artefact of the decision process in question, rather than an issue relating to the true nature of what was being measured. If on the other hand we look at assessment situations where no selection decision needs to be made – for example, a curriculum to be evaluated or the strengths and weaknesses of a particular learner to be assessed – then we would need to have a large number of different measures in order to produce an overall picture, and a single scale would be next to useless. Here we would construct a diversity of sub-scales. Although we may wish to know whether they are related, there would be no demand that they have any common element. These sub-tests would generally be presented as a profile, and examination of profiles of this type is very common where assessment rather than selection is the task in hand.

The functional model of the uni-dimensional nature of pass/fail decisions is particularly effective in practice. However, there are circumstances in which it breaks down, for example, where a judgement is made by a series of branching decision rules; for example, if the person has X then look at Y, if not then look at Z, etc. In these circumstances the strengths of the human interviewer are often rightly recognized. Traditional psychometric tests are necessarily rather rigid and are not generally able to take the individual circumstances of the candidate into account. But remember, interviews when used for selection are also psychometric procedures. That is, they need to be reliable, valid, standardized and free from bias. The handicap suffered by the classical pen-and-paper test is not its lack of humanity, it is after all designed by people, but its inability to model the complex social interactions that take place in an interview. Today, artificial intelligence and information technology is proceeding apace such that it is already possible to build computer programs that question the candidate more responsively and change their tack depending on the answers given. Interestingly, such software is functional by its very nature. Artificial intelligences as we know them today do not hold concepts in the way that humans do, and consequently any generalization that takes place is along a functional domain. The use of concepts, and more specifically traits, is an intrinsically human activity. When human experts are interviewed on how they make decisions about people, it is noticeable that much of their judgemental process is based on estimations of the person's personality and aptitude in general, and not on the very specific pieces of performance defined by the job specification itself.

Bridge building between trait and function

It is this focus on the actual thinking processes of the human decision-maker which has built the bridge between functional and trait-based psychometrics. Although, in principle, we can envisage a pure functional psychometrics in which everything in, for example, a selection test is based on what a person selected is expected to do, in fact, judgements about what is expected will be made by humans, and will be constrained by human psychology. These constraints will include the current classification and generalization systems of human folk psychology. Consider a parallel example. The need to reduce racial prejudice in society has occasionally led to the simplistic notion that it is possible to eliminate stereotyping altogether. Yet as soon as the realities of how people actually function are observed this becomes not so much an impossible as a meaningless task. Stereotyping has been shown by social psychologists to emerge from the need of individuals to make decisions in circumstances where data are inadequate. Thus when a person meets another for the first time, the only way to proceed is to work on the assumption that some of the person's characteristics are similar to those of people already known. It is difficult to imagine how humans could behave otherwise. The same applies with the folk psychological use of traits of personality and intelligence. These immediately become evident in practice when we look at how personnel experts trained in selection and counselling in fact identify the 'right person for the job'. The assessment of the intelligence and personality of others is a pre-existing part of human functioning within society. Although its mechanism is unknown, it reflects the behaviour of people as they actually are.

One valuable outcome of the recent ascendancy of the functional model in psychometrics has been the emphasis on obtaining a clear definition of the purpose of the assessment, and subsequently of the selection or assessment instrument. The initial definition of purpose should be simple and straightforward. A further outcome has been the increased emphasis on bringing the presuppositions and procedures for the construction of each test into the open so that they can be justified within the public domain. If the test is to be acceptable, to be seen as fair, and to be defensible in court, the purposes, once clearly formulated, need to incorporate adjustment for possible biases or irrelevancies. Issues dealing with any specific requirements – for example, the need within an organization to promote to senior level more members from a particular societal group in order to adjust for a pre-existing bias – need to be incorporated into the rationale at this early stage. For example, men had been preferred as truck drivers on grounds of the physical strength needed for steering. This no longer applies with the advent of powered steering. Similarly, analysis of police recruitment procedures in the UK was found to discriminate unfairly against members of shorter races under the height rule, a fault that has now been remedied. Unlike traditional trait-based tests, functional tests do not make an artificial distinction between statistics (being the job of scientists and technicians) and issues of implementation (being the job of politicians and lawyers). All who are involved in the requisition, design and construction of functional tests need to integrate these societal issues into their practice at each stage of this procedure.

Summary

Both the functionalist and the trait approaches have their advantages and disadvantages. Neither can be said to be wholly right or wholly wrong. What is important is that psychometricians should realize which set of assumptions they are using in a particular situation, and be prepared to justify this use.

Chapter 3

The process of test construction

Psychometric tests are composed of individual items, and the common characteristics of tests can more often than not be applied to individual items as well. Thus the simple question 'Are you interested in this job?' can be scored (1 for yes and 0 for no, or vice versa), can be unreliable (that is, some people may give different answers each time), can be invalid (the answers may be wrong), or it can be biased (such as when some types of people may be more likely to lie than others). It can also be administered by interview, it can be judged by observation, or it can be tested by a paper and pencil multiple-choice item (tick one box for 'yes', the other for 'no'). Although there are some cases where selection might be made purely on the basis of one question (for example 'What GCSEs do you have?'), this is unusual. More often there are many aspects we might wish to cover, especially as it is usually the case that the opportunity to ask one question provides an opportunity to ask many more. However, all tests are composed of individual items as their elements and so the success of a test depends on the success of its items.

Knowledge-based and person-based questionnaires

There are several important distinctions that are made between types of item, and these affect the tests that contain them. Items can be either knowledge-based or person-based. A knowledge-based item is designed to find out whether a particular person knows a particular piece of information, and such tests measure ability, aptitude, attainment and achievement. Knowledge-based tests generally assess maximum performance, while person-based tests assess typical performance. Most educational and intelligence tests as well as some clinical assessment instruments are knowledge-based. A person-based test is designed to measure personality, clinical symptoms, mood, interests or attitude. Examples of knowledge-based tests in the educational domain are the Wechsler Intelligence Scale for Children (WISC-III-UK) (Golombok and Rust 1992) which measures ability, and the Wechsler Objective Numerical Dimensions (WOND) (Rust 1996c) which measures attainment in mathematics. In the occupational domain, the Ravens Progressive Matrices (Raven *et al.* 1995) is often used to assess conceptual ability, having the advantage of being language-free. Tests of attainment assess what the respondent has learned in the past, while tests of ability assess their potential for learning or doing in the future. However, there is a great deal of conceptual overlap between the two as one of the best predictors of future ability to learn is the level of learning attained so far. Examples of person-based tests are Orpheus (Rust 1996e), a general purpose work-based personality questionnaire, the Golombok Rust Inventory of Sexual Satisfaction (Rust and Golombok 1986a), which measures clinical symptoms, the Beck Depression Inventory (BDI) (Beck *et al.* 1961), which measures mood, and the Strong Interest Inventory (Harmon *et al.* 1994).

One major difference between these two types of test is that knowledge-based tests are necessarily hierarchical and cumulative. The development of human knowledge moves in a particular direction from not knowing to knowing. Person-based tests on the other hand carry no such implication. Different personalities and different attitudes are just different, and there is no intrinsic implication that to hold one attitude is necessarily better or worse, or more or less advanced, than the holding of another. A consequence of this difference is that the scoring of knowledge-based items tends to be uni-dimensional, the person either gets the right or the wrong answer. The scoring of person-based tests on the other hand can go in either direction. Thus someone with a low score on an extraversion scale would have a high score if the scale was reversed and redefined as an introversion scale.

Objective and open-ended tests

The objective test item

A second distinction between item types is between the objective and the open-ended. The major type of psychometric item in use is the objective item, so called because its scoring is entirely objective. These items are usually either true/false, or multiple choice. The first of these occurs when the respondent merely has to say whether a particular statement, for example 'The capital of Brazil is Rio de Janeiro', is true or false. The multiple choice objective item gives a number of choices (for example 'The capital of Brazil is (a) Rio de Janeiro, (b) Brasilia, (c) São Paulo, (d) Bahia') and the respondent has to choose only one of the several possible answers. Items of this type are called objective because the author decides in advance exactly what defines the correct response, and thereafter responses are marked right or wrong against this standard. Thus as soon as the respondent has placed his or her tick on the response sheet, the rest of the process is automatic.

Comparing objective tests with essay tests

In educational settings, objective items of this type can be contrasted with the more traditional essay-type test, which is relatively open ended and therefore involves a certain amount of subjective judgement by the examiner in its marking. There are advantages and disadvantages in the use of both essay tests and objective tests and it can be instructive to compare them. It is often claimed that essay tests are able to measure originality, while objective tests are not. In fact this is probably an oversimplification. Originality itself, and creativity in particular, is in practice nearly always a matter of degree, particularly in education. Both the term originality and the term creativity turn out to be extremely difficult to pin down and operationalize in any application. Thus a 10-year-old who thought out Einstein's theory of relativity from first principles would certainly be being creative, but not original as Einstein got there first! It is because of distinctions of this type that it is in fact possible to construct objective test items that can measure creativity reasonably well, in spite of the seeming paradox. The claim for the superior ability of the essay test in measuring originality is also open to question. In practice, truly original answers are not particularly likely to achieve high marks, especially if they are written as an alternative to showing a straightforward knowledge of the taught syllabus.

Objective tests are claimed to have advantages over essay tests in their ability to ignore extraneous factors. It has been demonstrated in several studies that it is very difficult for the marker of an essay to ignore spelling, grammatical and punctuation mistakes in a text, even after being instructed to do so. This seems to apply to experienced and inexperienced markers alike. However, while objective-test enthusiasts often speak of the advantages of separating the qualities being measured, arguing that if spelling is of interest it should be tested separately, there are certain advantages in measuring the writing abilities of the respondent at the same time as the academic skills. In particular, if the respondent will eventually need to be able to write reports of any form there can be an advantage in testing this knowledge in an essay.

One clear advantage of an objective test is its reliability of scoring. There are three ways in which different markers may vary in how they award marks. They may differ in terms of the average level of marks given – some markers prefer to award high marks, either because they feel generous or because this can sometimes cover up a lack of rigour in marking, while others tend to prefer giving low marks. Markers may also differ in the variability of their marks, and taken together these factors can have a large effect. Thus marker A may give marks out of 100 with a mean of 70 and a standard deviation of 20, ranging between marks of 100 and 5, while marker B may give a mean of 40 and a standard deviation of 5, ranging between 35 and 52. However, both these forms of difference can be eliminated by standardization (see Chapter 5), where means and standard deviations of the two sets of marks are equated. A more serious problem is lack of inter-marker reliability. Essay marks are well known for their unreliability, and even when different markers are carefully instructed in the different points to look out for in a particular essay, the correlation between their sets of marks is rarely above 0.6. There is no way of adjusting for discrepancies of this type. Time of day and the order in which scripts are marked are also known to affect the marks. Objective tests on the other hand should, by definition, have an inter-rater reliability of 1.0.

Another advantage of the objective type of item is that, by requiring all respondents to attempt all questions within the whole test specification, it is possible to obtain information about which material the respondent does not know as well as what he or she does know. Essay-type tests necessarily allow the respondents to choose for themselves which aspects of the answer are important, so that there is often the possibility of avoiding the direct revelation of ignorance. Because the objective test covers the whole test specification and therefore presumably the whole curriculum, it is usually quite easy to identify the relative strengths and weaknesses of respondents from their answers. However, we can set against this the fact that it is impossible to guess the right answer in an essay test but that this can be relatively easy in an objective test.

Finally, the two forms of test differ in their relative construction and marking times. The proper construction of an objective test can be a long drawn-out process, with very careful consideration being necessary for defining the test blueprint, and the need for proper piloting. Essay questions on the other hand are relatively easy to set. When it comes to marking, these roles are reversed. Objective tests are very easy to mark, and in fact this process can now be done entirely mechanically, with optical scanners and computerized scoring. Essay marks, however, need individual human attention to be given to each script. The net effect of these differences is to favour essay tests where only a small number of candidates are involved. Here, the total amount of marking is small and the long time that would be required for constructing an objective test may not be justified. On the other hand where a test is given to a large number of respondents the particular strengths of the objective test are immediately obvious: it takes no longer to construct an objective test for 10,000 respondents than it does for 10, and while the marking of 10,000 essays would be a horrendous task, with an objective test this load can be taken over by a computer.

Open-ended tests in psychology

It is not only in education that open-ended psychometric items have been used. In psychology they have been suggested for use in creativity tests of the 'How many uses can you think of for a brick?' variety. Although an objective score can be defined in terms of the number of different responses, a subjective element creeps in whenever attempts are made to define 'different'. Thus 'To build a shop' and 'To build a church' should probably count as one response, but it is not really possible to define very precisely what counts as the same response. There is also a series of what are called projective tests in use in psychology, such as the Rorschach test, where the respondent has to report on what they see in an inkblot. Here again it is very difficult to be completely objective in the scoring.

Norm-referenced and criterion-referenced testing

Another important distinction has been made between items which are said to be norm-referenced and items said to be criterion-referenced. By far the major change that took place in psychometrics during the 1970s in the approach to constructing test items was due to issues surrounding this distinction. Until that time there had always been an emphasis on the need for psychometric test items to be selected in such a way that the test scores would have a normal distribution if administered to a large sample, and could be easily standardized. This achieved the aim of obtaining the maximum dis-crimination between individuals, and used the performance of the whole group of individuals as the standard against which each individual was judged. The response of a person on a test was then generally interpreted in terms of his or her relationship to the average. Although comparison against the norm can be useful, there are many situations where such comparisons are irrelevant, and where the performance of the respondent would be more appropriately measured against some outside criterion.

McClelland published a very influential paper that appeared in the *American Psychologist* in 1973. He argued that ability testing was completely ineffective as a tool for selection in employment settings. Following a review of the literature he surmised that neither ability tests nor grades in school predict occupational success, that tests were unfair to minorities, and that any relationships that had been found between ability and performance were spurious, resulting from social-class differences. He concluded that criterion-referenced 'competencies' would be better able to predict important behaviours than would 'more traditional' norm-referenced tests. This paper was particu-larly timely as it coincided with the anti-testing *Zeitgeist* of the early 1970s, and its influence is still present to this day. Indeed the emphasis on 'competencies' rather than ability is central to the model that underlies the NVQ assessment system. It also under-pins the popularity of work-sample tests in which candidates are asked to perform on a number of short pre-specified practical tasks that are felt to be typical of the job applied for. Such a test might be used, for example, in the recruitment of bank-tellers. However, the McClelland analysis was comprehensively debunked in a rejoinder by Barrett and Depinet in 1991. They carefully examined McClelland's literature review and data analyses, and concluded that none of McClelland's supportive arguments stood up to scientific test. They are particularly critical of his so-called alternative model of competencies, pointing out that the distinction he makes is largely semantics and that McClelland's tests are traditional tests, albeit rather inferior ones.

In the educational field, the work of Popham (1978) has been particularly important in the development of techniques for the construction of criterion-related items. Popham also argued that there had been too much emphasis on normative factors in testing. He believed that a normal distribution of test scores and the purported need for as large a spread of scores as possible to obtain maximum discrimination between individuals had been over-emphasized at the expense of fulfilling the purpose of the test. He pointed out that if, for example, we are interested in whether someone could ride a bicycle or not, then the performance of other people on their bicycles may well be irrelevant. Further, if we have a group of individuals, and wish to know whether they can ride bicycles, then we should be delighted if they all turn out to be able to do so, and not concerned that we do not have a wider spread of abilities. He suggested that there was no special need for the distribution of scores on a test to be normal. According to Popham, it is performance on the criterion that matters, even if all individuals obtain the same score.

When a test has been constructed with particular reference to performance on some objectively defined criterion it is said to be criterion-referenced, although the terms content-referenced, domain-referenced and objective-referenced are used by some authors. When the major characteristic by which the score of a respondent on a test is judged is comparison with the whole population of respondents, it is said to be norm-referenced. The issues raised by McClelland and by Popham led to a debate about the relative merits of norm-referenced and criterion-referenced testing. However, attempts to contrast norm- and criterion-referenced testing too strongly can be misleading, as the two approaches do have much in common. First, all items must be related to some criteria. Indeed, given that there is an intention that tests be valid, each item must relate to the purpose of the test itself. This purpose can only be judged in terms of criteria, and thus criterion referencing is a necessary aspect of validity for all tests, whether criterion- or norm-referenced. In fact, the situations in which it is possible to lay down strict single criteria for a task are extremely limited, and in practice the circumstances in which we are pleased if everyone gets 100 per cent on a test are unusual. This is not because people are less than delighted at success but rather that the only occasions in which this occurs seem to be those in which the information could probably be known with no testing at all. If we do go to the considerable task of constructing a classroom test we hope to gain some information from the results, and the conclusion from a 100 per cent success rate is more often that the test, and perhaps the curriculum, were probably too easy rather than delight in the success of teacher and pupils. Some information on any difficulty the pupils had in mastering the material, or on what the teacher found difficult to present, would probably be more useful. If all of the many applicants for a single job were tested and shown to be equally good, we would of necessity need to question our criterion. Of course, there are many instances where all we wish to know is whether a particular person can do a particular task or not. But this situation is not one that stands apart from traditional psychometrics; it is rather a special case within it.

Why is it that classical psychometrics has looked for normal distributions across a population in test scores, and has used the properties of this distribution to derive its statistics? This has not arisen because the normal distribution has some magical properties, which psychometricians have insisted human beings must meet. The normal distribution needs some demystification. It merely represents the distribution to be expected when large numbers of random factors can influence the score, and is indeed derived directly from probability theory. In any selection or evaluation processes error is always present to some extent, and if we wish to understand the performance of data in the presence of error, we must be able to quantify it. The estimation of error is made very much easier in situations where the data are normally distributed.

Minimum competency testing in education

The criterion testing movement has, however, had one particular, very important effect: it has led to a much-needed shift in emphasis from the properties of tests and towards the properties of items. By tackling the problem of defining criteria at the level of the individual item, the full complexity of item characteristics has been brought to light. One impetus for this process in both the UK and the USA has been a widespread concern for what has been perceived as a fall in school standards. Evidence to support these claims was given in the *Black Paper* in Britain, and in *A Nation at Risk* in the USA. The latter included the claim that, as a result of changed methods of schooling since the 1960s, 73 million Americans are functionally illiterate, that 13 per cent of all 17-year-olds in the USA are functionally illiterate, and that the College Board's Scholastic Aptitude Tests demonstrated a virtually unbroken decline from 1963 to 1980. Both of these publications led to widespread demands for some form of universal curriculum in the basic educational areas, largely in reading, writing and arithmetic, and to evaluate this universal curriculum there has been a demand for universal tests of these basic skills to monitor what is actually occurring in the schools.

A decline of basic standards, prima facie, seems to be a perfect situation in which to test the advantages of criterion referencing, for basic skills seem to be suitable for forming universally agreed criteria. If we take arithmetic as an example, we could say that every child must at a certain age at least be able to add up and multiply. This would be popular with many parents who feel it important for their children to know their times tables. But this on even superficial analysis turns out not to be simple at all. A child can be able to sing their times tables (rather like singing a French song) and not know about multiplication at all. Or they may be able to repeat that $6 \times 3 = 18$ but not know how to apply this; or they may know it for calculating purposes but not for enumerated objects and so on. These issues often turn on fine points of epistemology. The usual answer to this form of conceptual analysis is to make a call to popular consensus. It is argued that while many teachers and parents will have their own special views on what is important, they will generally be able in a series of meetings to produce a document that represents consensus. So long as such a consensus is available, then it should in principle be possible to devise appropriate tests. Once agreement has been reached on the appropriate curriculum for arithmetic and for the role of multiplication within it, then items to measure the achievement of these skills are possible.

Since the 1980s the use of sophisticated criterion-based techniques for assessing simple skills has increased, particularly in the USA, where Minimum Competency Tests have become mandatory in many states. These tests are designed to set minimum standards for schools and pupils in reading, writing, arithmetic and other learned skills. In a summary of survey findings in 31 states and 20 local districts, Berk (1986) summarizes the following common features of these programmes:

1   There is an emphasis on the acquisition of minimum skills or competence, usually academic skills (e.g. reading, math, writing) and/or life skills (e.g. following directions, filling out a job application, balancing a chequebook).
2   An explicit performance standard for pass–fail decisions is set, so that one can separate the competent from the incompetent.
3   The test results are used to make important decisions about individual students such as promotion to a higher grade (or retention at the same grade), awarding of a high-school diploma or a certificate of special recognition (or awarding a certificate of school attendance), or assignment to remedial classes.

However, the introduction of these testing programmes has not gone unchallenged, and many parents have taken the state education authorities to court on claims of unfair decisions based on test results. A series of cases has led to stringent attempts to demonstrate the reliability and validity of the tests used, and has also led to more openness in the definitions and establishment of criteria. Thus, for example, in the case of *Debra P.* v. *Turlington* (1981), the State of Florida carried out a large survey of instructional validity, and gathered a huge amount of evidence that the curriculum on which the tests were based was indeed taught in the classroom. This followed an earlier judgement that the state must demonstrate that the material on the test was actually taught in the classrooms to demonstrate content validity. A further development has been the widespread acceptance that there are no real objective standards available to define competencies, and that the selection of the most important skills for the purpose of testing is highly subjective. This has not, however, led to a rejection of testing but to the development of political procedures and public strategies to obtain the consensus of all interested parties such that the definition of the curriculum and requirements for minimum competency can have credibility and meaning. Berk argues that the trend towards minimum competency testing will probably intensify. Linn and Gronlund (1995) describe the techniques and provide guidance for the procedures necessary for the development of criterion-referenced tests.

Obtaining test scores by summing item scores

When a test is scored from its items it is usual to simply add up the number of correct responses. The main justification for this seems to be that it is normal practice, as there is no a priori reason why a test should be scored in this way. When we do this we are effectively assuming that all of the items are equally important in their contribution to the test. This being so, it would seem sensible to review the actual importance of each item, and to use a score that is weighted for 'importance'. For example, if item 1 is considered of importance 1, item 2 of importance 2 and item 3 of importance 4, we could weight item 1 by 0.5, item 2 by 1, and item 3 by 2, thereby achieving a test score which more accurately represented the actual contribution of the items. In practice, however, this is rarely done, probably for pragmatic reasons. A standard approach to scoring throughout psychometrics does have many practical advantages. In particular, it becomes easier to evaluate tests, to give instructions on scoring and to set standards.

Although a standard practice seems to have arisen in the manner in which item scores are combined to give a total test score, the interpretation of the relationship between item and total score has varied. From one point of view, items are seen as measuring-sticks of varying length. Imagine measuring the length of a table by holding sticks of different length against the table one after another. The length of the table will be given as the average length of the two sticks that were on either side of the actual table length, just shorter and just longer. Similarly, an individual's ability could be defined by the item which he or she just managed to pass and the item which he or she just failed. In practice, there would be some error in this approach, but we can see that the simple sum of items correct does give a fair estimate of test score. Another approach is to imagine a situation where all items have equivalent difficulty but where individuals with higher ability have a higher probability of getting each of these items right. Here again the simple summation of the number of correct responses gives an estimate of the individual's ability, which makes intuitive sense. Thus, whatever way we choose to think of the measuring process involved in the traditional item summation method, we achieve a match with the final score. It is this generality of the age-old technique that has given the traditional approaches to psychometrics so much staying power. Of course, all of these models assume that it makes sense to actually add the items, and, by implication, that the items are to some extent measuring the same thing or construct.

The correction for guessing in objective knowledge-based tests

One common concern with this traditional manner of looking at test scores has been that some respondents may artificially inflate their scores by guessing the answers. Thus, if we have a test composed of 100 statement-type items to which each of the respondents has to agree or disagree, a rogue who knew nothing could obtain a score of about 50 by answering at random while an honest person who knew nothing would get zero from being unable to answer any question. One way of reducing this effect is to use multiple choice items rather than true/false; however, even here there can be a guessing artefact. If there are five alternative responses within the multiple choice questions then the rogue still has a 20 per cent chance of getting the item right by guessing, giving a score of 20 on a 100-item test. A technique for tackling this problem is to apply a correction for guessing. There are several formulae for this in the literature but the following is most common:

$$C = (R - W) / (N - 1)$$

where C is the corrected score, R is the number of correct responses, W is the number of incorrect (wrong) responses, and N is the number of alternatives available. With true/false-style items the number of alternatives is two, so the formula reduces to 'number right' minus 'number wrong'. This formula has several interesting aspects. First, we can see that it is effective. The rogue who guessed all the items in the true/false test should on average get half right and half wrong, and the difference between these will be about zero, which seems appropriate. Second, we can fairly easily see the rationale for the formula: the 'number wrong' is effectively used as an estimate of the number of guesses, and when this number is estimated, the effect of the guessing can be eliminated. Thus, in a true/false test, if a respondent has 8 incorrect answers, then it is assumed he or she obtained these by guessing. As there was a 50 per cent chance of obtaining a wrong answer by guessing it is further assumed that the number of items guessed was 16, the expected number he or she would need to guess to obtain 8 wrong answers. The respondent has gained no advantage from the 8 wrong answers obtained by guessing, but has gained an extra 8 points for the 8 right answers, which are consequently deducted from his or her total score. A third aspect, however, leads to problems. What has effectively happened is that the respondent loses one scale point for each wrong item, that is, he or she is penalized for wrong answers. This information is often given in the test instructions when this type of correction is to be used, and there is no real penalization as the successful guesses effectively outweigh the unsuccessful ones. However, the formula assumes that a respondent either knows the answer to an item, or guesses. But in practice most guesses are inspired, and a person who guesses is more likely to be right than wrong. The formula therefore underestimates the amount of guessing and therefore undercompensates for it.

Let us now look at the effect of telling respondents that a guessing adjustment will be made. An honest person will take these instructions seriously and will avoid guessing, but the rogue who guesses, and who presumably makes some inspired guesses, will still achieve a higher score. The total effect of our formula, and our appeal to honesty, have thus had the net effect of giving an advantage to the rogue. Another difficulty with the use of guessing effects can be that they are viewed by respondents, particularly young children, as being unfair.

There is more to examinations than testing alone – they exist within a tradition that is an integral part of the social environment of personal advancement. Within this environment, successes or failures are often attributed to luck or fate. What may seem like error of measurement to a psychometrician, for example, where the answer to an item is known by a student because of some fluke, can be seen as a stroke of luck to a student. Thus, in a Latin unseen examination, if I know no Latin and yet appear to make a perfect translation from Latin to English because I already knew the passage in English and am able to identify it from the recognition of a name or two in the Latin text, then first I am very lucky but second my score on the test is psychometrically invalid. However, there is a general belief that people to some extent deserve their luck and have to put up with fate, and this can also be applied to the guessing situation. Thus, if a child guesses an item and gets the item right, this is not seen as an error that needs correction but a form of divine intervention. From such a perspective it seems churlish to remove it. This can be put another way. There are social conventions in the use of tests, and one of these is that the score on a test is the number of items a person has responded to correctly. This convention has a wide degree of acceptance, and it may be unwise to apply any form of transformation, which undermines this acceptance, however apparently psychometrically justified.

For these and other reasons corrections for guessing are to be avoided in testing as much as is possible. It is much more effective simply to instruct respondents that if they do not know the answer they should guess. This way all get an equal chance. The only disadvantage is that now effective scale points do not start at zero. However, this zero has no true meaning in any case. A scale that runs from 50 to 100 is just as useful and valid. Unfortunately, there are some forms of test, particularly timed tests, where this is not applicable. With a timed test it is not expected that everyone would be able to complete the test in the time allowed, and consequently most respondents will have no opportunity to make guesses of the later items. Thus with these tests it may be necessary to apply a guessing correction. However, it is also an argument against the use of timed tests where it is avoidable.

Summary

There are several types of test and test item commonly used in psychometrics. Knowledge-based tests and items can be distinguished from person-based tests and items. The former measure the extent of a person's knowledge, while the latter measure personality, clinical symptoms, mood or attitude. Norm-referenced items and tests are derived to see how a particular person's score compares with the population at large, while criterion-referenced items and tests attempt to relate the respondent's answers directly to some outside criterion, usually the ability to carry out a task. Finally, items can be either entirely objective, where the scoring criteria can be completely specified beforehand, or open-ended, as in essay tests or projective tests. For the latter it is impossible to eliminate the subjective element completely from the scoring process. All of these different types of item and test have their different uses, and which is to be preferred varies with the purpose to which the test is to be put.

Item analysis

In the stage of test construction following the construction of the test specification, we will be generating a large number of possible items. There is then the need to reduce these to a manageable number, and in doing so, to select the best. But how are we to make such a selection? The answer is provided by a procedure known as item analysis. Within the item analysis all the possible test items are subjected to a stringent series of evaluation procedures, individually and within the context of the whole test. This process takes place in two stages: first, a review by experts and second, a pilot study. In the first stage each item should be discussed with an expert, someone who knows and is familiar with the subject matter in question. The rationale for each item should be made explicit, and the stages of reasoning which the respondent may follow should be rehearsed. If the item is to be scored as right or wrong, then possible alternatives need to be explored, as it is occasionally the case that respondents may (correctly) be able to identify the distracters as correct under certain circumstances. The more care that is taken at this early stage the better, as once the test has been piloted we no longer have a completely free hand in making changes to the items, except by carrying out a re-pilot at further expense.

Item analysis statistics for knowledge-based tests

For the pilot study a sample of respondents should be obtained with similar relevant characteristics to those people for whom the test is intended. The test is administered to these respondents, and an item analysis is then carried out on their responses. Classical item analysis in knowledge-based tests has concentrated on two statistics, item facility and item discrimination.

Item facility

Item facility is obtained by calculating the ratio of the number of respondents who give the right response to the whole number of respondents. If all the respondents are right on an item, this statistic will be equal to 1; if nobody gets it right, the statistic will be 0. As the easier the item the higher the score, this statistic is generally called the item facility index (although, rather confusingly, the term 'difficulty value' is sometimes used).

The meaning of the facility index can be understood in two ways, a common-sense way and a statistical way. Looked at from a common-sense point of view we can ask, 'What would be the effect of leaving out an item of facility 0 from a test?' It can easily be seen that this would have no effect at all. As total test scores are calculated by adding up the number of items correct, an item that every respondent gets wrong will not have made any contribution to any of the total scores. Hence the total scores would have been the same had the item never existed, and it is therefore redundant. The same argument can be applied to an item with facility 1, although here there is the apparent effect that the existence of the item has caused all respondents' scores to be increased by 1. In fact, this increase is more imaginary than real. If it is found that a child obtains a score of 0 on a geography test, this does not mean that the child knows no geography at all, but rather that the test was at too high a level for him or her. In fact, all normative statistics – variances, standard deviations, standard scores, etc. – are not affected in any way when the same constant is added to all scores. In interval scale terms the addition of an item with facility value 1 to a test has no real effect.

Facility can be interpreted from a statistical viewpoint if it is viewed within the context of norm-referenced testing. One presupposition of norm referencing is that the purpose of the test is to spread out individuals' scores along a continuum, and it follows from this that the larger this spread the better. A larger spread is equivalent to a greater test variance, and thus one way in which items can be judged for suitability for inclusion in the test is by examining whether or not they make a contribution to this variance. The variance of a group of respondents' scores on a test is made up of two components, one related to item variance and another related to the correlations between the items. Thus an item which has large correlations with other items in the test and which itself has a large item variance will be making a large contribution to the total variance of the test. An item which is uncorrelated with other items and which has a small item variance will be making a relatively low contribution. All items will probably be making some contribution of this sort, but if in item analysis we select only those items which make the larger contributions, then the overall test variance will be large, and the test will be improved.

An item variance is simply the calculated variance of a set of item scores, all ones and zeros if the test item is scored as right or wrong. The item variance of an item with facility 0 is zero, as all the respondents have responded in the same way; and the same is true if the facility is 1. More usually some of the respondents will get the item right and some will get it wrong, and in this case the variance is obtained by letting the facility index equal p, and calculating it from the general formula for obtaining item variance:

$$\text{Variance of item} = p \times (1 - p).$$

Thus, if half the people get the answer wrong, the facility index is 0.5 and the variance of the item is $0.5 \times (1 - 0.5) = 0.5 \times 0.5 = 0.25$. In fact this is the largest possible value for the variance of an item; the value gets smaller as p gets either greater or less than 0.5, and reaches 0 at the limit where $p = 0$ or 1. Whether we use a statistical formula or our intuition we arrive at the conclusion that items which some get right and some get wrong are giving us more information than those items for which all respondents tend to respond in the same way. Maximum information from an item is obtained when the number right is equal to the number wrong.

When the facility value is known for each item, this information can be used to select items for the final version of the test. Before this is done, however, it is best to calculate the other item analysis statistics, so that each item can be judged in its entirety on a whole range of different criteria.

Item discrimination

The second item characteristic of classical item analysis is slightly more complicated, but it can again be looked at both from a common-sense and from a statistical point of view. Consider the case of an item which turns out to be such that those people who obtain a high score on the test as a whole tend to get the item wrong, while those who obtain a low score on the test as a whole tend to get the item right. Here it would be suspected that something was amiss – in all probability the wrong answer had been specified as being correct. In any event it is clear that the item is not behaving as the item writer intended, and therefore is no longer conforming to the original test specification. Such an item is said to have negative discrimination. A more common occurrence is for an item to have zero discrimination – that is, the people with low scores on the test as a whole are just as likely to get that item right as those with high scores. We would tend to say that such an item was idiosyncratic. Whatever it was measuring was unrelated to whatever the test as a whole was measuring. Viewed from the statistical perspective, such an item also fares badly. If it is uncorrelated with the total test score, then it is almost certainly relatively uncorrelated with most of the other items in the test, and therefore is making no contribution to the variance of the test.

There are various ways of calculating the discrimination of an item. If we have the data on a computer, the easiest way is simply to calculate the Pearson product-moment correlation coefficient of the item scores with the test scores. This will tell us the extent to which each item correlates with the overall scale. This can be interpreted as the extent to which the item is actually making a contribution to the scale. In the absence of a computer the discrimination can be estimated from the mean score on the test for those people who get the item right and the mean score for those who get the item wrong, and finding the difference between the two. While the figures yielded by this technique will not be absolute, depending on the number of items in the test, they will enable all of the items to be compared with one another in terms of their discriminability. If the difference is big and in the right direction the item is a good discriminator; if this difference is small, zero or negative, the item is a poor discriminator. There are many additional techniques for calculating discriminability, with different practitioners having their own special preferences.

Once the facility value and discrimination value are obtained for each item it is possible to begin to make a selection of good items and to eliminate the bad from the final version of the questionnaire. Items should be selected which have moderate facility, as this will ensure that the items chosen are ones which make a large contribution to the variation between the total scores and that room in the questionnaire is not wasted by the inclusion of relatively uninformative items. As an additional bonus it is a good idea to balance the number of easy items against the number of difficult items, so that the average score on the test is about midway between the highest and lowest possible scores. This balanced set is more likely to show a normal distribution in subsequent use of the questionnaire, which can be important, as most statistical tests assume that data are normally distributed. If the original test tended to be too easy (with most items having a facility greater than 0.5) or too difficult (with most items having a facility less than 0.5), this can be counteracted by selecting the same number of each, regardless of their original relative frequency. Similarly, all items with poor discrimination can be eliminated from the test by only choosing those items with higher discrimination values for the final version of the test. This exercise, however, owes as much to common sense and convention as it does to statistics, and in particular there is a need to bear in mind the original test specification. Clearly if an entire column or row were eliminated from the blueprint, the test would be changed and it would lose content validity. Thus it is important to ensure that the general pattern of item distribution from the blueprint is retained, even if this involves accepting some relatively poor items from some cells at the expense of good items from others. To demonstrate the danger here, imagine a test that repeated the same item twenty times where this item had facility of 0.5. On statistical criteria alone all the items in this test would seem ideal, with the right facility and almost perfect discrimination. It is only when this result is compared with the distribution in the blueprint that the error can be seen – all the items are within the same cell, and thus the new version of the test does not reflect the test blueprint – there is no content validity.

Item analysis for person-based tests

The procedure that has just been described for a knowledge-based multiple choice test is generalizable, with slight modification, to the construction of almost all forms of test.

Item facility

While the term 'facility' might seem only to apply to knowledge-based tests, where item responses are either right or wrong, the same approach can in fact be used for all forms of objective test. Thus, in a personality test for instance, if agreeing with a statement would give a person a higher score on the personality trait in question, the p value, the number who agree divided by the total number of respondents, gives an appropriate equivalent item analysis statistic. It is important to remember in these cases, however, that all items must be 'scored' in the same direction with respect to the trait. This is because, in personality tests, many of the items are reverse items. Thus in a schizotypal personality test the items 'I have no enemies' and 'Some people are out to get me' both measure paranoia, but in opposite directions. A high score on paranoia is thus represented by responding 'agree' to item 2, but 'disagree' to item 1. In practice it is often easiest when doing item analysis on these types of data to reverse all the 'reverse' items before the item analysis is carried out.

In a health questionnaire, for example, statements to which agreement indicates good health will be scored as 1 for 'agree' and 0 for 'disagree'. Statements for which agreement indicates bad health will be scored as 1 for 'disagree' and 0 for 'agree'. When the resultant scores are subjected to item analysis, the facility value will represent the extent to which endorsement of good health is positive or negative by the respondents in the pilot study, and again we would want to eliminate all items to which almost everyone agreed or everyone disagreed.

Within person-based tests there tend to be situations in which there are more than two response options, not just right and wrong, or agree and disagree. Here again 'facility' values can still be obtained, but these will be the mean value across respondents of the item scores. Thus, if the possible responses are 'strongly agree', 'agree', 'undecided', 'disagree' and 'strongly disagree', these may be scored as 0, 1, 2, 3 and 4 respectively. Here extreme facility values are represented by 0 and 4 rather than by 0 and 1. Such items can easily be reversed by subtracting the non-reversed score from 5, so that 0 becomes 5 (5 – 0), 1 becomes 4 (5 – 1), 2 becomes 3 (5 – 2) and so on. This situation should not, however, be confused with the four or five possible responses in multiple choice knowledge-based tests. Here one of the choices is right and the rest wrong, so that the item analysis still uses 0 and 1.

Item discrimination

The discrimination index for a person-based test would represent the extent to which the item was measuring the same concept as all of the other items in a particular scale of the questionnaire. It will therefore again be calculated from the Pearson product-moment correlation coefficient between the item score and the total score for each scale, and will represent the extent to which the item is in fact measuring the trait in question.

Item analysis in criterion-referenced testing

A claim that is often made in educational settings is that classical item analysis is designed for norm-referenced tests, and therefore does not apply to criterion-referenced settings (see Chapter 3). Although it is the case that the central idea behind the statistical rationale for classical item analysis is the paradigm for norm referencing, it does have relevance for criterion-referenced tests as well. Within criterion-referenced testing there remains the need to evaluate items to find out whether they are suitable for inclusion in the test. This means that all criterion-referenced tests need to be piloted, and the evaluation of criterion-referenced items still requires the examination of facility and discrimination as a first step. While a normal distribution of the eventual test scores is no longer necessary, it still remains useful for the items to be sufficiently challenging for the respondents, and therefore distributions are often found which, while not normal, are not extreme either. Berk (1984a) recommends that item analysis in criterion-referenced testing should be based on an evaluation of the difference between facility values obtained before and after a programme of instruction. If a large difference is obtained, this can be taken as evidence that the item in question is valid as a measure of the skill taught. If the difference is small or zero, then the item may be invalid. To calculate this pre-instruction/post-instruction difference, item facility both before and after the period of instruction needs to be found; however, the difference itself is a measure of item discrimination rather than item facility. Berk goes on to look at item homogeneity (his name for item discrimination calculated by the correlation between item scores and total test scores) as a possible statistic for use in criterion-related item analysis, and considers it is not of itself necessary in criterion-referenced testing. However, while it is true that it is not a priori necessary, it is usually the case that items in a test will be expected to relate to each other as part of our underlying conceptualization of what is being measured. If they fail to do so it may well cast doubt on whether we actually understand what we are doing. Berk places particular emphasis on the qualitative procedures of judgemental review of item objective congruence and content bias. These are both issues that benefit from increased emphasis, and apply to norm-referenced tests as well.

Psychological traits, true scores and internal test structure

The consideration of item analysis so far has been based on the assumption that in some sense there is a construct that the test is measuring. Item discrimination in particular seems to make the added assumption that this construct is unitary or unidimensional.

But suppose that there is no single underlying trait involved? What if, for example, in a geography test there is not one single underlying skill of achievement in geography, but that there are many independent skills such as map reading, memory, political understanding, and so on? This is a variety of the argument about the existence or otherwise of the true score within the theory of true scores previously considered in Chapter 2. It can further be argued that if the sub-components of a test are uncorrelated, then it makes no sense to add them up. It is only if we presume the existence of a true score on an underlying trait that it is possible to judge whether an item can 'contribute' to this trait. This latter point is a restatement of the rationale for eliminating items with zero discrimination, but it still leaves the question, 'To what extent are we justified in assuming a single trait to such an extent that items which fail to conform are eliminated?' It is at this point that differences appear in the item analysis process between the use of tests for selection and for assessment. If the eventual aim is selection then we are obliged in the end to reduce our data to a binary statement – pass or fail. Within this constraint we are therefore bound to select data which are summative. We must be able to combine any elements into a single decision, and it therefore makes sense to choose items that conform to this procedure, that is items that are correlated with the trait in question as estimated by the test score. Where the test is to be used for assessment, on the other hand, we may in fact be interested in various attainments or traits within the data. While these will be evaluated as a totality, there is no special need for them to be additive as a whole, but only for each item to correlate with the particular set of items that are measuring the same aspect. Our major interest in the item analysis is to eliminate items which tell us little, and, within our requirements, to obtain the simplest possible interpretative structure for the remainder, perhaps within a profile of several sub-tests. In fact there is far more information available from the pilot study data than the statistics of classical item analysis, and one way in which this can be utilized is through factor analysis.

Item analysis for more complex situations

The use of factor analysis

Factor analysis is a procedure, originally developed by Spearman in the early part of the twentieth century but since refined by statisticians, which enables us to investigate the underlying structure of a correlation matrix. A correlation matrix is generated whenever the relationship between more than two variables is investigated, and its contents increase rapidly with each additional variable. In a 5-item test, for example, there are $5 + 4 + 3 + 2 + 1 = 15$ correlations, as each item correlates with each other item. When there are 10 items in the test the number of correlations is $10 + 9 + \ldots$, etc., which equals 55 correlations. A correlation matrix of all correlations between items in a 100-item test is very large indeed. Spearman was originally interested in the various correlations between intelligence sub-tests (verbal, arithmetical, spatial and so on), and developed the technique of factor analysis to find his common factor of general intelligence.

Factor analysis can be particularly useful in item analysis. Where there is indeed one underlying construct being measured this should emerge as a first factor. It is then possible, in principle, to select items that correlate with this first factor, which provides an alternative to obtaining the discrimination index. In fact, factor analysis can be more useful than this. Where no simple first factor emerges it can also show possible alternatives, and should be able to tell us how many factors actually are needed to describe the data. Unfortunately the approach is often unable to give unequivocal results. Unlike techniques such as analysis of variance, there is still always a strong subjective element in its interpretation. Further, it has been abused by attempts to extract too much meaning from particular data sets, and can also be vulnerable to breaches of its own statistical assumptions. In spite of these drawbacks factor analysis is beginning to regain its former popularity. Log-linear models have clarified issues surrounding its assumptions, and in circumstances where it is used as a tool, rather than a technique for proving hypotheses, it is invaluable.

One example of its use is in the identification of response bias in the test, and in the selection of items which reduce this bias. A first factor will often be contaminated by acquiescence effects (the tendency of some people to always agree or disagree with everything), and a procedure called rotation can be carried out to find out what weightings (in this case functionally equivalent to item total correlations) would be obtained if this effect was eliminated. Other contaminating effects such as lying can be reduced by introducing 'lie' items into the pilot version of the test and rotating to a solution which eliminates these. Within tests designed for assessment it is often necessary to identify a number of sub-tests, and again factor analysis can indicate to us which types of sub-test should be used, and how these should be constructed. So long as factor analysis remains a tool, supplementary to but never overriding common sense, it continues to be one of the most useful statistical techniques available to test constructors. It is available within most statistical packages for computer, for example on the Statistical Package for the Social Sciences (SPSS) (Nie and SPSS 1983), indeed so much so that we can expect its use (and unfortunately abuse) to grow.

Latent trait models and item response theory

Another technique of item analysis that has recently become popular is based on latent trait theory (Birnbaum 1968), and is more generally known as Item Response Theory (IRT). This provides an alternative approach to item selection from that provided by the classical method. It is far more precise than the classical model and thus has the potential of utilizing this precision to generate more accurate and sensitive ways of selecting items. The IRT approach is based on the concept of an Item Characteristic Curve (ICC), which, for each item, relates the probability of getting the answer right to the respondent's ability.

An example of an item characteristic curve is given in Figure 4.1. It can be seen that the ICC takes the form of a normal ogive, that is, a cumulative normal distribution. There should be nothing surprising about this as the ogive is just another version of the normal distribution, and is therefore to be expected where the effects of random error are included in observed measurements, as in all models based on the theory of true scores. Each item has its own curve, and it will be expected to move in an upward direction from left to right, although the extent to which it does this is a property of the item. The starting point on the left-hand side of the ICC frame represents the probability

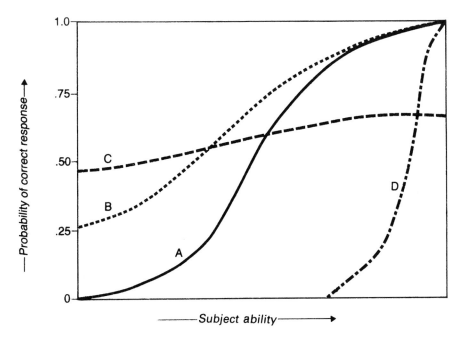

Figure 4.1 The Item Characteristic Curve (ICC)

Note: A: A normal ogive
B: ICC for multiple choice item with guessing effect
C: Item with poor discrimination
D: A difficult item

of a person with very low ability getting the item right. If the ability axis is started at a low enough level this might be expected to be always zero, but this only applies if there is no guessing effect. Thus if a person of very low ability guesses the answer to a multiple choice item with four choices he has a 25% chance of getting the right answer by chance and the curve for such an item would therefore be expected to begin at the 0.25 probability point of the y axis. If the ability axis is extended to a high enough level on the right-hand side of the ICC frame we might expect a probability of 100% that the response will be correct. However, even here this is not always the case. If the item is not in fact measuring what it is intended to measure, then even high ability respondents may not choose the item designated as correct, simply because from their point of view it is not so. There are other ways in which ICCs can vary. Some may be more or less flat while others may begin at a low level and follow this path for a while, and then show a sudden increase and flatten out again at the top of the frame. This latter shape would be expected where an item has very high discrimination. Correspondingly, the flat items are those with low discrimination. Another form of variation is defined by a bunching effect to either the left- or the right-hand side of the frame. If the item crosses the 0.5 probability level well to the left, then it means that the item is easy. Respondents of moderate ability have a high probability of getting it right. If on the other hand the curve crosses the 0.5 probability point well to the right, then the curve must be for a rather difficult item.

The aim of item response theory is to look at the fundamental algebraic characteristics of these ICC curves and to try and model them in such a way that a set of equations can be extracted that can predict the curve from some basic data. This modelling is the same as that involved in the more familiar process of obtaining the equation to a straight line. This is, you will remember, based on the equation $y = a + bx$, so that if a and b are known then so is the position of the straight line itself within the xy frame. When the ICC ogive is modelled in this way the situation unfortunately turns out to be somewhat more difficult, but easily achieved by computer, even a PC. There is a general consensus that four variables are required to define an ICC. These are one respondent variable (the respondent's ability) and three item variables (which are called the item parameters). The three item parameters map on to the traditional notions of classical item analysis, i.e. one of them describes item facility, another item discrimination, and a third the guessing effect. If the values of the three parameters are known, then it is possible to reconstruct the item characteristic curve.

In earlier days the model of the full process was too mathematically complex, time-consuming and expensive for the computers then available, and for these reasons attempts were made to simplify the full model by approximating the ICC with a lower number of parameters. The three basic models of item response which resulted have become known as the one-, two- and three-parameter models, depending on how many of the three variables needed to describe the item characteristic curve (item facility, item discrimination, and the probability of getting the answer right with zero ability i.e. the guessing effect) are considered. The main proponent of the one-parameter model has been Rasch (1980). The Rasch model became popular in the United Kingdom in the 1970s but has now fallen into disrepute as a result of its premature and rather ill-considered application on a wide scale. Rasch was able to show that if it is assumed that any guessing factor is held constant (as is the case if all items are of the same type), and if only items with equal discrimination are accepted, then some of the restrictions of classical psychometrics are loosened. In particular the model seemed to be able to generate, on computer, a single statistic for each item which enabled that item to be used in a wide variety of different situations, regardless of which other items were included in the test and of the particular respondents involved. This approach showed considerable promise in the calibration of item banks.

Item banks and the Rasch one-parameter model

An item bank, in its widest definition, is merely a collection of items accumulated over time and stored, perhaps in a filing cabinet. Such a bank would be built up wherever there was a repeated need for testing in the same area – for example, the many multiple choice items used in the British medical examinations, or in the Hong Kong school selection system. Item banks are used to store items that can then be used for new tests. As expertise in item construction developed, with item constructors generating thousands of items over the years, a particular style of item began to stand out, and be used again. When an item bank contains far more items than will be actually required on any one occasion, there is the temptation simply to withdraw a few items at random each time testing is required. However, even with large banks it is still important to check the items, to pilot them, and to establish their reliability and validity. Within the classical model it is the test, rather than the bank, which is the basic unit. Clearly there is some redundancy in this approach. After all, each time an item is used considerable information is gathered about its properties, and this tends to be ignored if the item happens to be chosen again. Attempts have been made to retain the information on the facility and discrimination of each item, and to find some algorithm that would enable this information to be used later. The main difficulty was that each group of items was different, and it was here that the Rasch model began to look attractive. Rasch was able to show that, as long as all the items in the bank had equal discrimination, it was possible to produce a single item statistic (parameter) which was independent of the respondents used to pilot it, and of the other items included in the pilot. For this reason he called his technique both 'respondent free' and 'item free'.

Let us consider how this would work. Assume we collect 1,000 items within a bank. To begin with none of the items would have a Rasch parameter. However, if we withdraw a set of 50 items at random from the bank and administer them to a group of respondents, each of these 50 will pick up some information towards its parameter. This will depend largely on its facility and will be tagged to the item within the bank. As further random groups of items are chosen then, so long as some of the pre-tagged items are included, the new items will also be tagged but with automatic adjustment made from any differences in the ability of the new group of respondents. This is possible as those items that were used in both the first and the second groups provide information on this difference. As more items are tested in this way we should eventually have an item bank in which all items are tagged. As items are drawn on again and again, their tags become more certain, since new information is gathered each time. To score a set of Rasch scaled items from the bank, the respondents' responses and the item tags are fed into a computer program based on the Rasch algorithm, and a score is generated with respect to the bank as a whole, not just to the particular items administered. The score should be the same (within the usual margins of error) whichever items are chosen, and it should not matter whether the original tags were generated on a group of respondents whose ability was different.

This technique, if accurate, would be exceptionally useful to educational testers, particularly those dealing with very large populations. In the 1970s it proved particularly attractive in the United Kingdom to a group set up by the Department of Education and Science to monitor academic standards, which became known as the Assessment of Performance Unit (APU) (Gipps 1986). It seemed that if an item bank of appropriate items for measuring, say, mathematics achievement at age 11, was available, then by taking random sets of items from the bank for different groups of 11-year-olds, it would be possible to compare schools, teaching methods and even, with the lapse of years between testing, the rise or fall of standards. However, this was not to be. It soon became apparent that there were several serious flaws within the model.

Problems with the Rasch model

First, it was noticed that a set of items identified as suitable for the finished test seemed to be more or less the same whether classical item analysis or the Rasch technique was used in selection. This generated a paradox. If the items in a classical test and in the Rasch scaled test were the same, how could it be that Rasch's claim that the test was item free and respondent free was justified in the one case, but not in the other? The success of the Rasch model depended on selecting a special set of items, those with equal discrimination, while this was not a requisite of classical item analysis, which merely required good discrimination. In particular, an item which correlated very highly with the total test score should be accepted by the classical method and not by the Rasch method. It was particularly important for the claim of 'respondent freeness' that the items should have the same discrimination as each other, as it was on this assumption that properties of the item for a group at one level of ability were extrapolated to a group at another level. If we find the two techniques accepting the same items, therefore, there is the implication that the test of equality of discrimination of the items is in fact not sufficiently powerful to eliminate items that are atypical in their discrimination. This indeed turns out to be the case. The test applied for parallelism within Rasch is a test of equivalent slope with acceptance based on proving the null hypothesis, a notoriously non-powerful statistic. If the test is not sufficiently powerful, then many of the items accepted into the bank will in fact not be parallel. If this is the case, then the claims of respondent freeness and item freeness fail. If the technique were to be used, public policy on schools would be based on mistaken evidence.

A further difficulty for the technique arose from its being treated as if considerations of content validity were not necessary. It may have been felt that so long as a wide variety of item topics was used, taking a consensus of all the views of various educational theorists and practitioners, parents, politicians, religious leaders, etc., into consideration, then the item banks on a subject should be fairly representative. However, it turns out that comparisons between different groups of respondents are particularly sensitive even to small changes in consensus, and not in a fashion that can be ignored. Imagine, for example, that we wish to assess national standards in arithmetic at age 11, and to monitor the change in these over a 10-year period. For the first testing session a consensus of views will be drawn up, and this presumably should relate to the agreed syllabus in arithmetic for children up to the age of 11 at that time. If we imagine 12 cells in the curriculum specification, then for good content validity the 12 cells in the test specification of the item bank will represent all of these. Items drawn at random from the bank will further be equally representative, showing no bias for or against particular cells of the blueprint. Random selections of items are administered to a random selection of 11-year-olds, and 10 years later a new random set of items is administered to a new random group of 11-year-olds. It is at this later date that the problems become apparent. Consensus views are particularly unreliable over time (consider popular views on teaching mathematics over the last 10, 20, 30, 40 and 50 years), and the consensus view on arithmetic would almost certainly be different 10 years on; and so, therefore, would be the arithmetic syllabus. New ideas will have been introduced, and old ideas dropped. The child taking the test at this later date will, however, be taking a test designed 10 years earlier. The child will be asked questions based on some topics that are no longer taught, and will not be asked any questions about the new inclusions in the syllabus. Thus the more the curriculum changes, for better or worse, the more disadvantaged the child in the second testing session. Testing of this sort must always, therefore, suggest a falling of standards, and more so when improvements are made in the curriculum.

The future of item response theory models

It was for reasons of this type that the use of Rasch scaling techniques was discredited in British education. The use of some of the sub-tests on the British Ability Scale (Elliot 1983) also seemed to be discredited as these similarly had depended on Rasch scaling techniques for their construction. However, the worldwide trend is towards an increase in the use of item response theory models, particularly in the USA under the lead of the Educational Testing Service in Princeton. Many psychometricians are coming increasingly to feel that reaction against the use of these models has been an over-reaction based on previous abuses, and on a premature exaggeration of their possibilities. One of the main drawbacks to these models in the 1970s was the complexity of the algorithms and the inability of the computers of the day to cope, making the procedure too expensive and time-consuming for most applications. This was one of the reasons why the relatively simple one-parameter model was preferred over the more complicated two- and three-parameter models. However, times have changed. Programs for carrying out analyses for the Rasch model are now available for personal computers (Bock and Mislevy 1982), and the three-parameter model no longer presents the challenge that it once did (Hambleton and Swaminathan 1985).

The technique has proved to be particularly useful within computerized testing, where the items to be presented can be chosen on the basis of responses already given, enabling dependable results from administration of 50 per cent fewer items (Haladyna and Roid, 1983). In these cases, the entire item bank is held within the computer, and as each item is presented to the respondent on screen and responded to, a calculation is made as to which of the remaining items in the bank should be given next in order to obtain the maximum information. The respondent's score is an ongoing calculation, based on the most likely ability for the subject based on the combined probability generated from responses to all items presented so far. As more items are presented this estimate becomes more accurate and testing is terminated once a pre-designed level of precision is achieved.

The use of item response theory models for comparing the scores of respondents who have taken tests at different levels of difficulty (related to Rasch's claim of respondent freeness) has additionally provided very useful. This might apply, for instance, when an easy and a more difficult version of the same examination system (such as within the GCSE in England and Wales) need to be combined to generate a common set of marks. The public need for this type of comparison, for example when an employer wishes to compare two applicants for a job with different types of qualification, cannot be ignored. As with many areas in selection, it is not so much a question of saying what ought to happen, as of ensuring that what does happen is done fairly and efficiently. It is important to point out that most of the criticisms of the Rasch model do not apply to the two- and three-parameter models. These make no assumptions about the equality of discriminability of the items, and the three-parameter model additionally takes into account the effects of guessing.

Summary

There are several models which have been put forward to help in the selection of good items for a test. The basic paradigm, however, remains that set by classical psychometrics: the identification of facility levels and discrimination power within norm-referenced knowledge-based tests. This technique is easily modified for use in person-based tests, or for application to criterion-referenced testing situations. Today, more sophisticated models have been proposed which take advantage of computer technology. These models are now beginning to come into their own. However, there is a need to use them with caution: they carry with them the same problems as those found with large statistical packages in statistics generally. It is important that those who use these more advanced techniques avoid being blinded by the computer, and retain a connection with the basic data. The impact of psychometrics on society is enormous, and those responsible must therefore know what they are doing. Responsibility cannot be delegated to a computer.

Characteristics of tests

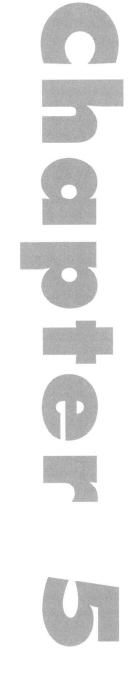

Within classical psychometrics, two of the most important aspects of a test are its reliability and its validity. Reliability has been defined as the extent to which the test is effectively measuring anything at all, and validity as the extent to which the test is measuring what it is purported to measure. If a test is unreliable it is impossible for it to be valid, so that it would be a logical impossibility to have a test which was valid but completely unreliable. On the other hand a test can be reliable but invalid.

Reliability

Reliability is often explained in terms of the measuring process in physics or engineering. When we measure, for example, the length of a table we assume that our measurements are reasonably reliable. We could check this out by taking several length measurements and comparing them. Even if we aim to be particularly precise it is unlikely that we will get exactly the same length each time. On one occasion the length of the table may be 1.989 metres, and on another 1.985 metres. But in most circumstances we would still be reasonably happy if the errors were only this small. In the social sciences on the other hand, unreliability of our measures can be a major problem. We may find that, for example, a pupil gets a score of 73 on a geography test on one occasion, and a score of 68 two weeks later on the same test, and we would probably feel that these figures were as close as we could reasonably expect in a classroom test. However, if the test in question was at university entrance, and the scoring system gave B for 70 and above, and C for below 70, and if the pupil was a university applicant who required B grades, we would certainly have cause for concern. It is because apparently reasonable levels of reliability for a test can have such devastating effects that we need first to make tests that are as reliable as possible, and second to take account of any unreliability in interpreting test results. All published tests are required to report details of reliability and of how it was calculated, and whenever a test is constructed and used, information on reliability must be included.

Test–retest reliability

There are several techniques for estimating the reliability of a test. The most straightforward is called test–retest reliability, and involves administering the test twice to the same group of respondents, with an interval between the two administrations of, say, one week. This would yield two measures for each person, the score on the first occasion and the score on the second occasion. A Pearson product-moment correlation coefficient calculated on these data would give us a reliability coefficient directly. If the correlation were 1, there would be perfect reliability, indicating that the respondents obtain exactly the same score on both occasions. This never happens (except perhaps by fluke) in psychological or educational settings. If the correlation between the two occasions is 0, then the test has no reliability at all: whatever score was obtained on the first occasion bears no relationship whatever to the score on the second occasion, and by implication, if the respondents were tested again, they would come up with another completely different set of scores. In these circumstances the scores are quite meaningless. If the correlation between the two occasions is negative, this implies that the higher the respondent's score the first time, the lower the second time (and vice versa). This never occurs except by accident, and if it does a reliability of 0 is assumed. Thus all tests can be expected to have a test–retest reliability between 0 and 1, but the higher the better. One advantage of using the correlation coefficient to calculate test–retest reliability is that it takes account of any differences in mean score between the first and second occasion. Thus if every respondent's score had increased by 5 points on the second occasion but was otherwise unchanged, the reliability would still be 1. It is only changes in the relative ordering or in the number of points between the scores which can affect the result.

Parallel-forms reliability

Although the test–retest method is the most straightforward, there are many circumstances in which it is inappropriate. This is particularly true in knowledge-based tests that involve some calculation in order to arrive at the answer. For these tests it is very likely that skills learned on the first administration will transfer to the second, so that tasks on the two occasions are not really equivalent. Differences in motivation and memory may also affect the results. A respondent's approach to a test is often completely different on a second administration (e.g. they might be bored, or less anxious). For these reasons an alternative technique for estimating reliability is the parallel-forms method. Here we have not one version of the test but two versions linked in a systematic manner. For each cell in the test specification two alternative sets of items will have been generated, which are intended to measure the same construct but which are different (e.g. 2 + 7 in the first version of an arithmetic test, and 3 + 6 in the second). Two tests constructed in this way are said to be parallel. To obtain the parallel-forms reliability, each person is given both versions of the test to complete, and we obtain the reliability by calculating the Pearson product-moment correlation coefficient between the scores for the two forms. Many consider the parallel forms to be the best form of reliability; however, there are pragmatic reasons why it is rarely used. When a test is constructed our main aim is to obtain the best possible items, and if we wish to develop parallel forms not only is there twice the amount of work, but there is also the possibility of obtaining a better test by taking the better items from each and combining them into a 'super test'. This is generally a more desirable outcome, and frequently where parallel forms have been generated in the initial life of a test, they have later been combined in this way, as for example in the later versions of the Stanford–Binet.

Split-half reliability

A more widely used approximation to parallel-forms reliability is split-half reliability. For this technique a test is split in two to make two half-size versions of the test. If this is done in random fashion, a sort of pseudo-parallel forms is obtained where, although there are not necessarily parallel items within each cell of the test specification, there is no systematic bias in the way in which items from the two forms are distributed with respect to the specification. It is a common convention to take the two forms from the odd and even items of the questionnaire respectively, so long as this does indeed give a random spread with respect to the actual content of the items. For each individual two scores are obtained, one for each half of the test, and these are correlated with each other, again using the Pearson product-moment correlation coefficient. The resultant correlation itself is not a reliability. It is, if anything, the reliability of half of the test. This is of no immediate use as it is the whole test with which we have to deal. However, we can obtain the reliability of the whole test by applying the Spearman–Brown formula to this correlation:

$$r_{\text{test}} = 2 \times r_{\text{half}} / (1 + r_{\text{half}}),$$

where r_{test} is the reliability of the test, and r_{half} is the correlation obtained between the two halves of the test. This tells us that the reliability is equal to twice the correlation between the two halves, divided by one plus this correlation. Thus if the two halves correlate 0.6 with each other, then:

$$\text{reliability} = (2 \times 0.6) / (1 + 0.6) = 1.2 / 1.6 = 0.75.$$

It is worth noting that the reliability is always larger than the correlation between the two halves. This illustrates the general rule that the longer the test the more reliable it is. This makes sense as the more questions we ask the more information we obtain, and it is for this reason that we will generally want our tests to be as long as possible, so long as there is time for administration and the respondents are co-operative. Of course, this only applies so long as the items are actually discriminating, that is, they are making a real contribution to the overall score (see Chapter 4 on item analysis).

Inter-rater reliability

All of these types of reliability relate in particular to objective tests, i.e. tests in which the scoring is completely objective. However, there are additional forms of reliability which are applicable where the degree of objectivity is reduced. For example, different markers of the same essay tend to give different marks, or different interviewers may make different ratings of the same interviewee within a structured interview. Reliability here can be found by correlating the two sets of marks or the two sets of ratings respectively, using the Pearson product-moment correlation coefficient between the scores of the two raters. These forms of reliability are known as inter-marker or inter-rater reliability.

Interpreting the reliability coefficient

From the theory of true scores a very simple formula for relating error to reliability can be derived:

$$\text{error variance} = \text{variance of test} \times (1 - r_{\text{test}}),$$

where r_{test} is the reliability of the test. The standard error of measurement is found as the square root of the error variance. Thus the error of measurement is equal to the standard deviation of the test, multiplied by the square root of one minus the reliability. If a test has a known reliability of 0.9, and a standard deviation of 15, then:

$$\text{error of measurement} = 15 \times \text{the square root of } (1 - 0.9)$$
$$= 15 \times \text{the square root of } 0.1,$$
$$= 15 \times 0.3 = 5 \text{ (approximately)}.$$

This is the standard deviation of errors associated with individual scores on the test. From this we have some idea of the distribution of error about the observed score. This enables us to calculate a confidence interval for the observation. A confidence interval sets an upper and lower limit within which we can have a certain amount of confidence that the true score actually lies. Confidence intervals vary depending on the amount of certainty that is required. It may be important that certainty is high: we may want to risk being wrong only 1 time in 1,000, and this would be called the 99.9% confidence interval. Or we may want just a rough and ready estimate such that the risk of being wrong was as high as 1 in 10 (the 90% confidence interval). The usual convention is to use the 95% confidence interval for most purposes, so that there is a 1 in 20 chance of being wrong. Although it is good to be accurate, the more accuracy that is required, the wider the confidence interval, and thus the greater the general uncertainty. For example, if a person had an observed score of 43 on a general knowledge test and we knew the standard error of measurement, we could obtain upper and lower limits for particular levels of confidence. The 95% level may give us the information that we can be 95% certain that the person's true score lies between 40 and 46, for example. If we need to be 99.9% certain we may have to say only that the true score lies between 35 and 50, perhaps too wide for useful application.

If it is assumed that the error of measurement is normally distributed, then the statistical tables for the normal curve (z tables), which relate each z score to a particular probability, can be used to find the confidence interval. The appropriate z value for the 95% probability is 1.96 (a statistic worth remembering as it occurs in many different circumstances). The 95% limits themselves are thus obtained by multiplying the error of measurement by 1.96.

With an error of measurement of 5 (obtained from a reliability of 0.9 and a standard deviation of 15), an observed score of 90, and a 95% confidence interval, we can say that the true score lies between 90 plus or minus 5×1.96, that is, between about 80 and about 100. We could tell from this that another person with a score of 85 would not be significantly different, given the known amount of error that we have obtained from our knowledge of the test's reliability. This might be important if we needed to decide between these two people. In fact this example could easily have been obtained from scores on the Wechsler Intelligence Scale for Children (WISC), which does indeed have a reliability of about 0.9 and a standard deviation of 15. We can see from this why so many psychologists are unhappy about using ability tests on their own when making decisions about individual children.

One of the major uses of the reliability coefficient is in the evaluation of a test. Generally different types of test have different acceptable reliabilities. Thus individual

IQ tests generally report reliabilities in excess of 0.9 and tend to average about 0.92. With personality tests reliabilities of greater than 0.7 are expected. Essay marking tends to produce notoriously low inter-rater reliabilities of about 0.6, even when complex agreed marking schemes are worked out in advance between the examiners. Creativity tests (e.g. 'How many uses can you think of for a brick?') are almost impossible to construct with reliability higher than 0.5. The lowest reliabilities are found in projective tests, such as the Rorschach inkblot test, where reliabilities of 0.2 and lower are not unusual. A test with such a low reliability is useless for psychometric purposes, but can be of use in clinical settings to provide a diagnostic framework.

When interpreting reliability coefficients, the spread of the scores of the sample under scrutiny must also be taken into account. This can only really be done by ensuring that the reliability has been calculated on a similar group to the one to which it is being applied. If a sample selected on some narrow criterion is used, such as university students, then reliability coefficients will be much smaller than for a whole population. This phenomenon is called the restriction of range effect. Generally the larger the standard deviation of the group the higher the expected reliability. Thus, if the reliability from the whole population were to be combined with the standard deviation of the narrower group, the calculated standard error of measurement would be a considerable underestimate and might lead to serious mistakes.

Forms of reliability and forms of error

Decisions about the form of reliability to be used in comparing tests cannot be made without a consideration of the nature of the error that is involved in each. There are two ways in which the reliability coefficient relates to error. First, there is a straightforward mathematical relationship between the coefficient itself and forms of error. Lord and Novick (1968) make an important distinction between error of measurement, error of estimation and error of prediction, and give different formulae for the calculation of each from the same reliability coefficient. The example above on the interpretation of IQ scores gives only the estimated error of measurement. Second, different circumstances will generate different reliability values for the same test depending on differences in the source of the error. If a test is administered with a one-week interval between two administrations, then the error is composed of random elements which may have increased or decreased the respondent's scores on the two occasions – lack of sleep, hunger, illness, revising the right or the wrong material, and so on. If the test is given in split-half mode, but at one sitting, the form of error is different. It is now error due to the different manner in which the two forms are sampled from the same domain. With inter-rater reliability the error is due to the different strategies and values of the raters, and is independent of the actual performance of the respondents. Which of these errors is appropriate and which reliability is correct? Thorndike (1947) defined five different forms of variance that would be found operating within a reliability coefficient:

1   Lasting and general: e.g. general test-taking ability.
2   Lasting but specific: e.g. knowledge or ignorance regarding a particular item that appears in one test form.

3   Temporary but general: e.g. buoyancy or fatigue reflected in performance on every test given at a particular time.
4   Temporary and specific: e.g. a mental set that affects success in dealing with a particular set of items.
5   Other, particularly chance success in 'guessing'.

All these sources of error can be operating at the same time, so it is to be expected that reliability coefficients will differ in different circumstances and on different groupings and samplings of respondents. Can these influences be disentangled? The answer is a qualified yes, the qualification being that to do so in practice can be a complicated matter.

Generalizability theory

Cronbach and his colleagues have carried out a thorough investigation of the analysis of different forms of error. Their approach has become known as generalizability theory (Cronbach *et al.* 1972). In this they use an analysis of variance model to relate the various reliability and validity test evaluation statistics directly to test application. Within multivariate analysis of variance and covariance models in particular, conceptions of the nature of error have changed considerably since the early days of the theory of true scores. This framework makes an immediate and clear distinction between, for example, the error term as estimated between a group of respondents and the within-subject error term which is obtained when repeated measures are taken on a single respondent. Empirical evidence as well as theory have now shown that these sources of error often show large quantitative differences. Similarly, error terms between groups may be different from those between respondents, and further estimated differences are found depending on whether the variation between groups is fixed or random. Cronbach and his colleagues were able to show that the classical techniques within the design, construction and application of psychometric tests could be treated as multi-level models within analysis of variance. As the mathematics of this latter area is very well developed, they were thus able to make its increased conceptual clarity and practical precision available to psychometrics. They further argue that the distinction between reliability and validity is a false one, being a matter of degree which can only have meaning in terms of how the tester intends to generalize from the test results. They further argue that it is only through this generalization that test scores can have any meaning whatsoever.

One particular innovation of the generalizability model is its full statistical underpinning of the functionalist approach. The test construction process is integrated within the same 'experimental' setting as the test application. Thus as well as identifying particular sources of error within the construction phase, the need for each such source is extrapolated backwards from the use to which the test is to be put. Cronbach identifies four different kinds of decision that may need to be made within this applied setting, and points out that the appropriate reliability and error term is different for each:

1   An absolute decision about whether an individual's score exceeds a predetermined cut-off point. This is assumed to be a generally criterion-referenced comparison.

2   Comparison between two courses of action for an individual. This type of decision is particularly common in guidance where the person may choose one curriculum rather than another.
3   Comparisons between persons or groups.
4   Conclusions about the relationship between a pair of variables, e.g. between creativity and the schizotypal personality.

The general advice given in Cronbach's book is exceptionally sound, but unfortunately the practical application of the approach has not been widespread. This is probably due to its complexity. To devise such models is difficult, time-consuming and expensive. Further, its extreme functionalism, which argues against the use of the same test in changed circumstances without serious revalidation, means that the full implementation of the generalizability approach is out of the reach of most practitioners who work in situations where resources are limited.

Cautions in the use of reliability coefficients

The interpretation of a reliability coefficient is no simple matter. Although most researchers would not wish to become involved in the complexity of the models generated by Cronbach's generalizability theory, a high degree of awareness of possible sources of bias is necessary. All published tests are required to report data on reliability, and this needs to be properly interpreted in terms of the samples used and the types of reliability coefficients obtained, as well as in terms of the intended use of the test. It would be inappropriate, for example, in the use of a test for an experiment with university students, to quote the reliability coefficient for the test on the population as a whole. The most important element in the use of reliability coefficients is human judgement.

Validity

The validity of a test also has many different forms. There are several categorization systems used, but the major groupings include face validity, content validity, predictive validity, concurrent validity and construct validity.

Face validity

Face validity concerns the acceptability of the test items, to both test user and respondent, for the operation being carried out. This should never be treated as trivial. If respondents fail to take the test seriously the results may be meaningless. For example, some adults with cognitive impairment may be expected to have the same overall score on intelligence tests as 8-year-old children, but they may well object to the use of childish material in a test designed for them. Similarly, applicants for a job may be disenchanted if presented with a test designed primarily for the detection of psychiatric symptomology. Evaluation of the suitability of a test must include consideration of the style and appropriateness of the items for the purpose in hand, in addition to any more formal test characteristics.

Content validity

The content validity of a test examines the extent to which the test specification under which the test was constructed reflects the particular purpose for which the test is being developed. In an educational setting, content validation will generally involve a comparison between the curriculum design and the test design. In the use of a selective test for employment, the content validity will be the extent to which the job specification matches the test specification. Content validity is thus the principle form of validity for the functional approach to psychometrics, and has sometimes been described as criterion-related or domain-referenced validity in circumstances where the test designer is using the criterion-referenced framework for skills learning and curriculum evaluation. Content validity is fundamental to psychometrics and is the main basis by which any test construction programme is judged. Content validity has to be judged qualitatively more often than quantitatively, as the form of any deviation from validity is usually more important than the degree. Essentially, if the test specification is not reflecting the task specification, it must be reflecting something else, and all else is a potential source of bias.

Predictive validity

Predictive validity is the major form of statistical validity, and is used wherever tests are used to make predictions. For example, the use of a test for job selection or for a programme of instruction where the test is intended to predict eventual success in these areas. Predictive validity is represented as a correlation between the test score itself, and a score of the degree of success in the selected field, usually called 'success on the criterion'. Thus, for example, in the use in England and Wales of GCE A Level grades to select candidates for university, it might reasonably be assumed that the number and grade of A Levels is related to degree of success at university. We could generate scores on the test by combining A Level grades in some way (e.g. for each person, grade A = 6, grade B = 5, grade C = 4, etc., the scores for all examinations being summed). Similarly a score of success at university could be generated by assigning 0 to a fail, 1 to a pass degree, 2 to a third-class degree, etc., with a first-class degree having the highest score. A simple Pearson product-moment correlation coefficient between A Level scores and degree-class scores would give a measure of the predictive validity of the A Level selection system. If the correlation was high, say, over 0.5, we might feel justified in selecting in this way, but if it turned out to be zero we would certainly have misgivings. This would mean that students' success at university had nothing to do with A Level scores, so that many people with one E grade, for example, could have had as good a chance of getting a first-class degree as those with three A grades. The A Level selection procedure would then have no validity.

One common problem with predictive validity is that individuals who are not selected do not go on to produce a score on the criterion (people who do not go to university have no scorable degree class), so that the data are always incomplete. In these circumstances, the calculated predictive validity will nearly always be an under-estimate. It is normal practice to use the data available, and then justify extrapolation downward. Thus if individuals selected with three C grades do worse than individuals selected with three B grades, it would be extrapolated that those with three Ds would have fared even less well. However, there must always be some uncertainty here.

Concurrent validity

Concurrent validity is also statistical in conception and describes the correlation of a new test with existing tests that purport to measure the same construct. Thus a new intelligence test ought to correlate with existing intelligence tests. This is a rather weak criterion on its own as the old and new tests may well both correlate and yet neither be measuring intelligence. Indeed this has been one of the major criticisms directed against validation procedures for intelligence tests, particularly when the conceptualization of intelligence in the later test is derivative of the conceptualization in the first, thus producing a 'bootstrap' effect. However, concurrent validity although never sufficient on its own is important. If old and new tests of the same construct fail to correlate with each other then something must be seriously wrong.

Construct validity

Construct validity is the primary form of validation underlying the trait-related approach to psychometrics. The entity which the test is measuring is normally not measurable directly, and we are really only able to evaluate its usefulness by looking at the relationship between the test and the various phenomena which the theory predicts. A good demonstration of construct validation is provided by Eysenck's validation of the Eysenck Personality Inventory, which measures extraversion/introversion and neuroticism. It was not possible for Eysenck to validate this scale by correlating respondents' scores on the extraversion scale with their 'actual' amount of extraversion. After all, if this were known there would be no need for the scale. However, he was able to suggest many ways in which extraverts might be expected to differ from introverts in their behaviour. On the basis of his theory that extraverts had a less aroused central nervous system he postulated that they should be less easy to condition, and this led to a series of experiments on individual differences in conditionability. It was shown that, for example, in an eye-blink conditioning experiment with a tone heard through headphones as the conditioned stimulus and a puff of air to the eye as the unconditioned, extraverts developed the conditioned eye-blink response to the tone on its own more slowly than did introverts. He suggested that extraverts should also be less tolerant of sensory deprivation, and that the balance between excitation and inhibition in the brain would be different between extraverts and introverts, which led to a series of experiments. He also suggested that the EEG would vary, with extraverts showing a less aroused EEG, and this again could be tested. And finally he was able to point to some simulations of extravert and introvert behaviour, for example the effect of alcohol that produces extraverted behaviour by inhibiting cortical arousal. The validation of the construct of extraversion consists of a whole matrix of interrelated experiments. From this Eysenck concluded that extraverts condition more slowly, are less tolerant to sensory deprivation, are less sensitive to inhibiting drugs and are generally different from introverts on a whole variety of other psychophysiological and psychophysical tests. He claimed that his theory that extraversion had a biological basis was supported as it was able to provide a unified explanation for all these findings. Construct validation is never complete, but is cumulative over the number of studies available, and has many similarities to Popper's (1972) idea of verification in science. It is thus a reflection of a particular view of the scientific process, and is integrated within the positivist and hypothetico-deductive view of science.

The multitrait–multimethod approach

Campbell and Fiske (1959) pointed out that construct validity demanded not only that a test should correlate highly with some other measures it resembles, but also that it should not correlate with measures from which it should differ. Thus, a test of mathematics reasoning that had a correlation of 0.6 with numerical reasoning, but of 0.7 with reading comprehension would be of dubious validity, although we could have been misled by the first correlation alone. He designated the first type of correlation 'convergent validity', and the second type 'discriminant validity'. Campbell and Fiske go on to describe a technique, the multitrait–multimethod approach, which, they argue, can demonstrate true construct validity. It involves the assessment of three or more traits using three or more different methods. Thus, in a personality-testing situation, extraversion, emotionality and conscientiousness could be assessed using self-report, projective techniques and peer ratings, producing a 9×9 correlation matrix. High predicted correlations between the same personality trait measured by whatever method should be accompanied by low correlations elsewhere.

Standardization

Once a test has been constructed it needs to be standardized. Standardization has two elements: first the need to obtain information on the test scores of the general population by taking appropriate samples, and second the need to obtain a set of principles by which raw data from the test can be transformed to give a set of data which has a normal distribution. This latter becomes particularly important if the scores need to be subjected to statistical analysis, as is usually the case. All parametric statistical tests, factor analysis, and most of the advanced techniques available make the initial assumption that data are normally distributed.

If the only information that is available following the administration of a test is one respondent's score, then it will tell us nothing about that person. For example, suppose we are told that Bernard scores 23 on an extraversion test. Is this high, or low?

Before we can make an interpretation we need to know what a score of 23 represents. This may be from norm-referenced information, given by knowledge of the general population mean and standard deviation for extraversion scores. With this extra information we can say how extraverted Bernard is in comparison with everyone else. Or it may be criterion-related – for example, there may be information from the test handbook to tell us that people with extraversion scores of 22 and higher like going out all the time, or have difficulty settling down to a quiet read.

Comparison or criterion information of this type must be made available when a test is published. Norm-referencing procedures are much more common than criterion-referencing, largely because they are easier to carry out, and because for many tests it is extremely difficult to give clear and specific criteria. In order to obtain comparison data for a norm-referenced test a population must be specified that is directly comparable to the population of intended use. Thus, a test of potential to do well in business, used to select persons for admission to business school, must be standardized on business school applicants. If the potential sample is large, then the information can be obtained by a process of random or stratified random sampling. For information on the whole population of adults in a country, a random sample might be taken from the electoral register. Comparison data may be presented in raw form, as for example in the Eysenck Personality Inventory, where we are able to read in the handbook that the average extraversion score is about 12, with a standard deviation of about 4. We can tell from this that a person with an extraversion score of 22 is two and a half standard deviations above the mean. As extraversion scores on the population are known to be approximately normally distributed, we can find from tables of the normal curve (z tables), that less than 1 per cent of the population has a score this high. The normal population data may sometimes be given separately for different groups, and this often enables a more precise interpretation. The extraversion norms, for example, are given for men and women separately, for different ages, and for different occupational groups. This information is important where comparisons are to be made within a group, rather than with the population as a whole. A situation where this might be useful could be in assessing mathematics ability among applicants for university places on mathematics courses. Here we would be interested in how applicants compared with each other, and the fact that they all performed in the top 50 per cent of ability in mathematics in the population at large would be relatively uninformative.

Standardization to z scores

The interpretation of scores in terms of percentages within the general population is easy to understand, and it maps very well on to the pattern of the normal curve. Thus, from z tables, which are available in nearly all statistical textbooks, we know that a person who is above average is in the top 50 per cent, a person who is one standard deviation above the mean is in the top 16 per cent, a person who is lower than 2 standard deviations below the mean is in the bottom 2 per cent, and so on. For this reason, the comparison of an individual's score with the norm is often given in terms of the number of standard deviations with which it differs from the mean. In the earlier example of Bernard with an extraversion score of 22, it was clear that with a mean of 12 and a standard deviation of 4, his score is 2.5 standard deviations above the mean. This score of 2.5 is referred to as the standard score, and is given more formally by the formula $z = (\text{score} - \text{mean score}) / (\text{standard deviation})$; in this case $z = (22 - 12) / 4 = 2.5$. The process of determining the population data and using this to provide a method for transforming raw scores to standard scores is called test standardization. This is normally carried out either by providing data on the mean and standard deviation of the test together with a formula, or by providing a transformation table or graph.

Standardization to T scores

Transformed z scores on a test normally range between $- 3.0$ and $+ 3.0$, and have a mean of zero. This is not a very convenient way to present an individual's score; schoolchildren in particular might tend to object if told that their score on a test was -1.3! There is, therefore, a set of conventions that are applied to these standard scores to make them more presentable. The most common of these are the T score, the stanine and the 'IQ' formats. For T scores we multiply the z score by 10 and add 50. Thus a standard score of -1.3 becomes $(-1.3 \times 10) + 50 = 37$; much more respectable. The advantage of this format is that it turns the scores into something that resembles the traditional classroom mark, which normally has a mean of about 50 with most scores lying between 20 and 80. Unlike most classroom marks, however, it is very informative. If told that someone had scored 70 on a classroom mathematics test, we would not have any information unless we knew the marking scheme – it might be that a particular teacher always gives high marks. However, if the scores had been transformed to T scores, then because we already know that T scores have a mean of 50 and a standard deviation of 10, it is immediately clear that a score of 70 is two standard deviations above the mean. This is equivalent to a z score of 2, and by working backwards through the z tables we can easily find that such a score is in the top 2 per cent of scores on that test.

Standardization to stanine scores

The stanine technique transforms the standard scores to a scale running from 1 to 9, with a mean of 5 and a standard deviation of 2. This standardization is widely used, as a set of scores from 1 to 9 (rather like marking out of 10) has much intuitive appeal. There are no negatives and no decimals, which are, by convention, rounded off either downwards or to the nearest whole number. The advantage of the stanine over the T score is that it is sufficiently imprecise not to be misleading. Most tests have only a limited precision. A T score of 43, for example, would be equivalent to a stanine score of 4, as would a T score of 41. The difference between 41 and 43 is much too small to be of any real significance but their bold statement within the T format does give a misleading impression of precision.

Standardization to IQ format scores

The 'IQ' format originated when the definition of Stanford–Binet IQ scores was changed from one based on the ratio of mental age to chronological age (the original meaning of 'Intelligence Quotient'), to the now widely used standardization approach. The IQ transformation is based on a mean of 100 and a standard deviation of 15; thus a standard score of -1.3 becomes an IQ score of $(-1.3 \times 15) + 100 = 80.5$ (or 80 when rounded off). An IQ score of 130 (that is $100 + (2 \times 15)$) is two standard deviations above the mean and, as two standard deviations means a z of 2, we can tell from z tables that such a score or higher would be obtained by less than 2 per cent of the population. Some IQ tests use different standard deviations – for example, Cattell uses 16 scale points rather than 15. IQ-style scores are best avoided by psychometricians today. They have become something of a cult, and their extrapolations bear very little relation to normal scientific processes. IQs of 160, for example, often appear as news items in the media, yet 160 would be 4 standard deviations above the mean. As such a high score would occur in the general population only 3 times in 100,000, we would need to have had a normal group of about 1 million individuals to obtain the relevant comparisons. Usually tests are standardized on less than 1,000. Even the WISC, with its standardization group of 20,000, had relatively few respondents at each comparison age. The behaviour of individuals at probability levels of less than 3 in 100,000 is not something that can meaningfully be summarized in an IQ score. The whole conception of a unitary trait of intelligence breaks down at these extremes.

Normalization

All of these standardization techniques (the z score, the T score, the stanine and the 'IQ' format) make the assumption that scores for the general population already have a normal distribution. There are often good reasons why a normal distribution might be expected, and it is common practice to carry out item analysis in such a way that only items that contribute to normality are selected. This can be done by selecting only the appropriate items within the item analysis (see Chapter 4). However, there are occasions when sets of test scores have different distributions (perhaps with positive or negative skew, or having more than one mode) and here alternative techniques for standardization are required. Statistical techniques are available to test for the existence or otherwise of normality. Perhaps the most straightforward of these is to split the data up into equal interval categories (say, about five) and to compare (using the chi-square test of goodness of fit) the actual number of scores in each with the number which would be expected if the data had a normal distribution. Tests of normality are not particularly powerful, however, so that if there is doubt it is best to attempt to normalize the data in one of the following ways.

Algebraic normalization

The easiest technique for normalization is algebraic transformation. If the distribution of scores is positively skewed, for example, with most of the scores being at the lower end of the scale, then taking the square root of each score will produce a more normal distribution. The square rooting process has a stronger effect on the large, more extreme, figures. With extreme positive skew, log transformations can alternatively be used. All of these techniques are particularly important if the data are to be analysed statistically, as most statistical tests assume a normal distribution. Once an appropriate transformation has been found, it is usual to present the results in a table so that any test user can read off the transformed scores directly, rather than have to carry out a complicated algebraic operation (see Table 5.1).

It has been argued that this transformation procedure is unnatural, and does not do full credit to the true nature of the data. However, this view is based on a misunderstanding. For norm-referenced tests, the data really only have a true nature in relation to the scores of other individuals, while even in criterion-referenced tests the data are rarely at the interval level of measurement, the minimum level required for distribution effects to have much meaning. Further, the data only have functional meaning in relation to the tasks to which they are put (e.g. t tests, correlations, etc.), and these generally require normally distributed data.

Graphical normalization

For some data samples (particularly where there is more than one mode), the deviations from normality of the raw population scores are too complicated to be eliminated by a straightforward algebraic transformation, but these situations can generally be dealt with by the construction of a standardization transformation graph, which makes a percentile to normal transformation.

For a standardization transformation graph (see Figure 5.1), the data are first arranged in order of size, and then cumulative percentages are found for each point on the rank. Thus, for a sample with 100 respondents, and in which the top two respondents score 93 and 87 respectively, we mark 99% at 93 and 98% at 87, and so on. With different sample sizes it will not be quite so straightforward, but the appropriate scaling can still achieve the desired results. We then plot the raw score (x-axis) against the percentile score (y axis). This may well be a rather messy curve, but we can use our

Table 5.1 Transforming raw scores to stanine scores

Raw score	Standardized score
16 or less	1
17 to 21	2
22 to 25	3
26 to 29	4
30 to 33	5
34 to 37	6
38 to 41	7
42 to 46	8
46 or more	9

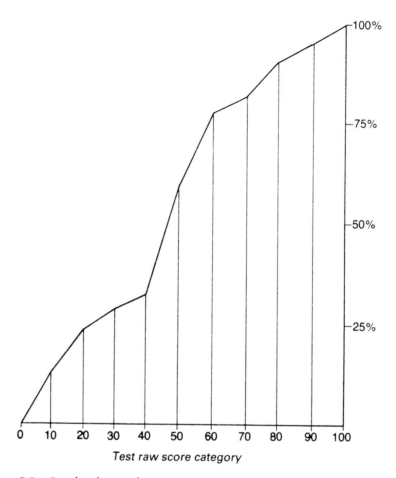

Figure 5.1 Graphical normalization

Notes: The graph is constructed from data by noting the percentage of respondents with raw scores of 10 or less, 20 or less and so on. Standardized scores can be obtained by reading the percentile associated with a particular raw score and translating this with z tables. Alternatively, the z values may be added to the y axis as scale points.

judgement to smooth it out, particularly in the areas where discrepancies seem to be due to few respondents. We can then use the known relationship between the z score and the percentile from the z tables to give us standard score equivalents for each raw score; $z = 0$ is equivalent to the 50% cumulative percentile, $z = 1$ to the 84% cumulative percentile, $z = -1$ to the 16% cumulative percentile, and so on. The recommended transformations will appear either as a transformation graph, with the percentile score axis stated as standard equivalents, or in transformation tables.

Summary

Once a test has been constructed it is necessary to be able to describe some of its general properties and to present the test in a form in which it can be easily used. The reliability of the test must be found, and quoted in a clear and precise form such that future users are able to obtain some idea of the amount of error which might be associated with the use of the test for their own particular purpose. Data on the validity of the test must be given for as broad a range of applications as possible. Data must be provided on the population norms, both generally and for particular subgroups that may be of interest. Finally, information should be given on the manner in which the data should be normalized and transformed to a common format to enable comparisons between the results of different studies.

Chapter 6

Bias in testing and assessment

It is important that all tests be fair and be seen to be fair in their use. However, fairness only makes sense when viewed within a wider social and psychological perspective. Taken from an individual perspective, unfairness occurs when a wrong decision is made about an individual on the basis of a test result. Yet wrong decisions are made all the time, particularly when an individual's score is near the cut-off. If, for example, a student needs a B grade to gain entrance to a degree course, and the examiners have decreed that a B is equivalent to 80% on the test, and the student has obtained 79%, then there must be a statistical chance of at least one in three that a mistake has been made. Now from the point of view of the examiners, who will be looking at the overall perspective, the best that can be hoped for is that mistakes will be kept to a minimum. Given the limited number of places available, and the lack of definitive knowledge of what makes for success in a course, it would be unrealistic to hope for any high degree of accuracy near the cut-off point. Yet it is unlikely that the unsuccessful student will find this argument acceptable. A consideration of this issue rapidly shows us that there exists a series of social conventions within society concerning what is considered as fair and unfair in these circumstances, and these conventions are informative as they often do not agree with conceptions of bias as viewed from the point of view of the statistician.

Bias and fairness

Consider for example a situation where half of the students taking an examination go, of their own volition, to a rather lively party the night before. Suppose all of these students scored on average five points less on the examination than all other candidates. In these circumstances it could be argued from a statistical point of view that the scores of the partygoers would be subject to statistical bias, and it would be reasonably easy to adjust for this bias – say by adding five points to the score of any person who was at the party. Now it is clear that this procedure, which may give a statistically better estimate of the true score, would be extremely unlikely to be accepted by the examinees or by society as a whole, and would probably even make the partygoers feel a little uncomfortable.

There is a general set of conventions about what examinees will accept as fair. If an examinee revises a set of possible examination questions which, although plausible, do not in fact occur in the examination, then a low mark will tend to be put down to bad luck rather than unfairness, even though a case for the latter could certainly be made. The ideology of these conventions is complex, as has been found by examination boards who attempted to make allowance for dyslexia. Generally the conventions allow exceptions for dyslexia so long as it is a medical condition, but do not make allowance for poor spelling, even though this is one of the major diagnostic criteria for dyslexia! A similar problem is found by schoolteachers who attempt to introduce a correction for guessing into their marking (see Chapter 3). In a true–false knowledge test, pupils who guess have a 50% chance of getting the right answer, so that if there are, say, 100 items then a pupil who knows nothing but guesses will have an expected score of 50. However, if the number of wrong responses is used as an estimate of guessing, then the score can be corrected. Children, however, do not take kindly to this procedure. From their perspective, if an item is guessed and the right answer is achieved, there is an entitlement to the mark obtained.

People will accept a certain amount of ill luck within testing procedures so long as it conforms to pre-existing social conventions, and this is not generally seen as unfairness. The major cases of perceived unfairness at the individual level are where items have been included in the testing procedure which are not relevant to the selection or assessment process involved. Thus, for example, it is seen as unfair if a bank excludes short people for service as tellers. Issues of relevance, however, nearly always involve issues of group membership, and thus issues of bias. Bias in a test exists if the testing procedure is unfair to a group of individuals who can be defined in some way. The major issues of test bias involve race, linguistic minorities, sex and cultural differences, although other categorizations are important in particular circumstances (e.g. social class, height, age, sexual orientation, physical attractiveness, etc.).

Forms of bias

It is crucial that tests used for selection should be free from racial bias, and indeed it is now illegal in most countries to select individuals on the basis of racial characteristics. In the UK, the 1976 Race Relations Act considerably strengthened the law affecting racial discrimination concerning employment, not just in terms of job selection but in promotion as well. The Sex Discrimination Act of 1986 followed in the steps of the Race Relations Act to disallow most cases of sex discrimination that resulted from inappropriate use of psychometric tests. Both direct and indirect discrimination are illegal under the Act. Indirect discrimination occurs when the chance of obtaining a job or a promotion is dependent on a requirement that is more likely to be met by one sex than by the other, such as would be the case if a psychometric test was used that was known to be biased. The Disabilities Discrimination Act of 1995 further strengthened the anti-discrimination legislation in this respect.

In addition to the Acts of Parliament themselves, statutory bodies have been established to oversee policy generally. Thus, since 1977 the Commission for Racial Equality has established guidelines of good practice, acted as an appeal body and carried out area reviews in order to achieve its aims. These are the eradication of discrimination and the promotion of equality of opportunity and better relations between different racial groups in the United Kingdom. The Equal Opportunities Commission provides a similar role for sex discrimination. It acts by supporting test cases and investigating employers suspected of discrimination, and provides guidelines for good practice.

All of the legislation in the USA and the UK has had a profound influence on how psychometric tests are used in both countries. In the USA many of the older tests were unable to meet the stringent requirements for fairness required by the courts. Indeed many intelligence tests, including the earlier versions of the Stanford–Binet and the Wechsler Intelligence Scale for Children (WISC), have been outlawed in many states within the USA. Test development since then has been far more systematic in its attempts to eliminate bias and new versions of tests, including the third revision of the WISC, have adopted stringent procedures to achieve fairness in use. There are three major categories of test bias: item bias, intrinsic test bias and extrinsic test bias.

Item bias

Item bias is the most straightforward in so far as it is fairly easy to identify and therefore to rectify. This describes a situation where the bias exists within the individual items of which the test is composed. For example, items developed in the USA that ask about money in terms of dollars and cents would not be appropriate for use in England. Linguistic forms of item bias are the most common, especially where idiomatic usage of language, such as the use of the double negative in standard English, are not allowed. This is a particular difficulty with a diverse and widely used language such as English. If a person learns international scientific English, rather than idiomatic English, they may well be perfectly fluent within a work situation but still be disadvantaged by items generated by users of English as a first language. Similarly, particular dialects that use different grammatical structures in, for example, the use of the double negative may again be vehicles for bias. This effect has been found in a comparison of the responses of black and white children in the USA to Metropolitan Reading Test items that incorporate the double negative (Scheuneman 1975). Of the 55 items tested, 10 involved some negative structure, for example 'mark the picture that shows neither a cat nor a dog'. Of the 7 items that were found to be biased, 6 were of the negative form. Scheuneman also discovered item bias against non-oriental children in the Otis–Lennon School Ability Test (OLSAT) for visual matching and embedded-figures tasks involving letters, numbers, letter-like forms and artificial letters. Eight out of 26 such items, of which 5 involved hidden letters, were found to be biased in this way. It was hypothesized that oriental children were more familiar with the use of ideographic written forms in their alphabet. Items of all of these types have often been included in IQ tests.

Identifying item bias

While item bias is simple to identify and eliminate in principle, it is unfortunately not checked as often as it should be. The easiest way to check is to carry out an item analysis separately for the groups involved. First an appropriate group substructure must be identified, for example men versus women, or speakers of English as a first versus second language. Once this has been done the facility values of each item in the item analysis are compared between the groups. This can easily be done if the items are placed in order of facility for one of the groups, so that the deviations can be recognized in the other. Let us suppose that items a, b, c, and d have facilities of 0.85, 0.76, 0.68 and 0.63 respectively in group 1, while for group 2 the facilities for these items are 0.87, 0.45, 0.63 and 0.61. We can easily see that item b is idiosyncratic, and once it has been identified it can be deleted or changed. While it is unlikely that the items will have exactly the same facility for the two groups, we have a rough idea of what to expect and a simple inspection will often suffice.

If deemed necessary, it is also possible to carry out statistical tests for the existence of item bias. There are many ways in which this can be done, but the most straightforward is probably a two-way (group by item) analysis of variance with the facility value as the dependent variable. The almost certainly significant main effect for items is not of any real interest, while any statistically significant difference between groups will represent other forms of bias than item bias. However, the group by item interaction will give a straightforward test of item bias, which can be repeated as the offending items are identified and eliminated.

Cleary and Hilton (1968) have pointed out that there is some error in this approach as facility value calculations are based on binary data (0 for fail and 1 for pass), and are consequently not normally distributed, thus breaking an assumption of analysis of variance. Angoff and Ford (1973) therefore suggest a transformed item difficulty model, where each item difficulty would be transformed algebraically to give a set of normally distributed equivalent values. This is done by finding the relative deviates that would cut off some proportion of the area under the normal curve. The distance from the common axis would then be plotted for the two groups (on a plot of group 1 against group 2) and used as an indicator of bias. Lord (1977), however, showed that this method was invalid unless the item characteristic curves are normal ogives and have the same discrimination (as in the Rasch model). Guessing also has a confounding effect.

An alternative approach to statistical tests for item bias is to compare the point biserial correlation coefficients between the item and the total score for the two groups, or to compare factor analyses for the two groups, but these approaches are still inexact where there are differences in the item characteristic curves (see Chapter 4). The chi-square approach (Scheuneman 1980) examines frequencies of correct response for two groups at different levels of test score, say by dividing into quartiles. This technique, although relatively free from error, is not particularly powerful. Finally, there are some exact models of item bias which carry out a direct comparison of the shape of the item characteristic curves obtained for each item within the two groups. All of these models are reviewed by Peterson (1980). In fact, where an item is clearly biased, it should show up whichever approach is used, and the models are likely to disagree only in borderline cases. When eliminating biased items, pragmatic considerations are usually more important than issues of whether the exact processes of the hypothetico-deductive model have been followed. Thus it may be advisable to use the easiest or more straightforward of these approaches (the analysis of variance or the chi-square), even where their conclusions may not be exact. The approach used by Scheuneman (1975) in her demonstration of bias in the Otis–Lennon School Ability Test and the Metropolitan Reading Test was the chi-square technique.

Item offensiveness

An issue related to item bias is that of item offensiveness. This is not the same thing, as many offensive items can be unbiased, and many biased items may appear inoffensive. Thus the well-known Stanford–Binet item where the child is asked to say which of two pictures of a girl or boy is ugly, and which attractive, can be offensive to people who are not conventionally attractive; however, it has not been shown to be biased in any way. There are very good reasons for eliminating offensive items other than the fact that they may interfere with performance on the subsequent items in the test. Items that may be seen as sacrilegious should obviously be avoided, as should items with irrelevant sexual connotations. Racism and sexism must be avoided, and it should be remembered that items that draw attention to prejudice can often be as disturbing as items that exhibit it. Examples here might be the use of anti-Semitic passages from Dickens or Shakespeare within English literature examinations. The use of stereotypes, for example men and women within traditional male and female roles, convey expectations about what is normal and should also be avoided wherever possible.

Intrinsic test bias

Intrinsic test bias exists where a test shows differences in the mean score of two groups that are due to the characteristics of the test and not to any difference between the groups in the trait or function being measured. It can be due to the test having different reliability for the two groups, or to group differences in the validity of the test (e.g. the same trait being measured in different proportions in the two groups, the measurement of an additional trait in one group, the measurement of unique traits in each group, or the test measuring nothing in common when applied to the two groups). Thus, for example, if a general knowledge test was administered in English to two groups, one of which was fluent in English while the other included people with a wide range of competencies in English language, then while the test may be measuring general knowledge in one group, it would be highly contaminated by a measure of competency in English in the other group. The validities in the two groups would thus be different.

Intrinsic test bias can also be due to bias in the criterion against which the predictive power of the test is validated. For example, if university degree class marks were biased against overseas students, then a selection test for admission to postgraduate courses that used degree class as the criterion for its predictive validation would also tend to be biased.

Differential content and predictive validity are the main causes of intrinsic test bias. Thus a test which has been constructed to match the characteristics of successful applicants from one particular group may not be so valid when applied to another. Differential content validity is the most worrying form of this bias as deviations in content validity are particularly likely to produce lower test scores in deviating groups. Any group on which the specification for a test has been constructed tends to perform better on that test than rival groups. This is because the cells of the specification, and thus items within the test, will have been drawn up with people from this group in mind. If for some reason a cell or items were not properly applicable to another group, then inevitably members of that group would be expected to get lower scores. Furthermore, positive and relevant attributes of the out-group that were not shared with the in-group would not appear in the test. Several statistical models of intrinsic test bias in selection have been produced to eliminate bias, and these were initially popular as they seemed to provide a rationale for positive discrimination programmes. There are two basic models of positive discrimination as seen from the statistical standpoint, first the use of different cut-off points and second the use of quotas.

Statistical models of intrinsic test bias

Cleary (1968) noted that a common regression equation usually underpredicted criterion scores for minorities, giving examples from data on black students' scores in integrated colleges in the USA. Cleary presented a model which allowed for different regression equations for each group when using the equation to predict, from test scores, the performance of two groups on a criterion ($y = A + Bx$, with A and B both being different for the two groups). This is illustrated in Figure 6.1. It was argued that true fairness had to be based on the use of the best predictor available. Effectively what was done was to equate the groups in terms of the cut-off point on the criterion, which, as the two predictive equations were different, produced different group cut-offs on the test score. Thus, suppose the cut-offs in the use of a test for selection for a course were 50 for group 1 and 60 for group 2. All persons in group 1 with scores higher than 50 would be selected, as would be all persons in group 2 with scores higher than 60. However, people in group 2 who obtained scores between 50 and 60 would not be selected, even though

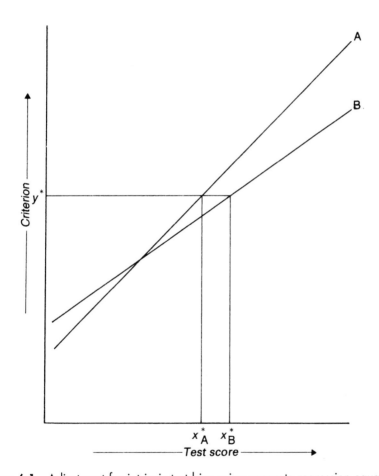

Figure 6.1 Adjustment for intrinsic test bias using separate regression equations

Notes: Equation A is represented by straight line A for Group A. Equation B is represented by straight line B for group B. The same performance on the criterion at y^* (the selection cut-off) is equivalent to scores above x^*_A for group A members, and to scores above x^*_B for group B members.

their colleagues with these scores in group 1 would be selected. They may well feel this was unfair, but the strong statistical argument here would be that they were mistaken and had failed to understand what selection was about. As the scores on the criterion had been equated, it would be argued, the score of 60 in group 2 was in fact equivalent to a score of 50 in group 1, and therefore no unfairness had occurred. Clearly here we have a difference of opinion based on the differences between the statistical and the traditional notions of fairness. Issues of this type have been widely tested in the US courts, where psychometricians representing the state or employers have been asked to put their case against lawyers representing clients who took recourse to definitions of justice contained in the United States Constitution. Thus in the case of *Bakke* v. *the Regents of the University of California Medical School* (1977), Bakke, a white student who had been refused a place in the medical school on the basis of a test score higher than that of some of his black fellow applicants, argued that his civil rights under the constitution, which guaranteed him equality regardless of race, had been breached. The case was carried by the Supreme Court of California, and eventually by the US Supreme Court, where a 5 to 4 majority verdict ruled in his favour. However, the judgement was not unanimous, and an appendix gave some clarification. It was ruled that, while the medical school had violated the equal protection clause of the US Constitution in this particular case, affirmative action programmes generally did not do so unless selection was merely on grounds of race. Had the medical school used a positive discrimination programme that looked at social or educational background rather than race, then the ruling would not apply. In the UK, positive race discrimination is illegal under the Race Relations Act (1976), although positive action, such as non-discriminatory training programmes to alter the balance or adjust for past discrimination, is allowed. Over the years the complex two-way interaction between the US courts and the test constructors has led to increased rigour and accountability in the use of tests, which are generally now of a much higher quality.

From the statisticians' viewpoint much of this legal argument might have been seen as irrelevant. However, this particular 'holier-than-thou' position was dealt a considerable blow by the development of alternative models of intrinsic test bias. Einhorn and Bass (1971) produced a threshold-loss function model for the prediction from the regression lines for the two groups, and argued that Cleary's mean-square-error function model was not appropriate. This model allowed for differences in error term between the equations for the two groups, as well as for the usual alpha and beta regression functions ($y = A + Bx + E$, rather than $y = A + Bx$, with E, as well as A and B, being different for the two groups). While this represented an interesting academic difference of opinion, its practical consequences were devastating to the statisticians' case. Had the statisticians had a single viewpoint to set against popular notions of fairness, they might well have persuaded people of the correctness of their position. However, it was quite different to expect people to accept that they might be selected for a job if psychometricians chose to use a mean-square-error function, but not if they used a threshold-loss function!

More new models confused rather than clarified the issue. Darlington (1971) produced the modified criterion model, which he claimed maximized validity and did not involve a quota system. Thorndike (1971) gave a constant ratio model in which groups were selected in ratio to their success on the criterion. He argued that the cut-off point should select groups in proportion to the fraction reaching specified levels of criterion performance. The conditional probability model of Cole (1973) based the probability of selection on the idea that all applicants who would be successful if accepted should have an equal chance of acceptance. Gross and Su (1975) produced a threshold utility model that used statistical decision theory to incorporate social factors directly into the decision process. This model accepted applicants with the highest expected utility. Utility was defined in terms of a statistical estimate of the social usefulness of having members of particular groups selected.

The models generally had no common criteria, and indeed some of the criteria were contradictory. It seems to be impossible to generate a model that is both fair to groups and fair to individuals. The fairer the models become with respect to groups the less fair they are for individuals, and vice versa. Some of the models resulted in a quota system, while others did not, and all could lead to some individuals being rejected who had higher scores than accepted individuals. A common tendency with them all was the identification of disadvantage with lower scoring on the test, the use of a mechanical formula, and the implicit matching of disadvantage with ethnicity rather than relying on direct measurement. Each of these characteristics has led to its own problems. The identification of disadvantage with low score causes particular problems where the disadvantaged group actually tends to have a higher score on the test. The use of the model in these circumstances, which are often found in cases of sex inequality, can lead to a decrease rather than an increase in the number of women being selected. Yet not to apply the formula or use the technique on a post-hoc basis in these circumstances would show the procedure to be an excuse for action, rather than the rational and systematic method that it is claimed to be. The matching of disadvantage with ethnicity has also generated problems in circumstances where such a match is partially invalid.

A further problem with the techniques for adjusting intrinsic test bias has been that, even with their use, the most disadvantaged were still not being selected. Interest in all of these models decreased as it was increasingly realized that, in most cases of serious discrimination, the source of bias was extrinsic to the tests themselves. Of particular importance was a meta-analysis of differential validity for ability tests with respect to groups of black and white US residents (Hunter *et al.* 1979). Thirty-nine studies were included in the meta-analysis, and no significant differences in validity were found between the two groups.

Extrinsic test bias

Extrinsic test bias is found when decisions leading to inequality are made following the use of the test, but where the test itself is not biased. It has also been described as 'adverse impact'. This can occur when two different groups have different scores on a test due to actual differences between the groups. Thus the use of the test, although itself unbiased, still results in a disproportionate selection of one group at the expense of the other. This situation is much more common in practice than intrinsic test bias, and is most often although not always the consequence of social deprivation. Thus an immigrant group that lives in a deprived inner city area where the schools are of poor quality is unlikely to generate many successes in terms of the academic qualifications of its children. The lack of these qualifications does not necessarily represent any bias in the examination but is more likely due to lack of opportunity. Where the community suffers deprivation for several generations the lack of opportunity is reflected in a lack of encouragement by parents, and a cycle of deprivation can easily be established. In other cases, adverse impact may come about as the result of differences between two schooling systems, say between Catholic schools and predominately Protestant state schools in Northern Ireland. Extrinsic test bias may result if selection tests are more closely geared to the academic syllabus of one of the school systems rather than the other.

Extrinsic test bias and ideology

There are two scientific and political groups likely to oppose the concept of extrinsic test bias. First, sociobiologists are likely to argue that differences in test scores between groups are in fact due to genetic differences between the two groups, and therefore do not represent bias so much as true differences. Second, extremely right-wing individuals may not see differences between cultural groups as undesirable, and are therefore unlikely to recognize them as bias. This controversy illustrates that bias is social and political in nature. What appears to be bias in one framework may not be seen as such in another. It would be pleasant to think that the issues could be rationally debated, leading to ideology-free notions of bias. However, the search for a completely atheoretical framework here is probably misconceived. Conceptions of unfairness, including conceptions of bias, are one of the cornerstones of ideology itself, and issues of ideology are implicit in any consideration of bias. Psychometricians need to be prepared to make a stand on these issues before they can proceed to offer solutions. Any ideological issues that are substantially involved in the selection or assessment process are relevant to the psychometrician's task, and any form of test bias that can result in social inequality must be a central concern.

Legal aspects of extrinsic test bias

As with issues of intrinsic bias, there have been many judicial cases, particularly in the USA, which have considered the various points of view on the use of tests in situations of extrinsic bias. The best known of these is that of *Larry P.* v. *Wilson Ryles*, Superintendent of Instruction for the State of California. This case came about as the result of the placement of seven black children into educational remedial classes on the basis of a WISC score of less than 75, a widely used criterion for the diagnosis of severe learning difficulties. The main case put forward by the parents was based on evidence that, while 9.1 per cent of the catchment area was composed of black people, the proportion of black children in educational remedial classes was 27.5 per cent. The ruling, in favour of the parents, included the principle that the burden of proof for non-bias rests with the test users, so that in these circumstances it was not up to the parents to prove that there was bias, but up to the California education department to prove that there was not bias. As a consequence no black children in California may be placed in educational remedial classes on the basis of IQ tests if the consequence is racial imbalance. In 1979, IQ tests that did this were ruled unconstitutional by the Californian courts. Another case, that of *Diana v. the California State Board of Education*, was settled out of court. Since 1979 the use of IQ tests has been outlawed in many American states, and has fallen into disrepute in most others.

What is particularly important about all of these cases is that they emphasize the need to make any sources of bias explicit, and to incorporate remedial factors into any selection or assessment programme. Extrinsic test bias can be identified by observing the existence of any form of disadvantage that is continuing or deteriorating in situations where testing has been involved in selection or assessment. Once extrinsic bias has been demonstrated, it is not sufficient to ignore its basis, or its role in a society that includes disadvantaged groups. One common solution is the introduction of special access courses to provide added educational input. An alternative approach is the reformulation of the curriculum objectives or job specification to eliminate biased components that may be irrelevant or relatively insignificant when set against the wider need for an equitable society.

The importance of test validity was also demonstrated by the case of *Griggs* v. *Duke Power Co.*, where it was ruled that the power station had failed to demonstrate that the Wonderlic Personnel Test they used in their promotion procedures was actually relevant to the tasks that employees were expected to carry out. Another relevant case is that of the *Albemarle Paper Company* v. *Moody*, in which it was again ruled that the test user must demonstrate the validity of the tests used; it was not up to the person being tested to demonstrate the evidence for invalidity. In the case of *Armstead et al.* v. *Starkeville School District*, the Graduate Record Examination (GRE) was ruled to be inappropriate.

Guidelines in cases of test bias

The US equal opportunity commission has issued guidelines for selectors in situations prone to extrinsic test bias. They argue that affirmative action programmes should in general de-emphasize race, and emphasize instead the educational level of the parents, the relative educational level of the peer group, the examination level, the quality of schooling and the availability of compensatory facilities. They further recommend job re-specification, the introduction of specific training programmes, and the equalization of numbers of applications by changing advertising strategies.

Summary

Three ways in which psychometric tests can be biased have been described. Item bias has proved to be the most amenable to direct amendment. Intrinsic test bias has received a very wide consideration by psychometricians and policymakers alike with the result that today the use of any test in the USA must be accompanied by positive proof that it is not biased in this way. Issues of extrinsic test bias have led to a much closer collaboration between psychometricians and policymakers generally, and to a recognition that ideological issues are of fundamental importance to the theoretical basis of psychometrics. The political links between psychometrics and popular conceptions of democracy continue to develop through the legal structure at both legislative and individual case level in many countries.

Factor analysis

Factor analysis is a technique that is widely used in psychometrics. It can be applied to any set of data where the number of subjects exceeds the number of variables, and is normally carried out on a computer. The variables involved in the use of factor analysis are usually item scores or sub-test scores. The analysis will provide a set of results that give an indication of the underlying relationships between the items or sub-tests. It will tell us which set of items or sub-tests go together, and which stand apart. Factor analysis identifies what are called 'factors' in the data. These factors are underlying hypothetical constructs that often can be used to explain the data. Factor analytic computer programs will give an estimate of how many such factors there may be in a set of data, and of how these factors relate to the items or sub-tests. By selecting items that relate to particular factors we are able to put together sub-tests of the construct that the factor represents. Factor analytic computer programs also give eigenvalues, statistics that are able to represent the relative importance of a factor, and can give estimates of the scores of individuals on any of the factors identified.

The correlation coefficient

One statistic that is fundamental to psychometrics and occurs again and again is the correlation coefficient. When a test is constructed, we correlate item scores with total scores to obtain discrimination in the item analysis (see Chapter 4), we calculate correlations to obtain the reliability (see Chapter 5), and more often than not we use them for validity estimation as well. In addition, if we have a series of sub-tests, the correlation between them is of interest as it is useful to know the extent to which they are measuring the same concept. This is also essential if we are to be able to make proper use of a profile analysis. And finally, the use of a test score itself often involves correlation with another variable.

The correlation matrix

Correlations are often summarized within a correlation matrix (see Table 7.1).

For an item analysis we can imagine correlations between all the items 'a', 'b', 'c', 'd', 'e', 'f' , and so on (rather as in Table 7.2). If we were to draw a matrix with both the

Table 7.1 A correlation matrix, representing correlations between the various components of an EEG evoked potential

	P2L	N2L	P3L	N3L	P2–N2	N2–P3
N2L	0.66					
P3L	0.07	0.18				
N3L	−0.04	0.09	0.25			
P2–N2	−0.04	−0.05	−0.29	−0.22		
N2–P3	−0.02	−0.06	−0.25	−0.14	0.86	
P3–N3	0.13	0.03	−0.21	−0.06	0.36	0.58

Source: From Rust (1975a)

rows and columns labelled 'a', 'b', 'c', etc., then where the rows and columns meet within the body of the matrix we could write a correlation. Thus where row 'b' crosses column 'c' we would have the correlation between 'b' and 'c', where row 'b' crosses column 'b' we would not have a proper correlation as it does not make sense to correlate a variable with itself, where row 'c' crosses column 'b' we would have the correlation between 'b' and 'c' again. In fact it is easy to see that all possible correlations between each of the items in the matrix would occur twice. That is why, in the example of the correlation matrix given in Table 7.1, only the lower triangle of the correlation matrix is shown, the upper triangle would merely duplicate. The statistical analysis of correlation matrices uses matrix algebra and forms the basis of much of multivariate statistics.

The basic structure of these matrices has been of interest to psychologists since the early twentieth century when Charles Spearman developed the technique of factor analysis, the first attempt to look for some underlying uniformity in the structure of correlation matrices. The example given in Table 7.2 illustrates his approach. Ignore for the moment all figures in brackets. First he arranged all the variables in what he called 'hierarchical order', with the variable that showed the highest general level of intercorrelation with other variables on the left, and the variables with the least correlation on the right. He then drew attention to an algebraic pattern in the relationship between such variables when arranged in hierarchical order. He noted that $rab \times rcd$ tended to be equal to $rac \times rbd$, and he observed that this could be extended to all the tetrads in the matrix; thus, for example, $rbc \times rde = rbe \times rcd$, and $rac \times rbe = rae \times rbc$. He measured the extent to which this rule held as the 'tetrad difference'. If the four corners of the tetrad are called A, B, C and D, then the tetrad difference is $AD - BC$. Thus, in the examples given from Table 7.2, the tetrad differences are $0.72 \times 0.42 - 0.63 \times 0.48 = 0$; $0.56 \times 0.30 - 0.42 \times 0.40 = 0$; and $0.63 \times 0.40 - 0.56 \times 0.45 = 0$. Spearman noted that such a pattern of relationships would be expected if a, b, c, d, and e were sub-tests of intelligence, and each represented a combination of two elements; general intelligence, which he called 'g', that contributed to each of the sub-tests, and specific intelligence that was unique to each. Thus, if sub-test a was a test of arithmetic, then the components of a would be 'g' and a specific ability in arithmetic. If sub-test b was verbal ability, this would be composed of 'g' and a specific verbal intelligence. He argued that it was the common existence of 'g' in all sub-tests that caused the correlation. He called this his 'two-factor theory' because each sub-test was composed of two factors.

By including the bracketed components shown in Table 7.2 within the calculation

Table 7.2 A correlation matrix, representing correlations between 5 items (a, b, c, d and e) in a psychometric test

	('g')	a	b	c	d	e
('g')	( )	(0.9)	(0.8)	(0.7)	(0.6)	(0.5)
a	(0.9)	(.81)	0.72	0.63	0.54	0.45
b	(0.8)	0.72	(.64)	0.56	0.48	0.40
c	(0.7)	0.63	0.56	(.49)	0.42	0.35
d	(0.6)	0.54	0.48	0.42	(.36)	0.30
e	(0.5)	0.45	0.40	0.35	0.30	(0.25)

of the tetrad difference he developed the first ever technique for factor analysis. For example, if x is the unknown value where the column 'a' and the row 'a' cross in Table 7.2 it can be obtained from the tetrad difference formula: $x \times rbc = rab \times rac$, that is $x \times 0.56 = 0.63 \times 0.72$, thus $x = 0.81$. He called this value the saturation value of 'g' on a, and deduced that the square root of this value would give the correlation of a with 'g', general intelligence. Thus, in Table 7.2, the column of figures under 'g' represents the factor loadings of each of the five sub-tests on general intelligence. We see that sub-test a is very highly saturated, while sub-test e is less so.

Of course, the example in Table 7.2 is artificial. In practice the arithmetic would never be this neat and the tetrad differences will never come to exactly zero. However, we can calculate such differences, find the average of the estimated values of x for each saturation and use this to estimate factor loadings on 'g'. Spearman actually took the process a step further. He used the loadings to estimate the values for each correlation were his two-factor theory to be true, and could therefore find the goodness-of-fit of his theory. He was also able to subtract the observed from the expected values of the correlations and carry out the process again on the residuals, this leading to the extraction of a second factor. Spearman's insight was brilliant, and it was many decades before the formal statistical procedures were established mathematically and able to catch up with his intuition.

Using graphical representation

Spearman achieved his factor analytic technique through the use of numbers alone. However, it was not really suited to either the extraction or the comprehension of more complex factorial models where more than two factors may be involved. This understanding did, however, become possible with the development of graphical techniques that could be used to represent what may be going on. These techniques (see Figure 7.1), which have produced visual representations of the process, have had a major impact on the development of psychometrics. These involve visualizations of the way in which variables relate to each other, and make the conceptualization of issues in psychometrics much easier. The basic ideas of factor analysis have emerged again and again in psychology, from multidimensional scaling in psychophysics to the interpretation of repertory grids in social and clinical psychology, but they are fundamentally based on the models provided by vector algebra. In vector algebra two values are ascribed to a variable: force and direction. Within factor analytic models, variables are represented by the 'force' element of the vector, which is held constant at value 1, while the angle between two variables represents the correlation between them in such a manner that the cosine of this angle is equal to the Pearson product-moment correlation coefficient. Thus, a correlation of 0.5 between the variables 'a' and 'b' (as in Figure 7.1) is represented by two lines 'oa' and 'ob' of equal length with an angle between them whose cosine is 0.5, that is 60°. A correlation of 0.71 would be represented by an angle whose cosine was 0.71 (45°). The translation between cosines and angles can be made using cosine tables, which appear at the back of many mathematical or statistical texts. Cosine to angle transformation is also a normal pushbutton option on most scientific calculators.

There are many useful characteristics that follow from this visual representation of the correlation. In Figure 7.1 we can see that one of the vectors 'ob' is drawn

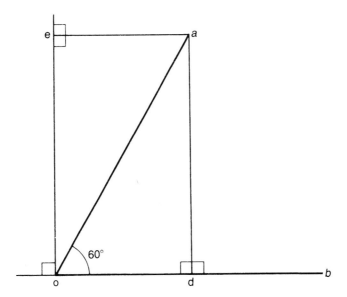

Figure 7.1 Spatial representation of the correlation coefficient

Note: A correlation of 0.5 between two variables *a* and *b* can be represented graphically by two lines of the same length which have an angle whose cosine is 0.5 (60°) between them.

horizontally, and the other 'oa' above it is drawn at the appropriate angle aob. A perpendicular 'ad' is then dropped onto 'ob' from 'a' to a point 'd'. If we assume that 'ob' and 'oa' have a length of 1.0, the distance 'od' will then be equal to the cosine of the angle between the vectors, and therefore to the correlation itself. Also in the figure we see that a vertical 'oe' at right angles to 'ob' has been drawn, and projected onto it is a horizontal line 'ae'. By Pythagoras we know that, as 'oa' has a length of 1.0, then 'od'^{2} + 'oe'^{2} = 1. This gives us a graphical restatement of the statistical formula $r^2 + (1 - r)^2 = 1$, which tells us how we can use the correlation coefficient to partition variance. To give an example, if the correlation between age and a measure of reading ability is 0.5, then we can say that 0.5^2, that is, 0.25 or 25%, of variance of reading ability is accounted for by age. It also follows that 75% of the variance in reading ability is not accounted for by age. This is represented graphically by drawing our lines 'oa' and 'ob' at an angle of 60° to each other as indeed is the case in the figure. The cosine of 60° is 0.5, and therefore, in our figure, the distance 'od' is 0.5. What is the distance 'oe'? Well, its square is 0.75 (1.00 − 0.25 by Pythagoras) hence 'oe' must be the square root of this, i.e. 0.866. This number can be seen as representing a correlation, but it is a correlation between reading ability and some hypothetical variable, as no vector 'oe' was originally given by the data. However, we can give a name to this variable; we could call it 'that part of reading ability which is independent of age'. We could estimate this value by partial correlation analysis, and we could use it in an experimental situation to eliminate age effects. While considering graphical representation of correlations, think about two special cases. If $r = 0$ the variables are uncorrelated. The angle between 'oa' and 'ob' is 90°, the cosine of 90° is zero. The variables are thus each represented by their own separate spatial dimensions; they are said to be 'orthogonal'. If $r = 1.0$, then the angle between 'oa' and 'ob' is zero (the cosine of 0° being 1.0) and they merge into a single vector. Thus the variables are graphically as well as statistically identical.

From this very simple conception we are able to demonstrate a fundamental idea of factor analysis: while the two lines 'oa' and 'ob' represent real variables, there is an infinite number of hidden variables which can exist in the same space, represented by lines drawn in any direction from 'o'. The hidden variable 'oe' represents an imaginary (or 'latent') variable, that part of 'oa' which is independent of 'ob'. If 'oa' were, for example, the weight of a human being, and 'ob' was the height of a human being, then 'oe' would be that part of the variation in the weight of human beings which was independent of height. It is thus a measure of 'fatness', not measured directly but by measuring weight and height and applying an appropriate algorithm. There are any number of circumstances in which these models can be applied. Another example relevant to psychometrics may have 'ob' as the score on a psychological test and 'oa' as a measure of the criterion against which it is to be validated; thus the angle between 'oa' and 'ob', representing the correlation between 'a' (the test score) and 'b' (the criterion), becomes a measure of validity, and 'oe' becomes the aspect of the criterion that is not measured by the test.

A flat piece of paper, being two-dimensional, is able to represent at most two totally independent sources of variation in any one figure. To extend this model to factor analysis we need to conceive not of one correlation but of a correlation matrix in which each variable is represented by a line of unit length from a common origin, and the correlations between the variables are represented by the angles between the lines. Taking first the simple case of three variables 'x', 'y' and 'z' (see Figure 7.2), and the

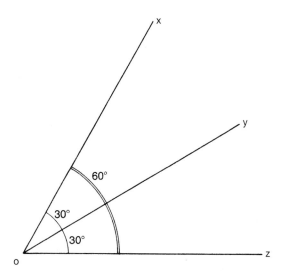

Figure 7.2 Figural representation of the correlations between three variables

Notes: Variables represented are x, y and z, where the correlations between x and y, and between y and z are 0.87 (cosine of 30°), and that between x and z is 0.5 (cosine of 60°).

three correlations between them, if the angle between 'ox' and 'oy' is 30°, that between 'oy' and 'oz' 30°, and that between 'ox' and 'oz' 60°, then it is quite easy to draw this situation on a piece of paper. This represents correlations of 0.87 (the cosine of 30°) between 'x' and 'y' and between 'y' and 'z', and a correlation of 0.5 (the cosine of 60°) between 'x' and 'z'.

However, if all these angles between 'ox', 'oy' and 'oz' were 30° it would not be possible to represent this graphically as two dimensions. It would be necessary to conceive of one of the lines projecting into a third dimension (in 3D) to represent such a matrix. With more than three variables it may be that as many dimensions as variables are required to 'draw' the full matrix, or it may be that some reduction is possible. Factor analysis seeks to find the minimum number of dimensions required to satisfactorily describe all the data from the matrix. Sometimes matrices can be reduced to one dimension, sometimes two, three, four, five, and so on. Of course, there is always a certain amount of error in any measurement, so this reduction will always be a matter of degree. However, the models used will seek solutions that can describe as much variance as possible, and will then assume all else is error.

Thurstone (1947) developed one of the techniques for carrying out factor analysis within the vector model that has just been described. He extracted the first factor by the process of vector addition, which is in effect the same process as that for finding the centre of gravity in another application of vector algebra, and is thus called the centroid technique. The centroid is a hidden variable, but it has the property that it describes more variance than any other dimension drawn through the multidimensional space, and we can in fact calculate this amount of variance by summing the squares of all the projections onto this vector from all the real variables. The square root of this value is called the eigenvalue of the factor. The position of the first factor can be described by reporting the correlation between it and each of the real variables, which are functions of the angles involved. The first factor within the centroid technique describes a basic fixing dimension, and when its position his been found it can be extracted from the multidimensional space so that further factors are sought only in regions at right angles to it. The cosine of an angle of 90°, that is of a right angle, is 0, and thus factors represented by lines drawn at right angles to each other are independent and uncorrelated. It is for this reason that factors are sometimes called dimensions, as figuratively they behave like the dimensions of space. A unidimensional scale is one that only requires one factor to describe it in this way. If further factors exist they will be described as the second, third, fourth and fifth factors and so on, and a unidimensional scale will not be adequate to fully describe the data.

There are many similarities between factor analysis and the process known as multidimensional scaling. Multidimensional scaling originally achieved popularity among psychophysicists, and proved particularly useful in practice for defining psychophysical variables. It was by this technique, for example, that the idea of there being only three types of colour receptor in the retina of the eye was generated, as it was found that people only required three colour dimensions to describe all colours. More recently, multidimensional scaling has provided a useful model for the behaviour of the hidden values in parallel distributive processing (PDP or connectionist) machines (Rumelhart and McClelland 1986). These models of parallel processing computation show similarities with the actual arrangement of the system of connections between neurones in the human brain (McClelland and Rumelhart 1987). It is likely that representational analogies of the type used in multidimensional scaling may turn out not just to be a convenient tool but also to tell us something about how the networks of neurons in the brain actually function. In much the same way in which multidimensional scaling models have provided a conceptual underpinning for psychophysics, factor analysis fulfils a similar role for psychometrics. Its success may be due to more than mere statistical convenience: it could be that the figural representation of factor analysis is so powerful because it mirrors the cognitive processes whereby human beings actually make judgements about differences between objects (or persons). One particular neural architecture, found within the brain, is capable of carrying out factor analysis when emulated within a computer. There is therefore the possibility that the brain itself uses factor analysis when trying to make sense of very large amounts of input.

The application of factor analysis to test construction

In psychometric test construction the factor analysis of all the item correlations in a questionnaire provides an alternative technique to item analysis, and also provides additional information on the conceptual structure of the test specification and on forms of bias in the test. With modern computer technology it is relatively easy to carry out factor analysis, and the majority of statistical packages carry it as one of their options. However, as factor analysis for psychologists has always been more of a conceptual tool than a statistical technique, there are dangers in the amateur use of these programs. When statistical packages run factor analysis automatically they use preset defaults that make assumptions about the data, many of which may be unwarranted in particular cases. Input from a skilled psychometrician is required, who needs to make informed decisions concerning the options available at the various steps of the process.

Finding the starting values for estimates of item error

In the absence of guidance the statistical programs operate default options, generally designed by statisticians rather than psychologists, and these can inadvertently mislead the user. The first set of these options provides the starting values for the iteration process used to fit the model. These starting values are normally estimates of the extent to which each variable is contaminated by error, and are thus estimates of reliability. If reliabilities are known they can be entered directly, but if not then the program will have to estimate them, usually either from the largest correlation of the variable in question with any other, or from the average of its correlation with all of the others. It is useful to check these starting values to ensure that they are not spuriously high or low. A good way to do this is to run a principal components analysis on the data first. This will usually be provided as an option within the factor analysis program. Principal components analysis has many similarities to factor analysis but was defined mathematically much earlier and does not give such a complete analysis. It is not strictly a statistical technique at all as there is no error term involved, and all variables are assumed to be completely reliable. If the principal components and factor analysis models produce more or less the same result then there is no special problem at this level. If on the other hand they give rather different results this will probably be due to large 'between item' variation in the estimates of item error. If this explanation makes sense then no adjustment to the factor analysis is necessary, but if it seems unrealistic it is probably advisable to insert better estimates of item reliability directly into the program. Most factor analysis programs allow this as an option.

Identifying the number of factors

The second point at which the default procedures intervene is the most troublesome: that of identifying the number of factors. The original factor analytic transformation generates as many factors as there are variables, and calculates an eigenvalue for each. The original set of variables defines the total amount of variance in the matrix, each variable contributing one unit. With a factor analysis of data on 10 variables, therefore, the total amount of variance present will be 10 units. The factor analysis rearranges this variance and allocates a certain amount to each factor while conserving the total amount. The quantity allocated to each factor is a function of a statistic called the eigenvalue, and this is such that the sum of the squared eigenvalues of all the original factors adds up to the total number of variables. With 10 variables, for example, there will be 10 original factors. The sum of the squares of the eigenvalues of these factors will be 10, but individually they may vary between about 5 and little above zero. The larger the eigenvalue of a factor, the greater the amount of the total variance it accounts for, and the more important it is. The first factor will accumulate a fair amount of this common variance within its eigenvalue, and subsequent factors progressively less, so that some way along the line factors will begin to have eigenvalues of less than 1. Eigenvalues of less than 1 indicate that the factor is only able to account for a small amount of variance, in fact less than is accounted for by a single variable. As the purpose of factor analysis is to explain a large number of variables in terms of an underlying structure with fewer elements, factor eigenvalues of less than 1 are often interpreted as being uninteresting and probably due to error.

The Kaiser criterion for selecting the number of factors

Most factor analysis programs as a default accept only those factors whose eigenvalues are larger than 1 as being of interest. This is sometimes called the Kaiser criterion, and indeed it makes intuitive sense. However, this is not always so and fails in about 50 per cent of cases. The major exceptions are (a) when there is too much noise in the system from too many unreliable variables, so that too many factors have eigenvalues greater than 1, and (b) when there are several factors with eigenvalues around the criterion level (usually 1). For example, it would not make much sense to use an eigenvalue criterion level of 1 where the eigenvalues for the first seven factors were 2.1, 1.8, 1.5, 1.1, 0.9, 0.6 and 0.5. Although the Kaiser criterion would here give us four factors, it might make more sense to inspect either the three- or the five-factor solutions.

The Cattell 'scree' technique for identifying the number of factors

An alternative to Kaiser is provided by the so-called Cattell scree test, which uses the metaphor of the shingle on a sea shore for the shape of a plot of eigenvalue against factor number, and suggests that a scree might be expected just at the point before the noise values become operative.

The scree is clearly visible in the data of Figure 7.3. However, most data produce no scree, so that other alternatives are needed. In fact the best guide to factor number is given by a conceptual analysis of the meanings of the factors extracted. Generally it is best to take as many factors as can reasonably be interpreted from an analysis of the pattern of item correlations for each factor. Thus factor I may be a general factor, factor II an age factor, factor III a bias factor, factor IV a potential sub-scale factor, and so on; eventually factors will be reached which are uninterpretable, and this is a good place to stop. An additional technique can be particularly useful where there are large samples, and this is to break down the sample into sub-groups and investigate the extent of similarity between the separate factor analyses. The number of factors that look similar across populations is a good guide to a suitable factor number.

Factor rotation

The third set of options available in factor analysis programs deals with rotation. The idea of rotating factors has been around for some time, and was of particular interest to

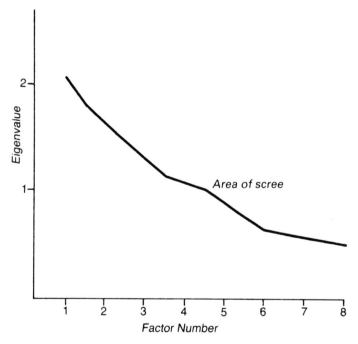

Figure 7.3 Plot of eigenvalue against factor number demonstrating a Cattell 'scree'

Thurstone in the 1930s. It arises only in situations where one factor is inadequate to fully describe the data and two, three or more factors are required. Factor rotation can most easily be explained within the visual representations model we have been using (see Figure 7.4); however, as we can only represent two dimensions on flat paper we are restricted to representing the rotation of factors to only two factors at a time. For the sake of simplicity we will consider a case where only two factors have been identified in a set of data. The first factor extracted will account for most of the variance, and the second will represent significant variance uncorrelated with the first factor. However, the actual position of these factors with respect to the underlying variables does not necessarily follow the arrangement that has the most psychological meaning. In fact there are any number of different ways in which we could define such latent factors within the two-factor space.

Consider as an example a situation where the loadings of six sub-tests of ability (arithmetic, calculation, science, reading, spelling and writing) on a factor analysis are 0.76, 0.68, 0.62, 0.64, 0.59 and 0.51 on factor I, while their loadings on factor II are 0.72,

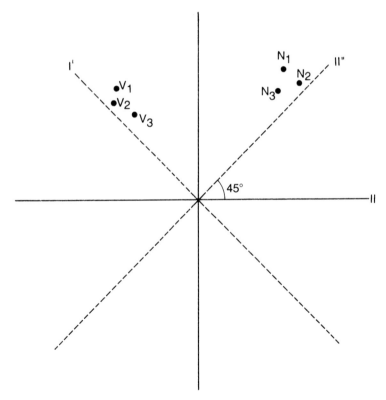

N1, N2, N3 are numerical sub-tests
V1, V2, V3 are alnguage sub-tests
Factor loadings are plotted

Figure 7.4 Rotation of orthogonal factors

0.67. 0.63, −0.65, −0.67 and −0.55 respectively. If a graph is drawn plotting these loadings on the two factors (I as the y axis and II as the x axis), then they form two clusters: in the top right-hand side we have mathematical abilities, while language abilities are in the top left-hand side of the graph. In this situation we could interpret factor I as a general ability factor, while factor II would contrast people who are good at mathematics and bad at language with people who are good at language and bad at mathematics. However, if we draw two new lines on this graph, both through the origin and at 45° to x and y respectively, we note that one of these lines passes through the mathematics cluster with no loadings on language, while the other passes through the language cluster with no loadings on mathematics. This could be interpreted as reflecting the existence of two independent ability factors, one of mathematics and one of language. Both these solutions are compatible with the same set of data! It can be seen that interpretation in factor analysis is never straightforward, and that to fully understand the results it is necessary to be fairly familiar with its underlying conception.

Rotation to simple structure

At one time, rotations of factor analytic data were carried out by hand, in the manner described above, and solutions sought by drawing lines on graphs which gave easily interpretable solutions. However, there was some criticism of this approach (although it is valid, merely open to abuse) on the grounds that it was too subjective. Thurstone therefore introduced a set of rules that specified standard procedures for rotation. The main one of these was 'rotation to simple structure'. The rotation carried out above on the mathematics and language data is such a rotation, and it involves attempting to draw the rotated factors in such a position that they pass through the major dot clusters. In practice the easiest way to do this algebraically is to require that as many of the dots as possible have zero loadings on the factors, so that rotation is defined in terms of the minimization of loadings on other factors, rather than of the maximization of loadings on the factor in question. This is the process that is carried out by the varimax procedure within a factor analysis program, and is the normal default option. In practice, data never behave quite as nicely as in our example, and there are occasions where the program finds it difficult to decide which fit of many poor fits is 'best'. There are other rotation solutions which can be tried in these situations, which give different weightings to different criteria. For example, if it is impossible to find a solution where the lines pass through one set of dots while other sets of dots have zero loadings, priority can be given to one or the other.

Orthogonal rotation

Generally, in factor analysis the derived factors are independent of each other, that is they are drawn at right angles to each other (this is called 'orthogonal'). There are good reasons for this. The factor structure, because it lies in 'possible' space, rather than the real space of the original correlations between the variables, needs to be constrained as there would otherwise be far too many possible solutions. This was after all one of the reasons that the rotation to simple structure was introduced as an algorithmic alternative to the subjective drawing of rotations. There is a further advantage of orthogonal factors in that they are relatively easy to interpret.

Oblique rotation

However, there are situations where the data do not sit happily about an orthogonal solution; and further situations where such a solution is artificial. It might be felt that there were good reasons why two particular factors would be expected to relate to each other. An example here might be sociability and impulsiveness as personality variables. In these situations there are procedures in most factor analytic programs for carrying out oblique solutions. These are more difficult to interpret as one of the main constraints has disappeared, and the factors found are not independent. The extent to which the orthogonality criteria can be relaxed can vary, and it is often found that different degrees of relaxation produce quite different solutions, so that a great deal of experience is required for rotations of this type. They are best avoided by people without experience of the technique.

Criticisms of the factor analytic approach

It is clear that factor analysis is a confusing technique that can easily produce contradictory results when used by the unwary. Generally, the analysis is particularly unsuited to testing hypotheses within the hypothetico-deductive model, as it can so easily be used to support almost any hypothesis from the same set of data. A common error is the assumption that if two variables have loadings on the same factor then they must be related. This is nonsense, as can be demonstrated by drawing two lines at right angles to each other, representing two uncorrelated variables, and then drawing a line between them at 45° to each, to represent a factor with 0.71 loading (the cosine of 45° is 0.71) from each variable! In early research major theoretical battles were often carried out on the basis of the results of different factor analytic rotations. For example, was there one factor of intelligence or many? These disputes were in the end seen as pure speculations; either position could be supported depending on how the data were interpreted. An important debate between Eysenck and Cattell about whether personality could be explained best in terms of two factors or sixteen turned out to be dependent on whether orthogonal or oblique rotations were used on the same data. Thus there could be two personality factors – or there could be sixteen, depending on how the situation was viewed.

A general dissatisfaction with factor analysis was widespread in the 1970s as a result of the apparent ability of the technique to fit almost any solution, and at this time stringent criteria were recommended concerning its use. In particular, it was felt that sample sizes had to be very large before the analysis was contemplated. In fact, the recommended samples were often so large as to render the use of factor analysis impractical. There were further constraints introduced in terms of the assumptions of the model, and in particular the requirement that the variables in the correlation matrix should have equivalent variance. This again produces a considerable practical problem as binary data in particular often fall short of this requirement, and item scores on psychometric tests are frequently binary.

An important distinction has been made between exploratory factor analysis of the type described in this chapter and confirmatory factor analysis. The latter, which makes use of structured equation modelling techniques has been developed specifically for testing hypotheses concerning factor structure. These may be that there are a particular hypothesized number of factors, or that two factor analyses carried out on different samples are the same, or that there is a particular patterning of variables with respect to factors. This could be important if, for example, it was felt that a population to which a test was to be applied differed in important ways from the population on which it was constructed.

Special uses of factor analysis in test construction

The reaction against factor analysis was carried to unreasonable extremes, which was unfortunate as it is a technique particularly suited to psychometrics. Much of the criticism has dealt with the inappropriateness of the factor analytic model within the hypothesis-testing situation specified by the hypothetico-deductive model of science, where assumptions of normality and probability limit the interpretation of results. However, within item analysis, the constraints of the hypothetico-deductive model are not generally relevant unless hypotheses are actually being tested, and pragmatics often have a much larger say in whether items are selected. In the same way that item difficulties and item discriminations together with the test specification are used to make informed judgements, so can various solutions using factor analysis be informative about the number of sub-tests which are appropriate, the extent of guessing, the respondent's selection of socially desirable items, or the possibility of forms of cultural bias; and the use of factor analysis as a guide can be used to reduce any adverse effects. In real life situations where tests are being used, it is better to be guided by a set of factor analytic solutions, even if only based on relatively small numbers of respondents, than not to be so guided. Factor analysis is now re-emerging as a pragmatic item-analysis technique, and this has been helped in part by the development of log-linear models within factor analytic programs that are able to make adjustments for binary data.

The use of factor analysis for test construction is best seen in terms of validity. If we imagine the vector for the task and the vector for the test lying within the same factor space (as with the two vectors representing variables in Figure 7.2), then these will never in practice be perfectly identical. After all, validity is always a question of degree and thus we never expect perfect correlation between a test and its validation criterion. But the various different directions in which the test vector slants away from the task vector represent different possible forms of invalidity, and while the task vector itself will never appear within the factor analytic space, there will be vectors representing forms of contamination. Consider, for example, a factor analytic solution of the item correlation matrix for a personality test in which all positively scored items load on one factor and all negatively scored items on another (a not uncommon situation in practice). It is fairly evident if this happens that each of these factors has been contaminated by the acquiescence artefact. This occurs when some respondents have a tendency to agree with all the statements whatever their content, while others tend to disagree with all the statements. To put the matter simply, some people tend to say yes to everything, while others tend to say no to everything, causing all the items to correlate positively with each other, regardless of content. If, however, we plot both of these factors on a piece of graph paper we will almost certainly be able to identify a rotation which gives the underlying test scale and the acquiescence effect as separate factors (probably not orthogonal). We can then use this graph in addition to our other item analysis data to choose items that effectively cancel out any acquiescence effect, an outcome that would be very difficult to attain without the factor analytic technique.

Another effective use of factor analysis in test construction is in the reduction of confabulation (the lying effect). By introducing a few lie items into the pilot study (such as the 'I have never stolen anything in my life, not even a pin' within the Eysenck Personality Inventory), we can obtain a factor that represents lying, and we can again choose items that rotate the prime test vector away from a contamination with this unwanted effect.

A further major use of factor analysis within test construction is for testing the adequacy of the unidimensional model. As discussed earlier, it is normally the purpose of a test that is important in determining whether a unidimensional single score or a multidimensional sub-score structure is required. However, there may well be situations, usually as a result either of ambiguities within the test specification or of a large number of unreliable or invalid items, where a simple unidimensional scale actually seems to misrepresent the data. Factor analysis will make this explicit and offer guidance for any decisions of principle that need to be made, such as whether to proceed with the attempt to construct a single scale and, if not, what the alternatives are. In other situations factor analysis can be used to explore the feasibility of a sub-scale structure for a domain that is reasonably secure and has been well explored. Such sub-scale structures can be particularly informative for further diagnosis, and are in wide use in profiles, such as the Minnesota Multiphasic Personality Inventory (MMPI) (Hathaway and McKinley 1965), or the Golombok Rust Inventory of Sexual Satisfaction (GRISS) (Rust and Golombok 1985, 1986a, 1986b). As sub-scales normally correlate with each other, their interrelations need to be known; otherwise conflicting interpretations would ensue. This is particularly true in the Cattell personality scales such as the 16PF (Cattell 1965), where sub-scales often have intercorrelations as high as 0.7. In these circumstances it is almost certain that if a respondent has a high score on one sub-scale then several other sub-scale scores will be high as well, with a consequent danger of over-interpretation. Factor analysis can also be used to ensure that sub-scales used are reasonably stable across different populations and different circumstances. Factor analysis of all the test items under different circumstances is particularly useful for deciding whether separate sub-scales are required, and whether they are valid. When used with caution, with insight and with pragmatism, factor analysis is an invaluable tool in test construction, although sometimes a dangerous one.

Summary

The procedures of factor analysis were developed very early in the history of psychometrics, and provide a useful way for workers in the area to make visual representations of the scales they are using. Although the technique is open to abuse it can, if used properly, be a considerable aid to test construction and be very informative about the underlying structure of a set of scores.

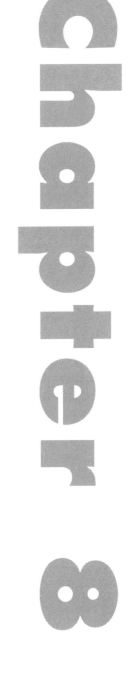

Chapter 8

Using psychometrics in educational settings

Questioning the examination system

The principal use of psychometrics in educational settings is in the development and evaluation of the examination system. Many of the principle questions in the field are psychometric ones, and some of these are addressed here.

Are examinations getting easier?

There has been some controversy concerning standards at both GCSE and A Level but also in universities. In the 1990s there was a massive increase in the participation rate in school examinations and in university education in the UK. This was accompanied by increased numbers of students passing examinations at a 'higher' standard. At the same time, academic staff in the old universities have been complaining about having to 'dumb down' their courses and employers have been expressing misgivings about the basic language and numerical skills not only of school-leavers but also of graduates. When this possibility is suggested to political figures, school heads and teaching unions it is met with a political 'I consider such a suggestion to be an insult to our teaching staff and students. The ever higher standards are due to their hard work.' What is going on here?

The facts of the matter are that participation rates as measured by numbers leaving school with GCSE or equivalent has increased from under 30 per cent to over 60 per cent in the past 30 years. The number of people going to university has increased from under 5 per cent to over 25 per cent in the same period. In terms of population statistics, the universities that were formerly selecting the top 5 per cent in ability are now selecting the top 25 per cent, where ability is measured by A Levels. In intelligence terms, therefore, university entrants were formerly expected to have an estimated IQ of at least 124 (that is, 1.65 standard deviations above the mean). Today they are expected to have an estimated IQ of over 110. These calculations are made by looking up the equivalent z-values for various percentages of the general population. We note, therefore, that the original 5 per cent with IQs over 124 are still there, but are joined by four times their number of less able cohorts. Also, the university curriculum has needed to be amended in such a manner that it can reasonably be followed by a person with an IQ of 110, and consequently the more intellectually challenging material from some courses has been much reduced. However, this does not mean that all graduates are now less able. We would be particularly worried if, for instance, doctors graduating today were less competent. Indeed we would hope that the opposite was the case. Also, there is no reason why some universities should not continue to maintain their high standards, leaving other university institutions to recruit the new type of student. Indeed, in the USA, the participation rate in universities has been higher than in the UK for a very long time, and no problems are found in differentiating between a high-level degree (say, from Harvard) and one from a community college. Thus, the problem in the UK is not with the increased participation rate, but rather with its novelty. University applicants and their parents, and indeed many school career guidance officers, do not have sufficient historical antecedents to be able to differentiate a good university from a poor one; a research university from a community college. All are called universities, and the significance of this term has been inflated by its former elitism. Unfortunately, political considerations have prevented educational managers from publicizing the changed status and its consequences, in particular the need for more rather than less selectivity.

The increase in the participation rate of universities could only have been achieved by an adjustment to the entrance requirements. Does this mean that standards have been lowered? Well, in one sense, yes. Today's selection criteria need to select people with estimated IQs of only 110, compared with 124 thirty years ago. Yet the required number and levels of A Level asked for by old universities has not changed to any great degree. Indeed this has been important politically to the universities, who have been able to increase recruitment considerably while claiming that their standards are the same. However, entry grades at A Level must now require an IQ of 110 compared with 124 in the past. As with the university examinations, this could only be achieved by a modification to the A-Level curriculum. This has happened in two ways. First, scores from continuous assessment have been used to augment the A-Level grade. Second, more difficult topics have been dropped from the syllabus. The consequence of the first of these measures is to make university education more accessible to students whose academic performance is better assessed by this method, and this will probably lead to the need for more continuous assessment in the universities themselves.

The dropping of more difficult topics from the A-Level syllabus has meant that those universities (e.g. Oxford and Cambridge) that wished to retain their old standards, have needed to modify the first year of their courses to include the material overlooked at A Level. Other universities might have wished to do this as well, but the scope for this was limited as the students who find these topics difficult or impossible at A Level will also find them difficult or impossible at university. Unfortunately, most universities had been encouraged by their managers to ignore the decrease in IQ equivalent of the same A-Level scores. This enabled many courses to expand while maintaining that standards had not been reduced. However, the only way in which standards could have been maintained would have been by increasing the A-Level grades required for entry. Those universities that failed to do this have been faced with the need to modify their syllabus to take account of the needs of the new type of less able student. The impact of this has varied from subject to subject. In psychology, for example, advanced statistics was always considered essential for a proper understanding of the subject. To maintain this view, however, would have led to large numbers of students failing their examinations. Furthermore, because of the expansion many more students than in the past are taking degrees in psychology, and there are no longer sufficient jobs as psychologists available to take more than a small proportion of those graduating in the subject. Many of those who do not become psychologists are able to apply their psychological expertise usefully, and in ways that do not require statistics. Also, if a university recognizes these developments, they are able to change, expand and develop in a way that can make them look very successful, and in an environment that is protected by the political taboo on the recognition of reduced standards. Indeed, by changing their teaching methods and bringing them more into line with those in schools, evaluations may show an increase in the standard of teaching that masks a decrease in the academic standard of the degree itself. Fortunately, professional bodies such as the British Psychological Society are able to monitor the standard of psychology in degree courses and keep the situation from running out of control.

It will clearly take many years before the system is able to come to terms not just with the changed situation but also with the fact of change itself. How, for example should an employer utilize examination results when selecting from a candidate pool whose ages range between 20 and 40? How does a candidate aged 40 with three Cs at A Level and no university degree compare with a 20-year-old graduate with a second class honours degree? It could be argued that in achievement terms, if not in ability terms, the latter is more qualified than the former. However, this might be unfair to the older applicant who was denied a place at university by the more stringent requirements of his or her time. Furthermore, given the extent of the changes in the intervening twenty years since his or her A Levels were achieved, it is possible that a topic crucial for the job in question (e.g. integral calculus) may have been included in her A-Level syllabus, and not have appeared in either the A-Level or degree course followed by the younger student. Additionally, the younger student may not in fact have the capacity to understand integral calculus. These age-related considerations, when taken together with the need to take into account not just the degree but also the university from which it was obtained have meant that employers are increasingly turning to psychometric tests as an alternative to school examination and degree results.

Does continuous assessment mean a decline in standards?

The increase in the participation rate for public examinations has been achieved partly through the introduction of continuous assessment. Formerly, all school and university examinations were by unseen written paper held under controlled conditions. This had the advantage of reducing the dangers of cheating by both pupil and teacher to a minimum. Today, while unseen papers are still a significant part of the process, marks achieved from work set during the year are also included in a final mark. Continuous assessment is clearly more vulnerable to cheating. Did the student, or his parent, do the assessed project? Did the student copy from a fellow or out of a book? Did the teacher give extra help to the student, knowing that he himself was also assessed in terms of the GCSE or A-Level marks achieved by his students? Do teachers have a vested interest in not detecting cheating by their pupils? All of these effects are possible, indeed likely, but could in principle be monitored. However, in spite of these dangers the advantages of continuous assessment are felt to outweigh the disadvantages. Those pupils who underperform in unseen examinations are given a better chance. Under-performance may be due to anxiety, or the fact that some people take longer to work things out, or that they have difficulty in the use of handwriting, or are dyslexic. Furthermore, continuous assessments can be devised to resemble lifelike situations more closely than the unseen examination, in the manner of the work sample test used by occupational psychologists. After all, sitting an unseen examination in three hours is not an activity representative of most jobs.

However, the major reason for the increasing favour of continuous assessment is its success. Since its introduction far more students are achieving examination results. Why is this? The success does not seem to primarily result from an increase in cheating, although it is only the disingenuous who deny this completely. Rather, it is because the examination by continuous assessment is paced. By breaking the assessment down into manageable units and assessing each independently it is possible to assign marks more effectively to those who achieve some minimum levels of performance. Continuous assessment is of particular benefit to slow learners. Thus a 40-week course could be examined through 40 separate assessments; each carried out in the week it is learned. Every person assessed with such a course should achieve some recognition, even if they drop out in the first week. Furthermore, with re-sits taken over several years, a slow learner could possibly achieve very high marks. Actually, there is a problem with this. Slow learners also tend to be quick forgetters, so that competence in the subject area at the end of the course could actually be zero in spite of the impressive-looking certificate obtained. It is not surprising that employers have some misgivings!

The introduction of continuous assessment does mean that far more students are able to leave education with some recognition of their achievement. The number of school leavers with no qualification whatsoever has decreased dramatically since continuous assessment was introduced, and this has had knock-on effects in terms of motivation and learning among the less able. The advantages to society in terms of an education system for all clearly outweigh any disadvantages that may be felt by those utilizing the examination results for selection purposes. The introduction of continuous assessment has led to a considerable shift from summative assessment to formative assessment within the education system. This is not a decline in standards per se. Indeed it is because the overall assessment is less challenging that the mass of students are actually learning more. It does, however, represent a change in emphasis that employers and universities need to take into account when interpreting the results of formative assessment as if they are summative.

How useful are school records of achievement?

Records of achievement were first conceived of as a method for ensuring that all children, particularly those who seemed to be unable to obtain any GCSEs at all, were able to leave school with something to record the skills they had achieved. Early attempts at developing pupil profiles laid particular emphasis on behavioural criterion-related items, which were seen as emphasizing what the child could actually do, rather than how the child compared with his or her peers. That is, they were criterion-referenced rather than norm-referenced. The City and Guilds of London was one of the first establishments to make use of profiles of this type. Their profiles provide a good illustration of the problem. One of their model profiles included sub-scale categories of communication (comprised of the sub-scales of talking and listening, reading and writing, and using signs and diagrams), social abilities (working in a group, working with those in authority, working with clients), practical and numerical abilities (using equipment, control of movement, measuring, and calculating), and decision-making abilities (planning, seeking information, coping and assessing results). In their sub-scale for calculating, for example, they have five categories representing five levels of achievement. These are: can count; can add and subtract whole numbers; can use multiplication and division to solve whole number problems; can add and subtract decimals and simple fractions; and can multiply and divide decimals and simple fractions. The criteria-relatedness of all these categories is admirable; however, there is one very immediate problem: while the profile indicates clearly what the pupil can do, it also makes all too apparent what the pupil cannot do. An employer reading the results from the criterion-related scale would tend to perceive that a person who can add and subtract whole numbers is also someone who is unable to multiply and divide or to deal with fractions and decimals. While in an ideal world the employer may think this irrelevant to the job in hand, it is unlikely to be ignored if other job applicants can achieve these additional skills. Consider also the five response categories for reading and writing: can read short sentences; can read and write messages; can follow and give straightforward written instructions and explanations; can use instruction manuals and can write reports describing work done; and can select and criticize written data and use them to produce own written work. There is a whole set of hidden messages in these categories. For example, does 'can read short sentences' in this context mean that the person is unable to write? And if so, has not the employer the right to be told this directly?

The attempts to include life skills and moral development within pupil profiles have been even more fraught. Very few authorities have taken the conception to its logical limit and included scales on honesty. One of the main problems with profiles of this type is in fact an ethical one. By increasing the capacity of the scheme to say something positive about everyone, we are also enabling more negative information to be conveyed. If it is desired that pupil assessments should give the opportunity for a person's honesty to be reported, then by default, if it is not reported there is the implication of dishonesty. There are two dangers here which are contradictory. If the assessment scheme is inaccurate, then there is the serious risk of injustice and libel; on the other hand, if the assessment scheme is accurate and known to be so, then what chances in life would a school leaver have if a reputation for dishonesty was included on their final school report? It is probably generally felt that there are some aspects of a person's performance, particularly during growing up, that individuals have a right to keep secret. As computerized databases come to have more impact on our lives, the dangers of abuse for the type of information provided by school-leaving profiles are considerable.

The main problem with reliable and valid psychometric pupil profiles was really that they were just too good. Far more information can be conveyed than is necessarily in the child's interest. Rather than considering the implications of this in an honest and straightforward manner, in practice various disingenuous strategies have unfortunately been developed for coping with these dangers of over-exposure. In the early 1980s there tended to be a denial of the necessity for psychometric techniques such as validation, as if data of the profile type, when criterion-related, somehow escaped the need to be reliable and valid. It was suggested that, with formative assessment in particular, the new subject of 'edumetrics' should replace the politically incorrect psychometrics of the past, and lead to a new science of assessment. There seemed to be a blindness to the fact that the need for reliable and valid data emerged from the need for reliable and valid processes. It is a complete nonsense to believe that, merely because the sociobiological approach to intelligence testing emphasized the reliability and validity of IQ tests, reliability and validity are somehow no longer an acceptable part of assessment. They are as central to it as they have ever been.

The second strategy involved attempts to report the data selectively. Thus an employer when given the results of the profile might merely be told that the pupil can read short sentences and can count. The further crucial information that he was unable to write or add up and subtract would not be given. Now of course an employer familiar with the scheme might be able to make this deduction; however, later developments in profiling attempted to prevent this by rewriting the information in the style of a personal reference rather than an examination result. This procedure can easily be computerized, with the positive items from the profile being transformed into various grammatical alternatives, the name of the pupil being substituted for X, and pronoun adjustments (his or her) being made automatically. Thus, the program might report, 'Maureen has ability at reading sentences, especially if they are short. She is also particularly good at counting.' This example is, of course, somewhat extreme but not an improbable outcome of this type of system. If such a scheme is introduced it is only a matter of time before employers become as proficient at reading these profiles as they currently need to be at interpreting written references and testimonials.

But is this the most productive direction for our examination system? In spite of the obvious difficulties of such an approach, the achievement of a national system of school-leaving profiles, now called 'records of achievement', is national policy in England and Wales. The purposes of the scheme as laid out in the 1984 Department of Education and Science Policy Statement, while including the recognition of achievement and the need for a short, clear and concise summary document valued by employers, emphasizes the role of the formative profile in motivation and personal development, as well as in curriculum and organizational review. In fact the use of profiles in formative assessment, by allowing for continuous monitoring across the whole range of activities, provided an ideal instrument of curriculum control for both national and local government alike. Formative assessment of pupils necessarily has to involve the teachers, and in the process of instructing teachers in its methods a great deal of control of the curriculum passes to their instructors. It is to this new ground that the curriculum control shifts as soon as final examinations are downgraded in their significance. The political debate between the left, who would like to see this control used to introduce a multicultural curriculum, and the right who would like to see a system of industrially orientated skills-training introduced, will no doubt continue for some years.

The standard profile contains one essential characteristic: it must include a series of measures or sub-scales. While the assignment to points on these sub-scales may often be criterion-referenced rather than norm-referenced, it must, if it is to be able to state what a person can do, by default tell us what a person cannot do. Incomplete reporting can obscure this but not eliminate it. In fact there are many instances of profile reporting which have not traditionally been seen as profiling. When an individual's GCSE and A-Level scores are reported, we have a set of scores on a series of sub-scales, and we make comparisons of clusters of successful and unsuccessful subjects. The manner in which we plan out a reference, deciding to say something about ability, how hard the person works, how they get on with other people, etc., is again an example of an implicit profile structure. This might suggest that profiling, rather than being a psychometric technique introduced by the advance of science, is merely an operationalization of folk psychological decision-making processes so far as they apply to judging and assessing other human individuals.

Do examination league tables achieve their purpose?

Examination league tables are used by government and public alike to judge the quality of schools. At face value this seems like a fair and objective process. However, not all educationists are satisfied with the results. What objections do they have? First, it is argued that the league tables are unfair to some schools, in particular those that pride themselves on their provision for special educational needs. Second, it is believed that most of the variation in league table scores is an indirect result of factors outside the schools' control, such as social and economic factors within the catchment area they serve. Third, league table scores may be the result of selection policies, either direct, such as the use of an entry examination, or indirect, such as the encouragement of applications from outside the immediate area.

All of these objections have some validity. If we consider, for example, an independent school that uses a very selective entry test such that all its pupils have IQs of over 130, then it would not be surprising if such a school did well in the league tables. They could achieve a good result even if they simply provided the students with syllabus and books and sent them home to study! At the same time a state school within a very socially deprived area may have achieved a miracle in obtaining GCSE passes for 30 per cent of its pupils. Any system that penalizes good teachers in difficult areas at the same time as allowing poor teaching in selective schools to go unnoticed must be questionable, particularly when the allocation of public funds is involved. Furthermore, league tables actually encourage schools to reject those very children for whom the new continuous assessment and examination system was designed. Thus, education policy as a whole is contradictory. However, schools do need to be judged, and we need to consider alternative strategies for evaluating their performance in terms of pupil output. One way of doing this would be to adjust actual examination results in terms of expected examination results. Schools could then be evaluated by considering whether their pupils have performed better or worse than expected. Thus, the highly selective independent school would be expected to have very good examination results, while the inner-city state school may have a much lower expectation. Clearly, before we can apply this method we need to have a reasonably foolproof method of calculating the expectation.

One way of doing this would be to compare like with like in terms of socio-economic factors. Thus the expected number and level of GCSE passes would be the mean of the performance of schools whose parameters were similar. Alternatively, different phenomena, such as school climate or management structure, could be used to evaluate schools. However, this does leave several questions open. It does seem reasonable to ask how well one could reasonably expect a particular child to perform in their examinations. This issue of baseline assessment has been a central concern of psychometrics since the early Binet tests in 1904, and brings us back to the question of how to measure ability independently of achievement in children. This question is of concern to special needs advisors and educational psychologists alike, particularly when assessing learning disability or diagnosing specific learning disabilities such as dyslexia.

Measuring ability in schoolchildren

The Stanford–Binet

The generally accepted statistic for the assessment of ability in schoolchildren is still the Intelligence Quotient (IQ). This term was originally introduced by Alfred Binet, and was calculated as the ratio of Mental Age to Chronological Age, multiplied by 100. Binet assessed Mental Age by administering tests of predetermined difficulty. There were six tests at each age. Testing might proceed as follows. Presented with a child aged 7 years 6 months, Binet would administer all the tests suitable for a 6-year-old child. If the child failed any of these tests he or she would be administered all the tests for a 5-year-old child. Otherwise he would be administered all the tests for a 7-year-old child, and then all the tests for an 8-year-old child, and so on, until a year for which he failed all the tests. Binet would then calculate the child's mental age by taking the child's 'base year' (the year at which the child passed all the tests) and crediting 2 months of mental age for each test passed thereafter. Thus a child aged 7 years 6 months who passed all the 5-year-old tests, five of the 6-year-old tests, two of the 7-year-old tests and none of the 8-year-old tests would have a Mental Age of 5 years plus 2×7 months = 6 years 2 months. His IQ would be $100 \times 6.17/7.5 = 82$. This system was widely accepted in education as it related the child's current ability level to that of a subjectively known quantity, the teachers' expectation of children's performance level at various ages. There were problems with older children as scores on some of the tests began to level off at around 13 years. Eventually, Terman, working from Stanford University, replaced the calculation with one based on norm groups and standard scores, although he retained the same format, using a mean of 100 and a standard deviation of 15. He found that this gave IQ scores that most closely resembled those found under the old ratio calculation. Terman's standardization is called the 'deviation IQ' and his development of the Binet scales the Stanford–Binet.

The Wechsler Intelligence Scale for Children (WISC)

The Stanford–Binet test proved so popular that it was used for the assessment of learning difficulties in adults as well as in children. However, many of the items were too childish to retain face validity in this population so that in 1939 David Wechsler developed a replacement that was first known as the Wechsler-Bellevue and later as the Wechsler Adult Intelligence Scale (WAIS). The adult test was itself so popular that in 1949 a children's version, the Wechsler Intelligence Scale for Children (WISC) was also developed. There is also a pre-school version of the test, the Wechsler Preschool and Primary Scale of Intelligence (WPPSI). The WAIS, WISC and WPPSI are all organized into Verbal and Performance sub-tests, there being at least five of each. Unlike the Stanford–Binet, all the sub-tests are applicable to the whole age range, although they have different standardizations for each age. Thus, in the vocabulary sub-test, the average 7-year-old may be expected to get 10 correct answers while the average 14-year-old will be expected to get 33 correct answers. The sub-tests themselves are standardized to a mean of 10 and a standard deviation of 3, while the main scales (Verbal IQ, Performance IQ and Full-Scale IQ) are standardized to a mean of 100 and a standard deviation of 15.

By the 1970s the WISC became the most widely used ability test for children throughout the world, particularly for the identification of those with special educational needs. It also came in for some criticism in terms of the Eurocentric nature of many of its items. Consequently a new version was developed in which groups representing various minority interests were involved in the design of items. In 1991 the third revision of the WISC was published, followed by its UK standardization in 1992.

WISC-III (UK) consists of 13 sub-tests, the 6 Verbal sub-tests being Information, Similarities, Arithmetic, Vocabulary, Comprehension and Digit Span, and the 7 Performance sub-tests being Picture Completion, Coding, Picture Arrangement, Block Design, Object Assembly, Symbol Search and Mazes. The WISC-III (UK) was standardized on 800 schoolchildren between the ages of 6 and 16. The children were widely sampled using a stratified random sampling approach. Thus, the land area of the UK was divided into 13 regions, e.g. Southwest, Scotland, East Anglia, etc., and appropriate proportions of children were selected within each. Similarly, sampling at each age was based on representative numbers of each of the ethnic minorities, of children living in rural and urban settings, and from each socio-economic class. Taking part in the project were 117 examiners and 60 schools.

The applications of the WISC include psychological assessment contributing to educational planning, resource provision and placement decisions; identification of unusual cognitive profiles relating to exceptional ability or learning difficulties among school-aged children; and clinical and neurological assessment and research. Of particular importance is the assessment of children whose educational progress is a cause for concern. Clearly there are many reasons why a child may not be progressing as expected and many factors need to be investigated in order to achieve a confident formulation of the child's situation. The most useful objectives of this assessment process will be concerned with decisions about future intervention in terms of management and resource allocation decisions. The particular strength of a standardized test like the WISC lies in the wide sampling of cognitive abilities provided by 13 different sub-tests and in the reliability of the scores provided. The WISC provides high-status objective information with considerable predictive validity concerning a child's capacity for learning. It also includes a factor structure that allows the psychologist to evaluate findings on a number of levels, from the simple index of a Full-Scale IQ through to detailed profile analysis.

Measuring achievement in schoolchildren

Reading tests, dyslexia and the diagnosis of specific learning difficulties

A child's ability always needs to be seen within the context of his or her current achievement level in school. Thus, if a child shows a particular level of achievement in reading, a teacher may wish to know whether this represents the expected level of achievement for a child of his or her ability. An average score on a reading test may represent over-achievement in a child of IQ 90, but will be a considerable underachievement if his or her IQ is 130. In the latter case we may well suspect a specific learning difficulty such as dyslexia, even though the child's achievement is well within the average range. In 1975, The US Government passed Public Law 94–142 that specified the legal framework for special needs diagnosis and provision within the USA.

Within Public Law 94–142, comparisons of intellectual ability with academic achievement serve as the key step in determining the presence of specific learning difficulties. It specifies that these exist if:

1   The child does not achieve commensurate with his or her age and ability levels in one or more of the areas listed when provided with learning experiences appropriate for the child's age and ability levels; and

2   The multidisciplinary team finds that a child has a severe discrepancy between achievement and intellectual ability in one or more of the following areas:
    (a) Oral expression
    (b) Listening comprehension
    (c) Writing skills
    (d) Basic reading skill
    (e) Reading comprehension
    (f) Mathematics calculation or
    (g) Mathematics reasoning.

The Wechsler tests of reading, numeracy and language skill

The US Department of Education established the Special Education Programs Work Group on Measurement Issues in the Assessment of Learning Disabilities in 1985. Their key guidelines for the development of tests of achievement in the assessment of over- or under-achievement were as follows:

1   National normative data should be provided for a large stratified random sample of children.

2   National normative data for the tests being contrasted must be highly comparable or the same.

3   The correlations between achievement and ability should be based on an appropriate sample.

4   Tests should be individually administered and provide age-based standard scores scaled to a common metric.

5   Measures should have a high level of reliability.

6   Other reliability and validity issues, particularly for performance-based measures of writing, should be addressed.

In 1991, The Wechsler Individual Achievement Test (WIAT) was published in the USA to meet these criteria. This formed the basis for the development of parallel tests in the UK (Rust *et al.* 1993; Rust 1996a). The Wechsler Objective Reading Dimensions (WORD) included the Anglicization and restandardization of three of the WIAT sub-tests assessing Basic Reading, Reading Comprehension and Spelling. WORD was standardized alongside WISC-III, that is, on the same children, in order to meet the above criteria. Subsequently two other sets of WIAT sub-tests were standardized and published in the UK. The Wechsler Objective Numerical Dimensions (WOND) includes the WIAT sub-tests of Mathematics Reasoning and Numerical Calculation. The Wechsler Objective Language Dimensions (WOLD) includes the Oral Expression, Oral Comprehension and Written Expression sub-tests. The various sub-tests of WORD, WOND and WOLD can also be combined to produce a Wechsler Quick Test score and a Wechsler Individual Achievement Test (UK) Overall score.

Ability–achievement discrepancy analysis

One of the major uses of the Wechsler scales is to compare a child's general ability level with his or her level of achievement. This comparison is the key step in determining the presence of specific learning disabilities. In the USA, Public Law 94–142 has specified that such disabilities exist where a severe discrepancy can be demonstrated between ability and achievement. The meaning of 'severe discrepancy' has been widely debated, and discussions of alternative definitions have been extensive (Reynolds 1990).

Methods and formulae for calculating ability–achievement discrepancies

The first step in choosing a discrepancy analysis method is to select the proper scaling procedure for test scores. Berk (1984a) and Reynolds (1990) have argued that grade equivalents, age equivalents, percentile ranks and ratio IQ scores all have statistical limitations that eliminate them from serious consideration as scaling procedures for discrepancy analysis. Only standard scores have been endorsed by experts (Reynolds 1985) as the acceptable scaling technique for calculating discrepancies. It is for this reason that standard scores are used in ability–achievement discrepancy analyses using the WISC with WORD, WOND and WOLD.

The second step in discrepancy analysis is to select a statistical method for comparing ability and achievement. The method determines the formula by which the two scores are contrasted. Two methods of discrepancy analysis that are widely used are the simple-difference method and the predicted-achievement method.

Simple-difference method

In the simple-difference method, an achievement standard score is directly subtracted from the IQ standard score. This method is often selected because it is easy to explain to parents, school boards, and other lay audiences. However, as Braden and Weiss (1988) have pointed out, the simple subtraction of standard scores ignores the relationship (correlation) between the two scores. As the correlation between two scores increases, the reliability of both their sum and their difference decreases. Also, unless the simple difference is tested for statistical significance, error of measurement is also ignored. The proper use of the simple-difference method therefore requires the user to determine whether or not the difference is statistically significant, and if it is, to determine how frequently the statistically significant difference occurred in the standardization sample (Berk 1984b). These are the same two steps used to interpret the difference between a WISC Verbal IQ score and Performance IQ score (Wechsler 1991). Reference to statistical significance provides an answer to the concern that measurement error in each test may produce a score difference merely by chance. The difference must be of sufficient size to minimize the probability of a difference occurring because of unreliability in the measures. Reference to the frequency of differences provides an answer to the concern that certain quantities of difference may not be rare in a normative population. Therefore, the difference should be of a size that is rare in the sample that links the two measures.

The formula for determining the statistical significance of a simple difference (Reynolds 1985; 1990) is:

$$A = vS\sqrt{2 - r_{xx} - r_{yy}}$$

where

A	is the size of difference required for significance
v	is the critical value from the normal curve that defines the boundary of the two-tailed significance test (1.96 for $p < 0.05$, 2.58 for $p < 0.01$)
S	is the standard deviation of the scores (15.0 for the Wechsler tests) and
r_{xx}	and
r_{yy}	are the reliabilities of the ability and achievement scores respectively.

Predicted-achievement method

A predicted-achievement method based on the correlation of ability and achievement was first advocated by Shepard (1980). Essentially, the ability score is used in a regression equation to calculate a predicted achievement value. Regression methods have been employed for many years, and the rationale has been explained by Thorndike (1963): 'It is necessary to define 'underachievement' as discrepancy of actual achievement from the predicted value, predicted on the basis of a regression equation between aptitude and achievement.'

The first step in the use of this method is to standardize both the ability and the achievement score by converting them to z scores. This is done by subtracting the obtained score from the population mean and dividing the result by the population standard deviation. In the case of the Wechsler scales the population mean is 100 and the population standard deviation is 15.

Next, the predicted-achievement z score is calculated by multiplying the achievement z score by the correlation between ability and achievement scores. This correlation is generally obtained from the manual of the achievement test being used, although other values for it may be available from any appropriate large-scale study in which both achievement and ability have been measured on the same respondents.

The predicted-achievement z score is then converted back into the same metric as that used for the achievement score. This is the reverse of the original process whereby the achievement and ability scores were converted into z scores, so you multiply by the standard deviation and add the mean. For Wechsler scales this means multiplying by 15 and adding 100.

The final step is to obtain the discrepancy by subtracting the actual achievement from the predicted achievement.

Because ability and achievement typically correlate in the moderate-to-high range (e.g. 0.40 to 0.75), the correlation is nearly always statistically significant, indicating that the prediction is reasonably accurate for most of the cases in a large group.

The formulae for determining statistical significance of differences between ability and predicted achievement are as follows (Reynolds 1985; 1990):

$$A = vS\sqrt{1 - r^2_{xy}} - wR$$

where

A	is the size of difference required for significance
v	is the critical value from the normal curve that defines the boundary of the two-tailed significance test (1.96 for $p < 0.05$, 2.58 for $p < 0.01$)
S	is the standard deviation of the scores (15.0 for the Wechsler tests)
r^2_{xy}	is the squared correlation between ability and achievement at a given age level
w	is the critical value for the normal curve that defines the boundaries of a one-tailed test (1.65 for $p < 0.05$ and 2.33 for $p < 0.01$) and
R	is the standard error of the residual. This needs to be calculated from the following formula.

$$R = S\sqrt{1 - r^2_{xy}} \sqrt{1 - D}$$

where

R	is the standard error of the residual (needed for the previous formula)
S	is the standard deviation of the scores (15.0 for the Wechsler tests)
r^2_{xy}	is the squared correlation between ability and achievement at a given age level and
D	is the reliability of the residual score. This needs to be calculated from the following formula.

$$D = \frac{r_{yy} + r_{xx}r^2_{xy} - 2r^2_{xy}}{1 - r^2_{xy}}$$

where

D	is the reliability of the residual score (required for the previous formula), and
r_{xx} and r_{yy}	are the reliabilities of the ability and achievement scores respectively
r^2_{xy}	is the squared correlation between ability and achievement at a given age level.

Simple-difference versus predicted-achievement methods

The advantages of the predicted-achievement method were summarized by Shepard (1980). He noted that 'expected performance is predicted from aptitude scores, so that children from the full ability continuum will be identified. ... Therefore, children with learning difficulties are clearly distinguished from slow learners' (p. 84). Some disadvantages of the predicted-achievement method were summarized by Berk (1984b), who pointed out the limitations of imperfect correlations (discrepancies are due to prediction error as well as true differences).

Given that there are both advantages and disadvantages for each method, researchers have conducted comparative studies to assess the empirical differences between the two models. Braden and Weiss (1988) have shown in data-based studies that the simple-difference method has a potential bias as compared to the predicted-achievement method. The simple-difference discrepancies correlated with ability level, resulting in larger differences for high-ability groups. Additionally, the simple-difference discrepancies appeared to be smaller for minority children. Because of the importance of eliminating potential bias in identification of learning-disabled children, the predicted-achievement method is recommended by the Dyslexia Association for use with WISC-III(UK), WORD, WOND and WOLD.

Case study

John is a 13-year-old who has a learning disability and who was referred for a re-evaluation in a special educational needs programme. John also has a history of reading difficulties. The results of an ability–achievement discrepancy analysis of his WORD, WOND and WOLD sub-test scores and WISC-III (UK) scores are presented in Table 8.1.

Table 8.1 Ability–achievement discrepancy analysis for a 13-year-old male, with WISC-III FSIQ score and WORD, WOND and WOLD sub-test scores

WISC-III scores: Verbal IQ score 104; Performance IQ score 107; Full-Scale IQ score 106

Achievement subtests	Predicted score	Actual score	Discrepancy	Sig.	Frequency
WORD					
Basic Reading	104	70	34	.01	<1%
Reading Comprehension	104	71	33	.01	<1%
Spelling	103	85	18	.05	4%
WOND					
Mathematics Reasoning	104	95	9	ns	15%
Numerical Operations	103	103	0	—	>25%
WOLD					
Listening Comprehension	104	102	2	—	>25%
Oral Expression	103	66	37	.01	<1%
Written Expression	103	70	33	.01	<1%

Note: The frequency scores in the last column are obtained from the respective test manuals.

123

For John, the discrepancies between ability and the Basic Reading, Reading Comprehension, Oral Expression, and Written Expression scores are all significant at the .01 level. Also, these differences occurred rarely (in less than 1 per cent of the linking sample). The discrepancy for Spelling is significant at the .05 level and occurred in about 4 per cent of the linking sample. John clearly qualified as having learning disabilities in more than one area. The four largest discrepancies are significant at .05, even after correcting for multiple comparisons (Reynolds 1990). Correcting for multiple comparisons consists of dividing the significance level by the number of comparisons. In this case the standard significance level of .05 is divided by 8 (the total number of sub-tests). The result, .00625, approximates .01. Hence, significance is indicated.

Limitations of ability–achievement discrepancy analysis

There are inherent limitations to the assessment of the academic achievement of young children. Children aged 6, particularly, have only begun their academic course of study. For example, some of these children have not been formally instructed in the reading of lengthy sentences or passages, so that the assessment of reading comprehension is inherently premature. For learning difficulties to emerge, the child must be exposed to multiple learning experiences, including both successes and failures. For these reasons, ability–achievement discrepancy analysis for young children should be conducted cautiously. Interpretations of the results always need to be tempered by the background and academic history of the individual child.

A related limitation is the precision of measurement that is possible for children who are at the extremes of the age range for the achievement test used. Because of a number of test-design considerations, such as curriculum specifications and optimum testing time, sub-tests are designed with a wide range of item difficulties. Thus, only a few items exactly match the functioning level of 6-year-olds who perform at the lowest levels of achievement on each sub-test. These 'floor' effects are present in the Reading Comprehension sub-test of WORD particularly and to a lesser extent in the Basic Reading and Numerical Operations sub-tests. Such floor effects also reduce the precision of measurement possible in determining ability–achievement discrepancies for young children. An analogous limitation is present for high-achieving older children (age 16), for whom few difficult items are present. This particularly applies to sub-tests of basic reading and numerical operations sub-tests. These 'ceiling' effects reduce the precision of measurement possible for older children and, in turn, the precision of determining ability–achievement discrepancies for them.

Reynolds (1990) discusses further limitations to discrepancy analysis, and cautions that 'determining a severe discrepancy does not constitute the diagnosis of learning disability; it only establishes that the primary symptom of learning difficulty exists'. Reynolds also stipulated the following.

1   Evidence separate from test results should indicate that the child has a 'failure to achieve' or lack of attainment in one of the principal areas of school learning.

2   Clinical evidence and direct observations by experienced professionals must indicate that the child may have some form of 'psychological process disorder' such as attention and concentration difficulties or problems of conceptualization, information processing or comprehension of written and spoken language.

3   The examiner must ascertain that observed behaviour, symptoms or deficits in the child's learning are not due to other factors such as sensory incapacity (visual or hearing impairment), mental retardation, emotional disturbance and educational and economic disadvantages.

4   Similarly, the examiner must determine that deficits do not result from factors in the medical or developmental history of the child. These factors include prenatal medical problems; delayed speech, hearing or visual development; brain injury or illnesses that cause neurological damage; difficulties with physical development or motor co-ordination problems; and many other risk factors.

Notwithstanding these difficulties and cautions, discrepancy analysis provides the best technique available for the diagnosis of specific learning difficulties such as dyslexia.

Summary

There is a demand for psychometric tests not only in selection but also in clinical or educational assessment. Within these latter settings additional criteria can apply to their construction and use. In educational settings the complex interaction between the curriculum and the test specification in situations where assessment is continuous has led to new understandings in the approach to both. Psychometrics also plays a major part in the diagnosis of specific learning difficulties such as dyslexia.

Personality theory and clinical assessment

A familiarity with psychological personality theory is a requirement of the British Psychological Society's Certification of Competence in Testing (Level B), and the subject is therefore covered here in some detail. Although the term 'personality' is widely used in everyday conversation, defining its meaning is not a simple task. We commonly talk about television 'personalities', or we may describe someone as 'being a personality' or as 'having a lot of personality' suggesting the kind of person who is typically lively, loquacious and who tends not to be ignored.

We also use the term 'personality' in relation to a person's most striking characteristics. For example, we may describe someone as having a jovial personality, or an aggressive personality, meaning that these are their most salient characteristics and that they tend to respond to a variety of situations in that particular way. It is hard to imagine, for example, someone who is usually shy suddenly becoming the life and soul of the party, or someone who is easily angered not rising to the occasion when insulted. So when we describe the personality of someone we know, we assume their characteristics to be fairly stable, not only in different situations but also over time.

Although the term 'personality' has different meanings in different contexts, it is a term that is generally well understood in everyday language. It may seem surprising, therefore, that psychologists cannot agree on a definition. Gordon Allport, one of the first contemporary personality theorists, identified almost 50 different definitions of personality in the literature as early as 1937. Here are just a few that have been put forward since that time:

Definitions of personality

the most adequate conceptualization of a person's behaviour in all its detail

(Menninger 1953)

a person's unique pattern of traits

(Guilford 1959)

the dynamic organization within the individual of those psychophysical systems that determine his characteristic behaviour and thought

(Allport 1961)

those structural and dynamic properties of an individual as they reflect themselves in characteristic responses to situations

(Pervin 1970)

the distinctive patterns of behaviour (including thoughts and emotions) that characterize each individual's adaptation to the situations in his or her life

(Mischel 1986)

Some theorists, notably Hall and Lindsey in their influential book on personality first published in 1957, *Theories of Personality*, start from the premise that '*no substantive theory of personality can be applied with any generality*'. Others have endorsed a more pragmatic approach, adopting a definition of personality that suits the purpose for which it is being used. With respect to psychological testing, the following parsimonious definition functions well in this respect:

> an individual's unique constellation of psychological traits and states
> (Cohen *et al.* 1988)

One reason for the lack of consensus is that definitions of personality are based on the theoretical perspective of the psychologist formulating the definition. A single, all-encompassing theory, and associated definition, of personality does not, nor is ever likely to, exist. Instead, the many different theories, each focusing on different but related aspects of human behaviour, contribute to a greater or lesser extent to our understanding of what personality is. The more influential of these are as follows.

Temperament   Although the term temperament has been used by personality theorists such as Allport and Cattell to refer to those aspects of adult personality that are considered to be largely inherited (such as impulsiveness), temperament is more commonly used in relation to infants and young children and refers to their tendency to behave in consistent ways across situations. Temperament is usually viewed as a genetic predisposition because differences in characteristics such as activity level and emotionality can be observed in newborn infants.

Motivation   Motivation is what drives us to do one thing rather than another. We may be motivated by basic needs such as the need to quench our thirst or relieve our hunger. In an occupational setting, some people are more motivated by a need for interesting work than by a need for money. For others, their primary motivation is a need for recognition of their achievements and the possibility of promotion.

Values   A value is an enduring belief about what should be important in our lives and how people should behave. Our values influence our choice of occupation. For example, a person who is deeply concerned about the effects of smoking is unlikely to apply for a job in the tobacco industry.

Attitude   The term attitude refers to how much a person likes or dislikes an object, person or idea, i.e. our positive or negative feelings towards an attitude object.

Belief   The term belief refers to the cognitive component of an attitude, i.e. what a person knows or assumes to be true. Examples are the belief in religion, and the belief that women make better secretaries than men. Beliefs may be held with varying degrees of certainty. They are distinct from attitudes in that they do not include an affective component; i.e. they do not include liking or disliking.

Ability   Ability refers to a person's knowledge or skill, and includes both aptitude (the capacity to learn) and achievement (acquired ability, e.g. ability in a foreign language).

Genetic versus environmental influences on personality

Whether our behaviour is genetically or environmentally determined is a question that has been, and continues to be, hotly debated by psychologists. Identical and non-identical twins have been compared in order to address this issue. The rationale for this approach is that identical twins have identical genes whereas the genes of non-identical twins are no more alike than those of ordinary siblings, and if identical twins are more alike than non-identical twins with respect to a specific personality characteristic this indicates that the characteristic under investigation is genetically determined. A number of studies have demonstrated that characteristics such as extraversion and neuroticism are inherited to some extent. However, it is now generally accepted that what we inherit is a predisposition to behave in particular ways, and that our experiences in the environment in which we live will either minimize or maximize our inherited potential. The question that psychologists are asking now is not 'Is characteristic X genetically or environmentally determined?' but is instead 'How does the environment interact with the genetic predisposition to enhance or diminish characteristic X?'.

To illustrate this point, let's take the example of male and female sex role behaviour. There is growing evidence that boys are born with a predisposition to be more active and aggressive than girls, as well as more interested in toys such as trucks and guns, and that girls are less interested in rough play and more interested in dolls and dressing up. The predisposition towards male sex role behaviour in boys is associated with the higher levels of androgens (male sex hormones) to which boys are exposed in the womb as a result of their Y chromosome. The function of the Y chromosome is to stimulate the testes to produce androgens. Girls' behaviour has been attributed to the lower levels of androgens to which they are exposed in the womb. As infants, small differences in the behaviour of boys and girls can be observed but, more importantly, large differences are found between the way in which parents treat their sons and daughters, encouraging them towards sex stereotyped behaviour. So what is the cause of the sex differences in behaviour that are apparent between boys and girls? It is thought that boys and girls are born with a predisposition to behave in sex-stereotyped ways, but that parents and others act on the small difference between the sexes to encourage boys and girls to follow different developmental paths resulting in significant sex differences in some aspects of behaviour. It is important to point out, however, that not all boys and girls behave in sex-stereotyped ways – there is a great deal of overlap between the sexes. There are also cultural differences in the expression of sex role behaviour – what is considered a male activity in one culture may be viewed as a female activity in another – and these cultural differences demonstrate the important influence of the environment in shaping the behavioural characteristics that an individual will exhibit. The attitudes and stereotypes to which we are exposed in our everyday life have a profound influence on how we behave.

Another characteristic that has received much attention recently is aggression. Whereas there is evidence from twin studies that a tendency to aggression is inherited, the extent and manner in which a person will exhibit aggressive behaviour is largely dependent upon that person's social environment. The family, in particular, is thought to inhibit or exacerbate aggressive behaviour in childhood and adolescence according to the reaction of parents. Studies have also shown that the wider social environment plays a key role. For example, boys who are raised in a subculture where aggression is acceptable are themselves more likely to engage in aggressive behaviour.

With the huge advances that have been made in recent years in identifying specific genes that are responsible for specific disorders such as Huntingdon's Disease and Cystic Fibrosis, attempts have also been made to identify single genes that determine specific behavioural characteristics. It has even been claimed that a gene for sensation-seeking and a gene for male homosexuality have been found. These claims await replication before conclusions can be drawn regarding their significance. Nevertheless, it should be remembered that most behavioural characteristics, to the extent that they are genetically determined, are thought to result from many genes and not just a single gene pair.

Theories of personality

The major psychological theories of personality are described below. Each theory has produced its own form of assessment. For example, questionnaires are derived from the psychometric approach, projective techniques from the psychoanalytic approach, behavioural rating scales from the social learning approach and repertory grids from the humanistic approach.

The various theoretical approaches differ fundamentally in their conceptualization of human personality. The psychoanalytic approach views personality as biologically-based, relatively unchangeable and determined by the need to control sexual and aggressive instincts. In contrast, humanistic psychologists emphasize the person's active role in shaping his or her own experiences, and believe that a psychologically healthy person is one who is striving for self-actualization rather than simply controlling his or her sexual and aggressive drives. Followers of the psychometric approach see themselves as scientists searching for facts, and criticize both psychoanalysts and humanists as being unscientific. Social learning theorists, like psychoanalytic theorists, are deterministic in their approach. Unlike psychoanalytic explanations of personality, however, social learning theory focuses on environmental influences on behaviour.

The psychometric approach

The psychometric approach to studying personality began with the work of Allport and Odbert (1936), who systematically selected all words from the dictionary that could be used to describe human characteristics. After laboriously omitting synonyms and terms that were rarely used or little understood, they were left with a list of approximately 4,500 words that they categorized according to their meaning. The guiding idea behind this enormous undertaking was that the dictionary contains all of the words that we use to distinguish between people, and thus provides a comprehensive record of our perceptions of the characteristics of others.

Following this early work, psychologists began to apply the technique of factor analysis to Allport and Odbert's word list to produce a smaller number of groups of related words. Factor analysis is a statistical procedure whereby items that are correlated with each other are combined to form overall scales, or 'factors'. Factor analysis

131

calculates intercorrelations between the responses of a large number of people to a set of items, and arranges the information in dimensions in order of importance. For example, the first factor of a set of personality items may relate to extraversion, and contain all of the items that have a strong association with extraversion. Some of these items may also relate to other dimensions and appear on these factors as well. In principle there can be as many factors as items in the questionnaire, but those towards the end will have little meaning. A major task of the factor analyst is to decide the point in the hierarchy beyond which the remaining factors are of no importance. Factor analysis is discussed in Chapter 7.

One of the most influential factor-analytic theorists was Raymond Cattell. By asking people to rate their friends, and themselves, on 200 words from the Allport and Odbert list, and submitting these ratings to factor analysis, he produced the following 16 personality factors (Cattell 1957; 1965):

Low-score description	*High-score description*
reserved, cool, impersonal	warm, easygoing, likes people
concrete-thinking	abstract-thinking
easily upset, emotional, impatient	emotionally stable, mature, patient
submissive, accommodating	dominant, assertive, opinionated
serious, sober, prudent, quiet	cheerful, expressive, enthusiastic
expedient, disregards rules	conforming, persevering, rule-bound
shy, timid, threat-sensitive	socially bold, unafraid, can take stress
tough-minded, insensitive, rough	sensitive, tender-minded
trusting, adaptable, accepting	suspicious, hard-to-fool, sceptical
practical, down-to-earth, conventional	imaginative, absent-minded, impractical
forthright, unpretentious, open	shrewd, polished, calculating
confident, self-satisfied, complacent	insecure, apprehensive, self-blaming
conservative, traditional, resists change	liberal, innovative, open to change
group-oriented, sociable	self-sufficient, resourceful, self-directed
undisciplined, uncontrolled, compulsive	controlled, socially precise
relaxed, composed, has lower drive	tense, restless, has high drive

A profile of a person's personality can be obtained by plotting on a graph his or her score (with a range of 1–10) for each of the 16 factors (Cattell 1986).

In the UK, Hans Eysenck has also used factor analysis, but instead of the 16 factors favoured by Cattell, he argued that the structure of personality is more usefully described by two dimensions that he called extraversion–introversion and neuroticism (emotionally stable–emotionally unstable) (Eysenck 1967a; Eysenck and Eysenck 1985). Whereas extraverts are sociable and like parties, introverts are quiet and introspective, and the dimension of neuroticism represents people who are anxious and moody at one end, and calm and carefree at the other. In fact, Eysenck's view of personality does not contradict that of Cattell as further factor analysis of Cattell's 16 factors results in Eysenck's 2 factors. To some extent factor analysis is a subjective procedure in that the outcome will depend on the measures that it is decided to include in the first place, as well as on the point at which it is decided to end the procedure. It is largely a matter of personal preference whether a researcher will opt for a larger number of factors to give a wider description of personality, or a smaller number to produce fewer factors that are more robust. However, in recent years, psychologists have come to favour five personality factors as the optimum number because the same five dimensions have repeatedly emerged from a large number of studies using a wide variety of measures (McCrae and Costa 1987). This model is discussed in more detail in Chapter 10.

Psychoanalytic theory

Sigmund Freud's psychoanalytic theory, based on the notion that an individual's personality is a manifestation of his or her underlying unconscious processes, has had a profound effect on the way in which human beings think about themselves. Although not a scientific theory, in that it cannot be tested empirically, Freud's work has led us to accept the idea of the unconscious and that much of our behaviour is motivated by impulses of which we are largely unaware. According to Freud, our adult personality is shaped by our thoughts and experiences in early childhood. But because these early thoughts are often unacceptable due to their sexual and aggressive nature, they are repressed. Although we cannot remember these early experiences as adults, they are assumed to play a critical role in our behaviour.

Freud conceptualized the structure of personality as comprising three parts: the *id*, *ego* and *superego*. Although these parts interact, each has a different function.

The *id*, which is entirely unconscious, is considered to be the innermost core of personality from which the *ego* and *superego* later develop. Freud argued that infants are born as pure biological creatures, motivated by intense erotic and aggressive desires, and that the psychological locus of these desires is the *id*. According to Freud, these desires build up in the *id* and produce tension, causing the *id* to function in an irrational and impulsive way. The seeking of immediate tension reduction is known as the 'pleasure principle'. It is postulated that in order to reduce tension, the *id* forms an internal image or fantasy of the desired object. For example, a hungry infant may fantasize about the mother's breast. But because the reduction of tension cannot be wholly achieved through fantasy alone, the *ego* develops to take over this function.

Soon after birth, part of the *id* develops into the *ego*, or conscious self. The formation of the *ego* allows the infant to cope with the desires of the *id* through rational thought. It has to differentiate between internal desires and the reality of the external world. The *ego* is governed by the 'reality principle', which requires it to test reality and delay the discharge of tension until the appropriate object is found. For example, the *ego* allows the infant to reason that although the breast is not available now, it will be available again at some point in the future. This is the early beginning of the ability to delay gratification, i.e. the ability to wait for something that we want very much. Thus the *id* seeks the immediate fulfilment of desires, whereas the *ego* mediates between the *id* and the external world, testing reality and delaying impulses for immediate gratification until the appropriate conditions arise. A major function of the ego is to channel erotic and aggressive desires into more culturally acceptable activities.

The *superego* develops from the *ego* and internalizes the moral standards set by parents and, indirectly, by society. By producing feelings of guilt, the *superego* restricts the attempts of the *id* and *ego* to obtain morally unacceptable gratification. According to Freud, a person with a well-developed *superego* will not succumb to immoral acts, such as violence or theft, even when no witnesses are present. Essentially, the *superego* is the conscience, differentiating good from bad, and right from wrong.

The *id*, *ego* and *superego* are considered to be in perpetual conflict, with the *id* trying to express instinctual desires, the *superego* trying to impose moral standards, and the *ego* trying to keep a balance between the two. Freud argues that an imbalance in this system will result in anxiety, and that in order to reduce this anxiety, defence mechanisms come into play. Defence mechanisms are unconscious processes that reduce anxiety by distorting reality. These include denial, repression and regression. Denial occurs when a person does not acknowledge the existence of some aspect of reality. Repression occurs when a person keeps anxiety-inducing thoughts from consciousness. Regression occurs when a person reverts to behaviours that are characteristic of an earlier stage of development.

From a psychoanalytic perspective, an individual's personality derives partly from the way in which conflict is resolved between the *id*, *ego* and *superego*, and partly from the way in which he or she coped in childhood with problems at different stages of development. Freud believed that we proceed through five stages of psychosexual development – oral, anal, phallic, latency and genital. During the oral stage (first year of life) infants derive pleasure from sucking. In the anal stage (second year of life), toddlers derive pleasure from withholding and expelling faeces. During the phallic stage (age 3–6 years) children derive pleasure from touching their genitals. It is at this stage that boys are believed to experience the Oedipal conflict, i.e. the conflict between their sexual desire for their mother and their resultant fear of castration by their father, a conflict which is resolved by identifying with their father. A parallel process is purported to occur for girls resulting in identification with their mother. The ages 7 to 12 represent the latency period during which children are less concerned with sexual desires. The final stage is the genital stage when children reach puberty and begin to experience adult sexual feelings.

A central tenet of Freud's theory is that a child who successfully progresses through each stage will reach the genital stage and become a mature adult. But if conflict is not resolved, development may be arrested or 'fixated' at an earlier stage, thus influencing his or her adult personality. For example, a person fixated at the oral stage may engage in excessive eating and drinking (oral personality), and a person fixated at the anal stage may be overly concerned with tidiness and saving money (anal personality). According to psychoanalytic theory, our personality is largely determined by our experiences in the first five years of life.

Although Freud has many followers, he was very intolerant of dissenting views. While agreeing with much of his theory, many of his closest colleagues took issue with some of Freud's ideas. Two of the most well known dissenters in Freud's day were Alfred Adler and Carl Jung. Contemporary Freudians, or neo-Freudians as they are known, have adopted an object relations approach to understanding human personality, i.e. they place more emphasis on the role of the *ego* and its independence from the *id*, as well as on the processes involved in attachment to, and autonomy from, parents.

Social learning theory

The social learning approach to understanding personality formation emphasizes the importance of the social environment in determining an individual's behaviour, i.e. that behaviour is learned through our experiences in interacting with the environment. Individual differences in behaviour are viewed as resulting from past differences in learning experiences.

According to social learning theory, behaviour is acquired in two ways: through reinforcement and modelling. The process of reinforcement is based on the principle that behaviour is modified by its consequences; behaviour that has favourable consequences (reinforcement) is more likely to be repeated, while behaviour that is not rewarded or is punished is less likely to be performed again. For example, sex differences in behaviour are thought by social learning theorists to result from the differential reinforcement of boys and girls. The consequences for children of many behaviours depends upon their sex; girls will generally receive a much more positive response than boys for playing with dolls, while boys are more likely than girls to be reinforced for playing with cars and trucks. And because these behaviours produce different outcomes according to the child's sex, they come to be performed with different frequency by boys and girls; girls more often than boys play with dolls, and boys more often than girls play with cars and trucks.

Although reinforcement has a powerful influence on shaping behaviour, social learning also occurs through the observation and imitation of others in the absence of reinforcement. This process is known as modelling or observational learning. To take sex differences in behaviour as an example once again, the modelling of individuals of the same sex is considered to be important for the process of sex role development. Children learn about both male and female sex role behaviour through observational learning. But they are more likely to imitate models of the same sex as themselves, not only because this is expected to yield more favourable consequences, but also because they come to value behaviour which is considered to be appropriate for their own sex.

While modelling is now generally viewed as an important aspect of social learning, the mechanisms through which this process operates appear to be rather more complex than previously thought. Contemporary social learning theorists, now called cognitive social learning theorists, believe that cognitive skills play a fundamental role in modelling. These include the ability to classify people into distinct groups, to recognize personal similarity to one of these groups, and to store that group's behaviour patterns in memory as the ones to be used to guide behaviour (Bandura 1977).

The influential social learning theorist Walter Mischel (1973; 1993) has also pointed to cognitive processes that influence behaviour such as selective attention to information in the social environment, and expectations about the consequences of different behaviours. According to Mischel, it is individual differences in cognitive processing that cause individual differences in behaviour among different people in the same situation. For Bandura, self-efficacy – our personal judgement of our capabilities – is a fundamental cognitive process that determines our behaviour.

Because social learning theory stresses the importance of the social context in determining whether a person will behave in a certain way, these theorists do not ascribe to the idea of personality traits, i.e. characteristics of an individual that are shown across all situations. Instead, individuals who are shy in one social setting (e.g. at work)

135

are not necessarily expected to be shy in another (e.g. at the gym). Although it is generally acknowledged that a person's social environment will influence his or her behaviour, the idea that there is likely to be little consistency in behaviour from one setting to another is now considered to be too extreme by most personality theorists and researchers.

The humanistic approach

The humanistic approach to the study of personality focuses on the individual's subjective experience. Unlike their psychoanalytic colleagues, humanistic psychologists start with the premise that people are basically well-intentioned, not products of sexual and aggressive drives, and that they have a need to develop their potential (self-actualization). From a humanistic perspective, self-actualization, rather than the need to control undesirable instincts, is the major influence on personality development.

One of the most influential humanistic psychologists was Carl Rogers (1951; 1970; 1980), who, like Freud, developed his theoretical ideas through work with patients or, as Rogers called them, clients. Rogers was the founding father of client-centred therapy, an approach to therapy, and to the understanding of personality, that expounded the fundamental nature of the individual's tendency to fulfil his or her potential. According to Rogers, the tendency to fulfil one's potential, or self-actualize, is a basic motivation of all human beings. The aim of client-centred therapy is, therefore, to help individuals change in a positive direction. Instead of proscribing a course of action, the role of client-centred therapists is, instead, to act as a sounding-board in order to help individuals decide for themselves which direction to take.

Fundamental to Rogers' theory is the notion of the self-concept. All experiences are believed to be evaluated in relation to a person's self-concept, and a person's perception of the self is believed to have a profound effect upon his or her thoughts, feelings and behaviour. For example, a man who believes himself to be attractive to women will behave differently in female company than a man who does not. A person's self-concept does not always reflect reality, however. Just because a man thinks that women find him attractive does not mean that this is necessarily the case. According to Rogers, a person whose self-concept is consistent with reality will be well-adjusted, whereas emotional problems such as anxiety will result when the two do not match. It was also Rogers who put forward the concept of the ideal self, i.e. the person we would like to be. A close correspondence between the real self and the ideal self is thought to lead to emotional well-being, whereas the consequence of a large discrepancy between the two is likely to be psychological distress.

Abraham Maslow (1967; 1970) was also a key figure in the development of humanistic psychology. Although similar in approach to Rogers, Maslow is probably most well known for his Hierarchy of Needs. According to Maslow, individuals are motivated by a series of needs beginning with physiological needs such as hunger and thirst, moving up through a hierarchy including the need to feel safe and the need to feel loved, and culminating in the need to find self-fulfilment and realize one's potential. It is only when needs at the bottom of the hierarchy are at least partly met that those higher up begin to motivate us to action. Maslow argues that we are unlikely to be motivated by a desire to understand our wider environment, or by a desire for beauty, if our energies are being consumed by the search for food. It is only when our basic needs are satisfied that we can turn our attention to higher levels.

Maslow was particularly interested in those who had reached the highest level, self-actualization, and carried out studies to establish what distinguished these people from others. He found that college students who had reached the stage of self-actualization were exceptionally well adjusted. He also studied eminent men and women such as Albert Einstein and Eleanor Roosevelt and found them to have the following characteristics.

- They perceive reality efficiently and are able to tolerate uncertainty.
- They accept themselves and others for what they are.
- They are spontaneous in thought and behaviour.
- They are problem-centred rather than self-centred.
- They have a good sense of humour.
- They are highly creative.
- They are resistant to enculturation although not purposely unconventional.
- They are concerned for the welfare of humanity.
- They are capable of deep appreciation of the basic experiences of life.
- They establish deep satisfying interpersonal relationships with a few, rather than many, people.
- They are able to look at life from an objective viewpoint.

Although humanistic psychologists would not deny that biological and environmental influences might contribute to personality development, their main emphasis is on the active role played by the individual. For psychologists such as Rogers and Maslow, self-actualization is the key to psychological health. A humanistic theorist who played a key role in the development of assessment techniques was George Kelly, whose personal construct theory led to the idea of the repertory grid.

Types versus traits

Type theorists propose that everyone can be divided into discrete categories that are qualitatively different from each other. Classifying people according to types dates back as far as Hippocrates in 400 BC, who proposed that there were four personality types associated with a predominance of one of the four bodily humours: black bile produced the melancholic (depressed) type, blood produced the sanguine (optimistic) type, yellow bile produced the choleric (irritable) type, and phlegm produced the phlegmatic (calm) type.

The origins of trait theory can be traced back to the development of the IQ testing movement, particularly to the work of Galton and Spearman. From the perspective of trait theory, variation in personality is viewed as continuous, i.e. a specific personality characteristic will vary in strength along a continuum. The advantage of a trait approach is that a person can be described according to the extent to which he or she shows a particular set of characteristics. In contrast, assignment to a type is an all-or-nothing manner; a person is categorized as either belonging, or not belonging, to a specific category.

In fact, the distinction between types and traits is not as clear-cut as it may seem. To illustrate the relationship between the two, Eysenck has demonstrated that the four personality types of Hippocrates can be represented by the two independent traits of extraversion and neuroticism, and that a person can exhibit each trait to a greater or lesser degree. Thus people can be extravert to a greater or lesser extent, as well as neurotic to a greater or lesser extent, and can be categorized as melancholic, sanguine, choleric or phlegmatic according to their position along these two dimensions.

One of the most influential type theories was proposed by Jung, and forms the basis of the Myers-Briggs Type Indicator (Myers and McCauley 1985). The four dimensions of the inventory are extraversion–introversion, sensing–intuition, thinking–feeling and judging–perception. Respondents are assigned to one side of each dimension, and their combination of dimensions determines which of the possible 16 types they represent. For example, those of the EIFP type (Extraverted-Intuitive-Feeling-Perceiving) are described as 'enthusiastic innovators' who are 'skilful at handling people'. Millon has also used a type approach in the Millon Index of Personality Styles to classify people as, for example, retiring or outgoing, individualizing or nurturing and complaining or agreeing.

In spite of appearing conceptually different, trait and type models are very similar in practice, and the same test can be treated as a test either of traits or of types. This is because test scores are open to two possible interpretations. We can either assume that the score on the test represents a person's *actual* score on a continuous trait (i.e. the extent to which the person exhibits the trait), or we can sssume that it represents a measure of the probability that the person fits into one type or another (depending on whether a person's score is above or below a specific cut-off point, that person is classified as belonging to one type or another).

For example, if a person obtains a score of 3 on a 24-point scale of introversion–extraversion (with a low score representing introversion, a high score representing extraversion, and a cut-off point of 12), then there is a high probability that he or she actually is an introvert type, and a low probability that he or she actually is an extravert type. A score of 12 shows that he or she has an equal probability of being either an introvert type or an extravert type. For those with a score of 11, there is a slightly higher probability that he or she is an introvert type than an extravert type. Thus a person's score on any extraversion scale may be used to represent their position along an introversion–extraversion dimension (trait) or as an indication of the probability that the person is an extravert or an introvert (type). In practice, however, scores on type measures are collapsed so that people are categorized as belonging to either the introvert or the extravert type.

Approaches to personality assessment

Self-report techniques and personality profiles

Self-report inventories comprise a series of items to which individuals respond according to how they view themselves. Paper-and-pencil questionnaires such as the Sixteen Personality Factor Questionnaire (16 PF) (Cattell 1965) are the most widely used self-report measures, although computerized self-report techniques are increasing in popularity. Orpheus (Rust 1996e), a work-based assessment of 12 personality traits, and Giotto (Rust 1997), an integrity test, can be administered either by paper-and-pencil or by computer. The advantages of self-report inventories are that they are quick and easy to administer, they can be administered to groups, the scoring is objective, and the responses are obtained directly from the person being assessed. Limitations may be that assessees may not have good insight about themselves, they may try to present themselves in the best possible light, they may try to present themselves according to what they think is expected or desired, and it is difficult to know whether the questionnaire has been completed with due care and attention.

The results of self-report psychometric personality tests are often reported as a personality profile. Within a profile, not one but many test scores are presented, but in such a way that they can be compared with each other. These are called sub-scales, and there can often be items from as many as 20 sub-scales existing in one personality test with their items randomly interspersed, the items only being brought together for scoring purposes. Raw sub-scale scores need to be standardized, and the set of standardized sub-scale scores are then illustrated on a profile sheet, which will have a sub-scale score as the y axis, usually with stanine scores ranging from 1 to 9 with 5 as the mid-point, and the various sub-scales laid out along the x axis. An example of a profile is given in Figure 9.1.

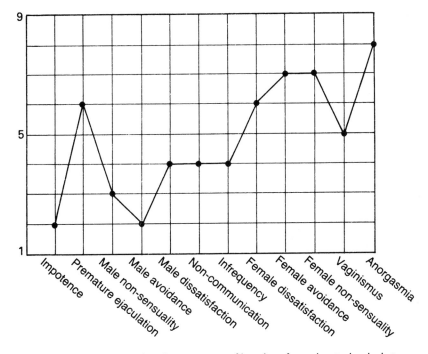

Figure 9.1 An example of a diagnostic profile taken from the Golombok Rust Inventory of Sexual Satisfaction (GRISS)

Note: Twelve sub-scales have transformed scores of 1 to 9, with 5 and above indicating a problem. This particular profile is for a couple attending a sexual dysfunction clinic.

One of the earliest profile systems developed was the Minnesota Multiphasic Personality Inventory (MMPI), which is still in use today and which provides a good general example of the technique. The MMPI was developed as a broad-spectrum personality test to be used on psychiatric patients, usually on admission to psychiatric hospital. It consists of over 400 personality-test-style items (of the type: Are you a nervous person? Do you sometimes hear voices? Are there enemies who are out to get you? etc.), which form a set of sub-scales within the overall questionnaire. Within the MMPI there are sub-scales of hypochondriasis, depression, hysteria, psychopathy, paranoia, psychoasthenia, schizophrenia, hypomania and masculinity–femininity. These sub-scales are each scored separately, and each is subjected to separate standardization. An individual's MMPI sub-scale scores are entered as points on a graph, and the points joined to form a profile. On such a profile, areas that are particularly problematic will appear as peaks on the graph, the higher the peak the greater being the disturbance. Psychiatrists who see large numbers of such profiles on their patients will soon begin to recognize common patterns, representing well-known conditions, such as for example paranoid schizophrenia.

Expert use of MMPI profiles can save a clinician a great deal of time. Obvious disorders stand out easily, difficulties are immediately made apparent, and the data are summarized in a standard and accepted way for all clinicians. While the ways in which profiles are used by professionals depend on the use of judgement, with the instrument as a tool for helping an essentially human process, the same principles of reliability, validity and proper standardization apply to each of the sub-scales as would apply to a single longer scale. Thus the proper psychometric construction of a profiling system is a much more complex and time-consuming process than constructing a single test.

Reports by others

These involve evaluation by someone who is familiar with the person being assessed. For example, an appraisal from a supervisor or more senior colleague. Rating scales are often used for this purpose. The advantages are that the report is independent of the impression that the assessee may wish to convey, and that the report is based on a person's actual behaviour at work. Limitations are that relevant criteria for judging successful performance are difficult to define; that the report is dependent upon how well the assessor knows the assessee; that the assessor's report may be influenced by how much he or she likes or dislikes the assessee, or by personal knowledge of the assessee, such as previous qualifications; that the assessor may have a vested interest in the assessee obtaining a positive or negative evaluation; that the assessor may not be competent to evaluate the assessee; that the assessor may have a tendency to give positive, neutral or negative evaluations of all assessees; that the assessor may hold stereotypes (for example about women in the workplace) that may influence the report; that the assessor may be reluctant to commit negative evaluations to paper; or that the assessor may be biased against unpopular assessees even if good at their job.

Situational assessments

Situational assessments may be conducted with individuals or groups, and refer to the evaluation of a person's behaviour, or the behaviour of the group, in circumstances that are similar to the work environment. The situation may be 'real life' or simulated for the purpose of assessment. For example, an essential element of the selection process for astronauts involves subjecting potential recruits to simulated spaceship conditions to assess their behavioural tolerance for the particular stressors that they would experience on an actual mission. The advantage is that it gives a sample of a person's actual behaviour in a relevant situation. The limitations are that it is time-consuming and costly; that assessees' behaviour may be influenced positively or negatively by the knowledge that they are being assessed; that assessees may perform differently in an artificial situation; that the stress of engaging in a situational assessment may interfere with optimal performance; that the method is dependent on the skills and integrity of observers; and that inter-rater reliability can be poor.

Projective measures

Projective tests involve the presentation of ambiguous stimuli, such as inkblots or pictures, on which individuals can 'project' their inner needs and feelings. It is assumed that whatever structure is attributed to the stimulus is a reflection of the respondent's personality. Probably the best known projective measure is the Rorschach Inkblot Test comprising ten inkblots to which individuals are asked to respond according to what they see. The test is scored by taking account of factors such as the content of the response, the part of the inkblot used to produce the response and the time taken to respond. The Thematic Apperception Test (TAT) uses pictures as projective stimuli, and respondents are asked to tell what events led up to the scene in the picture, what is happening in the picture, and what the outcome will be. The advantages are that it is an indirect assessment of personality therefore it is less obvious what a socially desirable response should be, or what might be expected; that individuals are free to respond in any way they wish, they are not constrained by standard response options; and that the responses are thought to represent unconscious as well as conscious processes. Limitations are that no clear consensus exists about the meaning of responses; that the procedure has a lack of validity against external criteria; that responses are open to situational influences such as the characteristics of the test administrator; that scoring is dependent on expertise of test administrator; that scores are unreliable, particularly of test–retest reliability, as responses are situation-dependent.

Observations of behaviour

This involves the systematic observation of a person's behaviour, often with a focus on the antecedents and consequences of the behaviours of interest and with a view to the development of an intervention programme. Behavioural observation is most commonly used in clinical settings to assess behavioural problems. For example, a person suffering from agoraphobia may be observed at the supermarket or on public transport in order to assess factors associated with the onset of anxiety and the consequences of the person's response to an anxiety-provoking situation. In the workplace, observation of behaviour might be used to assess how well a person can communicate information or give feedback. The advantage is that it gives a direct assessment of actual behaviour and thus provides information on whether a person can actually do something rather than just say they can. The limitations are that it is time-consuming; it only assesses samples of behaviour; and that behaviour may change as a result of being observed, i.e. may show what a person *can* do, not what he or she *will* do when not observed.

Task performance methods

Task performance assessment involves assessing a person's ability to conduct a relevant piece of work, and is similar to a situational assessment. A widely used example in the assessment of leadership ability is the 'leaderless group', whereby a group of people are required to carry out a task without anyone being put in charge. The behaviour of each person, and of the group as a whole, is monitored by an observer and rated according to a set of criteria of interest which may include a person's ability to work in a team, to communicate or to take control. Another example of the use of performance methods in organizations is the 'in-basket' technique. The person is presented with an in-basket filled with a variety of letters, memos, etc. to deal with in a limited period of time, and assessed according to criteria such as decision-making and problem-solving ability. The advantage is that it gives a sample of a person's actual behaviour in relevant work tasks. The limitations are that it is time-consuming and costly; that assessees' behaviour may be influenced by the knowledge that they are being assessed; that assessees may perform differently in an artificial situation; that stress produced by being assessed may interfere with optimal performance; that it is dependent upon the skills and integrity of the observer; and that inter-rater reliability can be poor.

Psychophysiological measures

Physiological measures used in the assessment of personality include pulse rate, blood pressure, respiration, brain waves and galvanic skin response (changes in electrical resistance of the skin associated with sweating). Most commonly, these indices have been used to assess reactivity to stressful situations. However, controversial 'lie detector' tests are also based on physiological measures. The 'lie detector', or polygraph, produces a graphic representation of a person's physiological state (for example pulse rate and galvanic skin response) in response to detailed questioning. It is claimed that lying causes changes in physiological responses that can be detected from the graphic output of the machine. The advantage is that the assessees cannot easily fake their responses. The limitations are that there is no clear evidence that a machine can detect lying as opposed to changes in emotional state for other reasons; that there is a risk of the assessee being accused of lying when telling the truth due to false positive results; that it is dependent on the expertise of the assessor; that it is dependent on the psychological state of the assessee; and that the assessee's responses may be influenced by the behaviour of the assessor.

Repertory grids

The repertory grid technique stems from personal construct theory, a framework for understanding and assessing personality developed by Kelly (1955). This approach is based on the assumption that everyone interprets (or constructs) events differently, and aims to elicit the specific constructs that are commonly used by individual people to understand their world. A construct is deduced by asking a person to state the ways in which two people (elements) are alike but different from a third. For example, from a list of significant people in a particular man's life, he may be asked how his father and brother are alike but different from his sister. As this is repeated for different groups of three people, the constructs he uses to organize information about others (i.e. the way he sees his own environment) begin to emerge. These may be tense vs. relaxed, loud vs. quiet, or hard-working vs. lazy. The idea that people may vary according to, for example, how tense or relaxed they are would then be considered as one of that man's constructs. The Role Construct Repertory Test (the Rep Test) is an example of a measure that has been designed to identify personal constructs in relation to a variety of roles such as 'boss', 'disliked co-worker' and 'liked acquaintance'. The advantages are that it can be tailored to a specific person and a specific situation; and that it is not immediately obvious what constitutes an acceptable response. Limitations are that expertise is needed to use it effectively; that there is always a need to make new versions for different purposes; that reliability and validity need to be determined for each version; and that it requires collaboration from the client in selecting relevant elements.

Sources and management of sabotage

Sabotage in personality assessment can be either deliberate or unconscious. For example, a person may agree with the lie scale item 'Throughout my life I have always returned everything I have borrowed', either because they are lying or because they genuinely (but mistakenly) believe this to be true. Management of sabotage can be considered from the point of view of test construction, test administration and scoring. Test manuals should always be consulted in order to establish the steps that have been taken to minimize the possibility of sabotage or distortion. Because of the dangers of sabotage, evidence from outside the testing situation, such as corroboration by others, should also be considered. Sources and management of sabotage are described below.

Self-report techniques

Sources of sabotage are:

(a)   lying;
(b)   presenting oneself in a favourable light;
(c)   responding according to how one thinks a successful candidate would respond;
(d)   responding randomly;
(e)   omitting questions or endorsing more than one allowed response, e.g. yes *and* no;
(f)   changing the questions and responding accordingly; and
(g)   answering in the same way (e.g. 'disagree') to long sections of the questionnaire.

It can be managed by

(i)   the use of a questionnaire with a built-in lie detector;
(ii)   the use of a questionnaire that has eliminated items to which people commonly lie;
(iii)   informing respondents that the test is able to detect lying;
(iv)   using a questionnaire that has balanced favourable with non-favourable aspects of each personality characteristic being measured;
(v)   using a questionnaire that has items for which the preferred responses are not obvious;
(vi)   using a questionnaire for which random responses generate a neutral score or profile;
(vii)   informing respondents that the test is able to detect random responding;
(viii) using a questionnaire for which items likely to be omitted or wrongly answered have been screened out during development;
(ix)   using a questionnaire with a scoring system that substitutes estimated values for missing values (but this can only be done for a maximum of about 5% of questions);
(x)   using a questionnaire for which items that tend to be altered have been eliminated during development;
(xi)   using a questionnaire with a scoring system that treats altered items as missing and substitutes estimated values for missing values (but this can only be done for a maximum of about 5% of questions); and
(xii)   using a questionnaire with a scoring system that rejects completed questionnaires with the same response throughout and re-administer the questionnaire.

Reports by others

Sources:

(a)   assessors may present assessees in a favourable light because this reflects posi-tively on themselves, e.g. if they have been responsible for training the assessee;
(b)   collusion between assessor and assessee, e.g. asking assessees to assess themselves;

(c)   the assessor may give a negative evaluation of someone they do not like, or a particularly good evaluation of someone they do like; or

(d)   the assessor may not follow the instructions on the assessment forms, e.g. omits sections.

It can be managed by

(i)   developing specific assessment criteria;

(ii)   thorough training of assessors in accuracy and fairness;

(iii)   careful monitoring of assessments;

(iv)   obtaining assessments from more than one person;

(v)   the use of independent assessors;

(vi)   ensuring that assessors understand the purpose of the assessment process and their responsibility within it;

(vii)   ensuring that the assessor is informed that self-assessment is not acceptable;

(viii) allowing the assessee to vet assessors;

(ix)   monitoring the integrity of assessors;

(x)   training assessors to give an independent assessment and

(xi)   ensuring that assessment forms are constructed and piloted by experts.

Situational assessments

Source: the assessee will not treat assessment seriously. This can be managed by independent monitoring of attitudes towards assessment.

Projective measures

Source: non-cooperation, e.g. censoring responses to give only socially acceptable ones. This can be managed by using experienced test administrators who can identify non-co-operation; and by training test administrators in how to build up rapport with the assessee in order to facilitate open responding.

Observations of behaviour

Source: the assessee will be on best behaviour. This is managed by observing the assessee for longer periods of time, or at random.

Task performance methods

Sources:

(a)   assessees present themselves in the expected role (e.g. giving instructions in the 'leaderless group') rather than in the role to which they may be most suited (e.g. following instructions);

(b)   assessees may undermine others who are competing in the task;

(c)   assesses may do what they think is required (e.g. make tough decisions during the 'in-basket' procedure) rather than what they would actually do in practice (e.g. fail to make tough decisions when necessary); or

(d)   assessees may present what they *can* do (e.g. be industrious during the 'in-basket' procedure) rather than what they *actually* do in practice (e.g. be really lazy).

This can be managed by

(i)   making the task as real as possible;

(ii)   using experienced and well-trained assessors;

(iii) monitoring the assessee's contribution to the functioning of the group as a whole rather than just leadership;

(iv)   ensuring that the preferred responses are not obvious; and

(v)   lengthening the task and ensuring that it is challenging.

Psychophysiological measures

Sources: (a) assessees can learn to control psychophysiological responses for example clenching fists to produce a galvanic skin response to each question; and (b) assessees can generate inappropriate thoughts to mislead the machine, e.g. think relaxing thoughts rather than concentrating on the questions. This can be managed by careful design of interview to enable the detection of deliberate manipulation, e.g. to see whether an increase in galvanic skin response occurs in response to a neutral question.

Repertory grids

Sources: (a) presenting oneself in a favourable light; and (b) responding according to how we think a successful candidate would respond. This can be managed by careful piloting involving simulation of attempts at distortion so that these can be recognized; and by ensuring that the test is devised by experts trained in the identification of misleading responses.

Informal methods of personality assessment

The types of bias outlined above result from deliberate distortion by the assessee or from the assessor. Other types of bias that can be produced by both the assessment and the assessor include racial bias, gender bias, bias against those with special needs, as well as biases such as ageism, classism and heightism.

Carefully constructed assessment procedures should have taken account of these forms of bias during the development process, eliminating their effects or reducing them to a minimum. It is always important to confirm that this has been done by checking the test handbook or the relevant research literature. The possibility of bias resulting directly from the assessor should always be actively considered, and assessors should be screened and trained, ideally within the context of the organization's equal opportunities policy. Assessment procedures should also be monitored, e.g. gender monitoring in selection for senior posts, so that inequalities can be identified and rectified.

It is important to recognize that bias is not unique to formal assessment methods; it is a part of social interaction in everyday life. Nevertheless, there is a tendency to evaluate bias in an assessment instrument against a perfect world where bias does not exist. Instead, the bias in assessment instruments should be compared to the bias that exists with other assessment procedures. The question should not be 'Is this test biased?' but 'Is this test more or less biased than the alternatives?' In fact, formal assessment methods often offer *greater* opportunity to reduce bias than less formal procedures such as interviews, as questions that produce differential responding, for example between men and women, can be identified and excluded. During an interview, however, male and female candidates may be questioned differently due to the underlying stereotypes of men and women held by the person doing the interviewing. These stereotypes are pervasive in our social world and, although they may evolve and change, are unlikely to disappear. A major strength of objective assessment techniques is that they provide a mechanism whereby the biases that result from social stereotypes can be monitored and reduced.

State versus trait measures

Some measures assess a person's current psychological state at the time of testing (state measures) whereas others assess their general pattern of functioning, i.e. how they usually are (trait measures). A polygraph measure is an example of the former, and personality questionnaires such as the 16PF and Orpheus are both examples of the latter. Some assessments comprise both state and trait measures, allowing a person's current state to be interpreted in the light of his or her general trait. An example is the Spielberger State–Trait Anxiety Inventory, a measure of anxiety for which one form (the State Anxiety Inventory) asks respondents to grade statements such as 'I feel calm' according to how they feel right now, and the other form (the Trait Anxiety Inventory) asks them to answer the questions according to how they feel generally.

It is usually assumed that trait measures, because they are assessing an enduring underlying characteristic, are unaffected by the respondent's current state. However, it is always important to be aware that a person who is, for example, particularly happy or sad at the time of assessment may respond, to some extent at least, according to his or her mood state.

Ipsative scaling

Ipsative scaling involves the use of items for which the respondent is required to choose one of two options. In a vocational preference scale, a person may be asked if they want to be an engineer (non-ipsative) or, alternatively, if they would prefer to be an engineer or a chemist (ipsative). This approach is particularly useful in differentiating between career possibilities within the same general area, e.g. architect vs. interior designer. The Jackson Vocational Interest Survey (Jackson 1977) requires respondents to choose between options such as 'Acting in a school play' and 'Teaching children how to write', and produces scales such as job security, dominant leadership and stamina. Another example is Giotto, an ipsative test of integrity for use in occupational settings. Respondents are presented with alternative adjectives, such as 'tolerant' vs. 'secure', and asked to select the one that most applies to them. Giotto's scale scores are designed to identify the strongest and weakest aspects of the respondent's character. A major benefit of the ipsative format is to reduce 'faking good' by forcing individuals to choose between options that are similar with respect to social desirability.

With ipsative tests, the endorsement of an item relating to one scale necessarily means that the comparison scale is not endorsed, and thus the total score obtained for each scale is not independent of the scores obtained for the other scales. Scores on ipsative tests are best interpreted in relation to scores on the other scales in the same test for the same person, rather than as absolute measures that can be compared between people (normative tests). The strength of the normative test is that all scales are independent of each other. Normative tests are favoured by statisticians because the independence of the scales allows a wide range of statistical procedures to be used in data analysis, such as correlation analysis for the assessment of reliability, and because the dimensions can be interpreted independently of each other. However, with a normative test it is possible for respondents to obtain a high score for all of the scales. The advantage of an ipsative test is that it forces the respondent to rank some characteristics as more or less important than others.

The danger of interpreting an ipsative test as if it is normative is illustrated by the following example. Person A who obtains a score of 8 for interest in engineering and 12 for interest in chemistry would by advised to pursue chemistry, whereas person B who obtains a score of 15 for chemistry and 20 for engineering would be advised to follow an engineering route. The fact that person B obtained a higher score than person A for interest in chemistry is obscured by the use of an ipsative procedure.

Spurious validity and the Barnum Effect

Face validity is more important for personality assessment than it is for the assessment of ability. If questions are not viewed by respondents as measuring what they are purported to measure, then the respondents may not co-operate with the test. If asked, for example, about their sexual orientation or their religion as part of a questionnaire designed to select them for a job, many people would feel this to be inappropriate and not answer the question. In the USA, employers have been sued for using questionnaires that include such questions.

One test of the face validity of an instrument is whether its name, and the names of the scales, are acceptable to those who are required to complete it. For example, a scale labelled 'neurotic' is more likely to be offensive to respondents than a scale labelled 'emotional'. For this reason, an attempt is generally made to label scales in as positive a way as possible. Similarly, feedback to respondents generally emphasizes their positive characteristics rather than their negative ones, and this is also true of computer-generated interpretative reports (narrative descriptions in everyday language of what a person's scores mean).

Although the process of presenting a test positively does not necessarily detract from its true validity, often this is exactly the outcome. For example, the interpretations given to respondents may be so vague as to be meaningless – although very positively received! This phenomenon is known as the 'Barnum Effect', after Barnum the circus owner's famous saying, 'There is a fool born every minute'. The statement 'You are the kind of person who may have successfully overcome difficulties in the past' is a good example of the Barnum Effect. It gives the impression of being meaningful but, in fact, is true of everyone who reads it.

It is the Barnum Effect that is responsible for the success of horoscopes, and many people believe that graphology is also dependent on this phenomenon. Just as people recognize themselves in horoscopes, so they can recognize themselves in feedback from personality tests. It is important to be aware, therefore, that a respondent's belief in the accuracy of his or her feedback may bear little relationship to the validity of the test.

Similarly, just because people like the feedback they receive from an instrument does not mean that it is a valid measure. A good instrument may well produce home-truths that are unacceptable to the respondent, whereas a test may be adopted enthusiastically by managers and candidates alike because the feedback is appealing, even in the absence of evidence of other types of validity.

The test developer may be influenced by the Barnum Effect in the choice of scale labels. Consequently, assessors must be trained to avoid taking these labels at face value. It is always necessary to read the handbook carefully to find out what the scale is actually measuring, i.e. aspects of personality that are not obvious from the label, as well as aspects that are implied by the label but that have not actually been assessed. For example, some scales labelled 'neurotic' include questions relating to anger whereas others specifically attempt to exclude anger items.

Assessment in clinical psychology

Clinical psychologists may use personality-testing techniques for research or for diagnosis. Scores on personality questionnaires such as the Beck Depression Inventory (BDI), for example, can indicate the severity of a patient's depression, or can be used to compare groups receiving different treatments in the evaluation of those treatments. Clinical objective and standardized assessments can also be made of behaviour or of situational parameters, such as the ability of a patient to cope when living on their own.

Neuropsychological assessment

More frequently, clinical psychologists will be called upon to make assessments of a patient's comparative levels of cognitive performance. This may happen, for example, when someone has suffered brain damage following a road accident. Such tests are called neuropsychological and normally take the form of a profile. The use of neuropsychological profiles in this context grew out of a practical need by the medical community to describe more completely the behavioural effects of brain damage. These behavioural data could then act as part of the diagnostic assessment of the severity and localization of brain lesions. As a further advantage it was non-obtrusive, and it could also provide a technique for monitoring improvement after treatment. There have traditionally been two major systems in use, the Halstead–Reitan Batteries (Reitan 1955), and the Luria–Nebraska Neuropsychological Test Battery (Golden *et al.* 1978). The Halstead–Reitan Batteries were almost completely functional and quantitative in their origin, and amounted to a formalization and agreement among clinicians on the set of sub-tests that were appropriate for diagnosis of brain damage. The battery included existing scales, such as the Wechsler Adult Intelligence Scale (Wechsler 1958) as well as new or adapted tests. The sub-test domains include concept formation, abstraction and integration; tactual discrimination, manual dexterity, kinaesthesis, incidental memory, spatial memory, verbal auditory discrimination, auditory visual integration, phonetic skills; non-verbal auditory discrimination, auditory perception; motor speed, visual scanning, visual motor integration, mental flexibility, integration of alphabetic and numeric systems; and motor speed dexterity. Adjunct tests often used were the WAIS or WISC, the MMPI, and tests of lateral dominance. The interpretation of these complex profiles to produce a diagnosis was traditionally carried out by expert judgement, and would also take into account adjustments for age, socio-economic background, sex, chronicity and any other factors which were felt to be relevant. However, in spite of the strong judgemental element in the interpretation, psychometric criteria were of prime importance in establishing the reliability and validity of the sub-tests themselves.

It was felt by the 1960s that many of the tests included in the Halstead–Reitan Battery were rather ad hoc, and the sub-tests of intellectual functioning in particular reflected a hotch-potch of often contradictory underlying theories. While the profile had been found to be effective for diagnostic purposes, advances in brain science generally were suggesting that a battery based on an overall understanding of brain functioning was now a plausible possibility. The first major diagnostic system to involve such a global theory was that of Luria (1973); however, this was qualitative in nature. After several aborted attempts at quantification the Luria–Nebraska System was the first to gain widespread acceptance. Luria's model distinguishes areas of motor function, an acoustic-motor rhythm scale, a higher cutaneous kinaesthetic tactile scale, spatial visual functions, a receptive speech scale, an expressive speech scale, and scales of reading, arithmetic, memory and intellectual functioning.

Both these batteries form an important part of the diagnostic work of neuropsychologists, brain scientists and clinicians. They have been particularly successful in diagnosing brain damage in 18 to 45-year-olds. Difficulties are encountered with children (where the constant presence of developmental change always makes medical diagnosis difficult) and in older people, where the effects of brain damage become confounded with the mental deterioration of the normal ageing process.

Summary

There is a demand for psychometric tests not only in selection but also in clinical or educational assessment. Within these latter settings additional criteria can apply to their construction and use. In educational settings the complex interaction between the curriculum and the test specification in situations where assessment is continuous has led to new understandings in the approach to both. In the clinical setting, the power of psychometric procedures within a single diagnosis has led to a high degree of sophistication and refinement in particular techniques, such as profiling.

Chapter 10

Psychometric assessment of personality in occupational settings

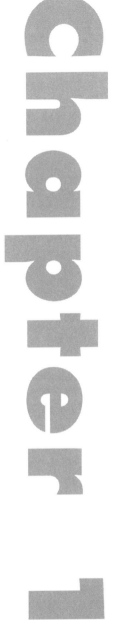

Prior to the 1990s the use of personality tests in occupational settings was widespread but controversial. Some occupational psychologists argued that there was no evidence that assessment by personality questionnaire had anything to offer over and above the assessment of specific competencies using, for example, work sample tests within assessment centres. However, at a folk psychological level there can be no doubt that interviewers are generally very interested in the personality of interviewees, and often find themselves working from job specifications that are very specific in their demand for particular types of personality. Furthermore, certain posts, such as those at the front-end of sales, seem to cry out for some form of personality assessment. Clearly the issue could only be settled by research specifically investigating the validity of personality tests in the workplace.

Personality tests are more difficult to validate than ability tests because each is measuring something different. All ability tests correlate to some extent and assess 'general intelligence' or 'g'. However, there is no such thing as 'general personality', and each claim for validity is consequently specific to particular traits in particular job settings. Because so many different tests were in use it was rather difficult to come to an overall picture. Notwithstanding this, a series of meta-analyses were carried out in the early 1990s that now seem to have settled the issue (Barrick and Mount 1991; Tett *et al.* 1991; Schmit and Ryan, 1993). These studies all demonstrate a sometimes small but nearly always consistent validity for the use of personality tests. This advance was made possible by the adoption of the big-five model of personality as the unifying force for the field.

The big-five model

Questionnaires associated with trait models of personality vary enormously in the number of scales they generate. Some, such as Eysenck's EPQ (Eysenck Personality Questionnaire), target a very few highly stable traits, whereas others, such as Cattell's 16PF, generate a plethora of interrelated and relatively unstable measures. This over-abundance of scales has always presented a problem for occupational psychologists in their attempts to make comparisons and choices among different models and instruments. In recent years, one particular five-trait model has emerged as the favourite and has become the industry standard in terms of making comparisons among instruments with differing numbers of scales. This is the model used in the seminal studies by Barrick and Mount (1991), Tett *et al.* (1991) and Schmit and Ryan (1993) in summarizing the validity of personality tests throughout occupational psychology.

While Thurstone (1934), using the factor analytic approach, was probably the first to suggest a specific five-factor model, it is more usual to attribute its origin to Fiske (1949). It is he who first noticed that with five factors it was possible to obtain similar factor definitions when different assessment techniques, such as self-ratings, peer ratings and observer ratings, were used. Tupes and Christal (1961) analysed results from peer ratings, supervisor ratings, teacher ratings and clinical assessments carried out in colleges and in military training and found five strong and recurrent factors across all these domains.

Knowledge of the field was advanced further by Norman (Norman 1963; Passini and Norman 1966), who returned to the origin of personality assessment in psychology

– the natural-language trait descriptor. This concept owes its origin to the Lexical Hypothesis of Galton (1884), who suggested that any important individual differences between people would have become encoded throughout history in single linguistic terms that would occur in all the world's languages. He identified about 1,000 such personality descriptors. Later, Allport and Odbert (1936) carried out a systematic survey of the English language, and listed about 4,500 words in four categories – personal traits, temporary moods or activities, judgements of personal conduct, and capacities and talents. Of these, just under 5,000 'neutral terms designating possible personal traits' received particular attention by psychologists (among them R.B. Cattell (1943), who used the list as the basis for his work on the 16PF). Norman argued that earlier studies were flawed as computers, prior to the 1960s, had not been sufficiently powerful to analyse all of the descriptors and had therefore had to rely on smaller sub-sets. Norman's initial very extensive work was followed up by Goldberg (1982), who factor analysed 1,710 of Norman's trait adjectives. In a number of different studies he found that, across a variety of samples, there was a very considerable consistency for the five-factor solution, even when different methods of item extraction, rotations and factor numbers were used (Goldberg 1990). Work by Digman (1990) and by John (1990) also supported the fundamental role of the big-five model. Costa and McCrae (1992) argue in favour of the big-five that the model is supported in four ways (1) the five traits have high stability and are identified using different assessment techniques (e.g. both self-report questionnaires and peer ratings); (2) they are compatible with a wide variety of psychological theories including psychoanalytic, psychometric and folk-psychological; (3) they occur in many different cultures; and (4) they have a biological basis. There is good evidence for the first three, and the fourth, while debatable, is not essential to the model.

Orpheus: a work-based personality questionnaire that assesses the big-five

Orpheus (Rust 1996e) is an example of a psychometric test battery that utilizes the big-five model of personality. Within Orpheus, the big-five model is re-conceptualized as a domain theory of personality, i.e. each of the big-five factors is considered to be unique to a particular psychological domain. The five domains are the social, organizational, intellectual, emotional and perceptual, all of which are essential parts of our psychological life. Thus, individuals live their daily life in a social world comprising their relationships with other people at the personal level. They also live in an organizational world in which hierarchies of social status determine their position. They exercise their judgement within an intellectual domain involving the use of reason and knowledge. They are driven moment to moment by their emotions. How they view the world, and what becomes significant in their perceptual field, will determine the framework for their actions. Once we know a particular person's position with respect to each of these five domains we have an almost complete description of the functioning of his or her personality.

The Orpheus trait names for each of the five domains are given in Table 10.1, together with the trait names in most frequent use by other big-five researchers.

Stability of the big-five model

While considerable evidence has accumulated to show the five-factor solution is more stable than any other number of factors, it should always be remembered that this is essentially a consensus. A minority of studies, which may be under different circumstances with different items and different populations, find other solutions provide a better fit, so it is not the case that for every data set the five-factor solution will always emerge. Rather, the five-factor solution is merely the most frequent and ubiquitous. Although it represents the highest level of agreement among experts, there is considerable scope for differing minority views, particularly in populations where special circumstances may apply.

Similarly, the intrinsic nature of each of the big-five traits also represents a consensus. Again there is wide agreement concerning the general area covered by each trait. But the specific names given to each trait, and the particular slant placed on them by the researcher, varies from study to study. Table 10.2 lists some of the names that

Table 10.1 Domains and trait specification for the five Orpheus major scales

Domain	Orpheus	Big-five trait
Social	Fellowship	Extraversion vs. introversion
Organizational	Authority	Tough-mindedness vs. agreeableness,
Intellectual	Conformity	Conventionality vs. openness-to-experience
Emotional	Emotion	Neuroticism vs. confidence
Perceptual	Detail	Conscientiousness

Table 10.2 Names given to big-five traits in the literature (the source is given alongside the trait name in brackets)

Social domain
Extraversion (Eysenck 1947)
Surgency, Talkative, Assertive, Energetic (Tupes and Christal 1961)
Impulsiveness, Sociability (Eysenck, 1970)
versus
Introversion (Eysenck 1947; Myers and McCauley, 1985)

Organizational domain
Aggression (Murray 1938)
Tough-mindedness (James 1907)
Moving-against tendency (Horney 1956)
Inhibition (Strelau *et al.* 1990)
Narcissism (Freud 1957)
Hostility (Dembroski *et al.* 1988)
Coronary proneness, Type A behaviour (Costa *et al.* 1989)
Indifference-to-others, Self-centredness, Spitefulness, Jealousy (Digman, 1990)
Authoritarianism (Adorno *et al.* 1950)
Hostile non-compliance (Digman and Takemoto-Chock 1981)

Table 10.2 Continued

Antagonism (Graziano and Eisenberg 1993)
Thinking (Myers and McCauley 1985)
versus
Abasement, Nurturance (Murray 1938)
Trust (Erikson 1950)
Self-monitoring (Snyder 1974)
Good-natured, Co-operative, Trustful (Tupes and Christal 1961)
Altruism, Nurturance, Caring, Emotional-support (Digman 1990)
Friendly-compliance (Digman and Takemoto-Chock 1981)
Friendliness (Guilford and Zimmerman 1949)
Tender-mindedness (James 1907)
Feeling (Myers and McCauley 1985)

Intellectual domain
Dogmatism (Rokeach 1954)
Sensing (Myers and McCauley 1985)
versus
Openness-to-experience, Creativity, Divergent thinking (McCrae 1987)
Understanding, Change, Sentience, Autonomy (Murray 1938)
Experience-seeking (Zuckerman *et al.* 1993)
Flexibility, Achievement-via-independence (Gough 1971)
Artistic interests (Holland 1985)
Private self-consciousness (Buss and Cantor 1989)
Culture (Norman 1963)
Intellectual, Cultured, Polished (Tupes and Christal 1961)
Differentiated emotions, Aesthetic sensitivity, Need-for-variety, Unconventional values
(McCrae and John 1992)
Intuition (Myers and McCauley 1985)

Emotional domain
Anxiety (Taylor 1953)
Neuroticism (Eysenck 1947)
versus
Emotional stability, Calm, Not neurotic, Not easily upset (Tupes and Christal 1961)

Perceptual domain
Achievement, Order, Endurance (Murray 1938)
Persistence (Windel and Lerner 1986)
Competence (White 1959)
Will-to-achieve (Digman and Takemoto-Chock 1981)
Superego strength (Cattell 1965)
Locus of control (Rotter 1966)
Character (Hartshorn *et al.* 1929)
Achievement-motive (McClelland *et al.* 1953)
Dependability, Conscientious, Responsible, Orderly (Tupes and Christal 1961)
Perceiving (Myers and McCauley 1985)
versus
Judging (Myers and McCauley 1985)

have been suggested in the literature as epitomizing each of the big-five, either by the original author or by subsequent literature reviews by other personality psychologists.

In spite of the consensus that five factors are optimal, for many of the factors there is rather less agreement about what the constructs mean. Why are some of these factors so difficult to tie down? There are several reasons for this. The first arises from the grounding of the big-five model in the statistical procedure of factor analysis. In spite of the widespread use of factor analysis in psychometrics there are important differences between the factor-analytic model and more traditional forms of item analysis. The classical personality test is based on the traditional model of assessment, derived from the idea that a score on a test represents the number of correct responses. It identifies a unique set of items that are used to construct each scale. Factor analysis, on the other hand, constructs traits each of which make use of all the items in the questionnaire. While it could very reasonably be argued that an improved scale could be made from a more sophisticated use of the factor scores that emerge from factor analysis, rather than insisting that each item be used in only one scale, there are good reasons why the classical model is normally preferred. In test construction psychometricians generally use factor analysis as a tool to advise them in their selection of the best possible items for each scale. Once this selection of items has been made, then it is the scale, and not the factor model, which will need to be defended in terms of standardization, reliability, validity, bias and other psychometric properties. Factor-analytic solutions to data sets may well, for a particular data set, provide factor scores with a better fit than the classical raw sums of item scores. However, with different populations and different circumstances the actual loadings on the factors would be different, and each would need to be defended separately.

Independence of the big-five traits

One particular issue, which has received particular attention in the construction of Orpheus, is the degree of independence between the big-five traits. It is often assumed that, because the big-five are based on a five-factor solution to an orthogonal factor analysis, any scales constructed to measure the big-five will be independent from each other. This is not the case and independence can only be achieved with considerable difficulty. A failure to recognize the difference between psychometric scales and factor scores underlies much of the confusion concerning the degree of independence of big-five scores obtained from questionnaires. The five-factor solution on which the big-five model is based is an orthogonal one – that is, it produces five independent factors. If factor scores were used in place of scales they would necessarily be independent, if only for the population on which they were based. However, this is achieved by using all the items in the questionnaire five times – each item will have a loading on each of the big-five although the size of these loadings will depend on the nature of the item in question. Independence in this orthogonal solution is achieved by a very careful balance between the various aspects of all five scales. If only those items which had high loadings on a factor were selected, however, the delicate balancing achieved by counterbalancing the other scales would be lost, and the big-five scales so derived would no longer be independent of one another. In fact, some of them would have a significant degree of intercorrelation. Attempts to redress this within the factor analysis itself are more likely than not to make matters worse. One solution, for example, would be to use synonyms of certain aspects of each of the big-five (sometimes called 'bloated specifics'). But this solution would not be the big-five. This is because the big-five solution, by its very nature, balances the different aspects of each of its component traits to achieve independence. Simply because the factor analysis generates orthogonal factors it does not follow that the primary traits suggested by each factor will be independent from each other when they are measured separately.

Coping with response bias

A further complexity of five-factor solutions to analyses of personality-trait descriptors needs to be considered. This involves the role played by two other elements in all personality questionnaire data sets. These are the response bias effects described as social desirability and acquiescence (Furnham 1986). Social desirability describes the tendency to fake good or fake bad in questionnaires. Job applicants in occupational settings will often succumb to the temptation to be economical with the truth to some degree. This is not as reprehensible as it may sound as all of us have been encouraged by careers counsellors and others to 'make the most of ourselves' in applying for a job. In clinical settings, patients who wish to see a doctor to obtain a sick leave certificate, or to cash in on an insurance policy, will often fake bad. The effect of social desirability is ubiquitous, affecting responses to most of the items in one way or another (Paulhus 1984). Consequently, it will always have some effect on the data set and will always influence the factor analysis. This phenomenon is well known to psychometricans, who are constantly struggling to eliminate or neutralize these effects. Unfortunately it is impossible to do so completely and consequently test users always need to be made aware of how social desirability effects may have influenced results. Acquiescence, the other major form of response bias, represents the tendency of some people to agree with every question or statement, and of others to disagree (Couch and Keniston 1960). This phenomenon can also affect every item in the questionnaire, and will often emerge as the first factor in a factor analysis. Again psychometricians have techniques for reducing its influence, usually by balancing the number of positive with the number of negative items for each trait being measured. For the factor analysis itself, however, both phenomena will always be present to some extent.

The effects of response bias on factor structure are not consistent but vary from sample to sample. Thus, students filling in a questionnaire for a research professor are less motivated to lie than are job applicants in a very competitive market (Schmit and Ryan, 1993). Some forms of bias will be affected by the nature of the job being applied for. Thus, those applying for junior positions would be likely to view different responses as being socially desirable than those looking for managerial responsibility. The perceptual, emotional and organizational domains are particularly likely to be influenced in this way. For example, applicants for sales positions are more likely to bias their responses in the social domain. All forms of response bias affect factor structure, and consequently the nature of the factors will themselves vary depending on the nature of the data set and the respondents' motives in agreeing to participate. This is another reason why it makes sense to treat the big-five structure as a consensus, rather than a scientific discovery concerning the nature of human personality (Vassend and Skrondal 1995). It describes the most frequent solution under the majority of circumstances. The particular loadings that occur form a complex family of related items, but one that is bound to be chaotic to some degree and that cannot be completely determined.

Many of the existing questionnaires that measure the big-five tend to have quite substantial correlations between their scales. These correlations tend to be under-reported, perhaps because the belief that the five-factor solution produces five independent scales (as opposed to five independent factors) is so widespread. While the reason for the intercorrelations between big-five scales has been explained above, the existence of these intercorrelations is undesirable as one of the main arguments put forward in favour of the five-trait model has been the independence of its domains. This is particularly important if we are to argue, along with Mershon and Gorsuch (1988) that models with smaller numbers of factors are superior, from both a theoretical and a practical point of view, to models with more traits. Cattell (1995) for example has argued that the big-five model does not address the full complexity of personality, and that a more extensive model, such as his 16PF, is required to dredge this valuable detail.

The advantages of uncorrelated traits

One argument against having many factors concerns the large degree of association among the traits in these models, which creates a great deal of redundancy within the personality profile. If two traits are highly correlated, they are also conjoined. That is, when one is high then, invariably, so is the other, and vice versa. We could obtain the same information more reliably by simply combining them. Hence we may just as well have measured only one. With independent traits, on the other hand, our ability to interpret profiles is maximized. A two-factor solution using only Extraversion and Neuroticism, for example, can produce four basic profiles: High Extraversion High Neuroticism, High Extraversion Low Neuroticism, Low Extraversion High Neuroticism and Low Extraversion Low Neuroticism. Eysenck argued that these are related to the four traits identified in classical Greece – the Melancholic, Choleric, Phlegmatic and Sanguine personalities respectively. With three traits we would have more possible combinations, eight in fact if we use all three dimensions. We can also generate further interpretations by taking the three combinations of two traits with the other held constant – producing fourteen interpretations in all (the three traits alone, the three traits in combinations of two and the eight ways in which all three can be combined). With five factors there are, in principle, seventy-four different profiles, each of which could receive an interpretation. Thus, if true independence among the primary scales can be attained, the five-factor model can provide more information than a questionnaire that claims to assess 70 oblique factors!

Table 10.3 shows some common interpretations that have been made for particular big-five profiles. It can be seen that some of these combinations overlap with trait descriptors that have been put forward for single big-five traits in Table 10.2. This should not be particularly surprising, as all the big-five solution provides are generalized clusters that fall within a broadly bounded factor space. The generality, however, is a fuzzy set within a mathematical system that represents data that is essentially chaotic. As soon as an attempt is made to tie down the general characteristics of a particular

Table 10.3 Interpretations of specific five-factor profiles that have appeared in the literature

Dependency	High Emotion, High Conformity, Low Authority
Social Leadership	High Fellowship, Low Emotion
Intellectual	High Fellowship, Low Conformity
Submissive	Low Fellowship, Low Authority
Need for recognition	High Emotion, High Fellowship
Defensive attitude	High Emotion, Low Authority
Exhibitionism	High Fellowship, High Authority
Autonomy	Low Emotion, Low Fellowship, Low Conformity
Harm avoidance	High Conformity, Low Authority
Supportiveness	High Fellowship, Low Authority
Achievement	Low Conformity, High Detail
Impulsiveness	High Authority, Low Conformity
Authoritarian	High Authority, High Conformity

domain to specifics at an adjectival level then there must necessarily be some degree of contamination from the remaining four domains. The 'true' latent trait of the domain is an abstraction (Loehlin 1992) which by its very nature eludes precise specification.

One other issue needs to be addressed before we turn to the structure of Orpheus itself – this is the question of whether the latent traits of the big five could represent real entities that may actually be related. Remember that the completely orthogonal nature of the big-five solution is imposed by the factor-analytic technique. However, while it may be the best-fitting orthogonal solution, it is possible that the data could be better explained if a less constraining oblique rotation was used – one which allowed the factors to retain some degree of relationship to each other. While this avenue has frequently been explored, it has not been found to be particularly productive. Once the constraint of orthogonality is abandoned we have lost one of the elements of common ground among our studies – the very one which gave privilege to the five-factor model in the meta-analytic studies. It is not merely a simple question of orthogonal vs. oblique, because, short of the complete independence represented by the orthogonal solution, there are no grounds for preferring any particular degree of relationship over any other. To put this another way, if we are no longer specifying targeting a correlation of 0.0 between the factors, should we target a between-factors correlation of 0.1? or 0.2?, or 0.5? or any other degree of relationship (in practice the degree of relationship between oblique factors is specified by the delta coefficient rather than by correlations). Without the rigour provided by the demand for complete factorial independence there is no fixed standard whereby to judge the appropriateness of any particular factorial solution.

While the exploration of the true nature of the relationship between the five domains represented by the big-five model is of scientific interest, it is not the issue of most importance to the practitioner. Similarly, we can safely bypass any controversy concerning whether the five traits are biologically based. While it has previously been argued that psychophysiology provides a mediator between personality and biology (Rust 1975b) there is no necessary link between the two. Readers who are interested are referred to Costa and McCrae (1992) for a recent review of supporting evidence for a biological basis for the big five. From the practitioner's point of view all we require is a convenient structure within which to arrange and summarize our knowledge and experience of personality theory as it applies to occupational settings. This will apply at all levels, from everyday practice to sophisticated meta-analytic evaluations of validity.

The Orpheus scales

Fellowship assesses the big-five trait of extraversion/introversion. High Fellowship scorers are generally happier working with others or in a team. Low Fellowship scorers generally prefer work that requires a degree of independence.

Authority assesses the big five trait of tough- vs. tender-mindedness, sometimes called 'agreeableness'. High Authority scorers can make tough decisions. Low Authority scorers generally adopt a more co-operative approach.

Conformity assesses the big-five trait of 'openness-to-experience'. High Conformity scorers are likely to have a preference for traditional ways of doing things and to respect established values. Low Conformity scorers often wish to do things differently, and to seek out alternative solutions to problems.

Emotion assesses the big-five trait of neuroticism. High Emotion scorers, while often being of a nervous disposition, are likely to be sensitive to the feelings of others. Low Emotion scorers are likely to be more able to perform under stressful conditions but may lack caution.

Detail assesses the big-five trait of conscientiousness. High Detail scorers generally excel at mundane tasks that require particular care, although they may become over-involved in minutiae. Low Detail scorers have less patience for routine tasks and prefer to see the wider view.

The Orpheus scales were constructed progressively and incrementally from core attributes of their traits which had been predefined for items with the use of markers (Golombok and Rust 1993a, 1993b; Goldberg 1992). As the scales emerged, they were carefully balanced for positive and negative items to avoid acquiescence effects (Paulhus 1991). Positive items are those that are summed directly into the scale, negative items are reversed before being summed into the scale (e.g. ' I am sociable' would be a positive item, and 'I am not sociable' would be a negative item for a scale of sociability). Scale intercorrelations were also continuously monitored as well as item/total correlations and alpha coefficients to ensure both breadth and diversity in trait coverage. The five major scales were modelled around the big-five template with the additional criterion that no two big-five traits should have intercorrelations above 0.3, and that the correlation with a previously constructed interim social desirability scale should also be as low as possible.

Given this development process, how might we expect the five major scales from Orpheus to differ from other questionnaires that have utilized the big-five model? First, the requirement that scales should be as independent as possible from lie and social desirability effects will help to identify any meritorious personality characteristics which may be associated with individuals who obtain 'undesirable' scores on a scale. While it is widely believed that the big-five model is non-evaluative, inspection of the scales shown in Table 10.2 will demonstrate that contamination with social desirability is rampant throughout the big-five literature. Given the labels used in many questionnaires, there seems to be little support for the claim that the big-five structure is non-judgemental.

The requirement that correlations between each of the big-five scales be less than 0.3 addresses a set of common problems. One of these has been the degree of concordance between extraversion and openness-to-experience. While extraversion almost invariably includes a social aspect, different extraversion scales vary in the extent to which impulsiveness items are included. The disagreement owes its origin to Eysenck (1947), who, in the earliest versions of the EPI (the Maudsley Personality Questionnaire), focused on the independence of extraversion and neuroticism. Two-factor solutions always provide the simplest model for the use of factor analysis in personality test construction. While the nature of the two factors that will emerge from this model will always depend to some extent on which items are in the pool, it has long been known that for any wide-scale sampling of natural-language trait descriptors the most likely two factors resemble extraversion and neuroticism. Either is likely to emerge as the first factor, and once it has been identified it is relatively easy to construct an independent second scale from prudent balancing across the remaining items in the pool.

Unfortunately, as soon as the number of factors is increased beyond two, this structure is liable to disintegrate. Eysenck himself was only able to generate an independent third factor of psychoticism by removing impulsively items from his earlier extraversion scale (Claridge and Birchall 1978; Rust 1987, 1988, 1989). When the number of factors is further increased from three to five, impulsiveness tends to transfer to openness-to-experience rather than to psychoticism. Within Orpheus, the constraint on the size of the correlation between Conformity (Openness-to-experience) and Fellowship (Extraversion) has produced both Fellowship and Conformity scales less contaminated by impulsiveness, which is now picked up by the High Fellowship, Low Conformity profile.

Another common confound has been between the big-five traits of Detail (conscientiousness) and Authority (agreeableness). This has largely come about because almost all the development work on the big-five was carried out in academic institutions using students as respondents. The friendly and conscientious student is highly valued by staff and fellow students alike and the benefit of this trait is seen as self-evident. However, although people low on 'agreeableness' may not make ideal students, there are a very large number of them – and many are very successful in their careers. The experience of many occupational psychologists is that those with low scores on agreeableness and/or conscientiousness are not always the ne'er-do-wells that have been implied. Successful senior managers, and human resource managers in particular, very frequently have this profile, so that its positive qualities do need to be addressed. By focusing on low correlations between Authority and Detail, and by reducing the mediating effect of social desirability, Orpheus has achieved a good degree of independence between these traits.

Within the Orpheus structure, an 'agreeable' and altruistic outlook at work is seen as more appropriate for high-performing junior staff and not necessarily a suitable quality for those who have to direct the activities of others. People who have heavy managerial responsibilities may often see themselves as tough-minded or even 'disagreeable'. With the conceptualization of 'disagreeable' respondents as High Authority it is possible to give recognition to their positive qualities, in particular their ability to make tough decisions and their will to succeed. The distinction between the Social and the Organizational domains also helps to disentangle the social quality of agreeableness which otherwise tends to relate its friendliness aspect to extraversion. By treating 'agreeableness' as a characteristic of those possessing less onerous responsibilities it is possible to distinguish well meaning and kind but introverted individuals from their more demonstrative and ostensibly helpful colleagues.

There has also been a tendency within working populations for low agreeableness (tough-mindedness) to correlate with high openness-to-experience. This is very likely an artefact introduced by the relationship between status and education. High Authority individuals are generally more senior and also more educated – often at degree level. Such people tend to be more intelligent, which in turn relates to lower scores on Conformity. The relationship between openness-to-experience and intellect in the form of divergent thinking has been widely explored in the literature. However, it is a mistake to treat openness-to-experience as merely a surrogate for intelligence. In fact the relationship with IQ scores, although usually present, is not particularly straightforward. By targeting lower correlations with Authority and by placing the trait in the intellectual domain, Orpheus deliberately emphasizes its relationship to the process of reasoning rather than its behavioural attributes. The concept assessed by Conformity should be seen in the context of epistemology and the philosophical theory of knowledge rather than the more prosaic psychological concepts of intelligence. Low Conformity scorers aim to change their own ways of thinking, High Conformity scorers are more willing to take things on faith.

Orpheus interprets conscientiousness as attention to detail, and thus places its trait of Detail within the perceptual domain concerned with how and where we focus our attention. While the relationship between conscientiousness and attention to detail is well documented, relatively little attention has been paid to the attributes of low scorers on this trait as can be seen from the relative paucity of descriptors it receives in Table 10.2. Where trait descriptors for Low Detail scores have been negative they have invariably been portrayed as extremely undesirable, using such terms as unreliable, lazy, hedonistic, and lacking in self-control and moral principles. In spite of this, persons with scores at this end of the Detail scale often seem to be fully functioning and successful individuals! It is hoped that the Orpheus framework will address this injustice and emphasize their ability to 'pan out' from the narrow focus of the highly conscientious individuals. Low Detail scorers may be more able to use their intuitions and more able to make use of a gestalt style of perception, recognizing that the whole is often more than the sum of its parts. They epitomize the impressionist in contrast to the photographic mode of perception.

The psychometric characteristics of Orpheus

Piloting

The pilot version of Orpheus was administered to 274 employees in a variety of occupations, ranging from junior technical and clerical staff to senior managers and professionals. A broad sample of work settings were sampled, including a major automobile manufacturer, a major police force, an industrial petro-chemical concern, a retail chain and a city financial institution. Item analysis of these data, together with those already available in the item bank, gave twelve scales – the big-five plus seven minor scales designed to assess integrity. The five major scales of Fellowship, Authority, Conformity,

Emotion and Detail all had intercorrelations of less than 0.3, and each had a correlation less than 0.3 with an interim social desirability scale specifically constructed for this purpose from social desirability items that had been included in the pilot.

Standardization

Orpheus was administered to 423 respondents in a variety of occupations within over 20 companies in the UK. The sample included 275 males and 138 females, and the mean age of the sample was 30.67 years with a standard deviation of 11.01. The respondents were from a broad range of educational levels, from no qualifications through City and Guilds to PhD. The proportion of ethnic minority respondents was the same as that in the general working population. The accumulated data from all the respondents in the standardization study provide the general population norms for Orpheus. These are used to produce the standardized stanine scores that are used in the narrative report.

The data were standardized within each respondent. That is, for each completed questionnaire the mean and the standard deviation of all item responses was calculated, and the standard score for each item was computed using the z score formula $z = (x - \text{mean})/\text{s.d.}$ This was carried out in order to eliminate response bias effects resulting from acquiescence. Item analysis, reliability analysis and validation were conducted with data that had been pre-transformed in this way.

Reliability

The split-half reliabilities for the Orpheus big-five scales from the 423 respondents in the standardization sample are all greater than 0.73 and fall within the range 0.73–0.81.

Validity

One of the most straightforward ways in which content validity can be reported is to give those items that have the most extreme loadings on each scale in both positive and negative directions. A positive loading means that the item has a large positive correlation with that scale, while a negative loading means that the item has a large negative correlation with that scale. With Fellowship for instance (see below), High Fellowship scorers tend to agree with the item 'I am the sort of person who can easily be the life of a party' and to disagree with the item 'I hate being the focus of attention'. Low Fellowship scorers, on the other hand, tend to disagree with the item 'I am the sort of person who can easily be the life of a party' and to agree with the item 'I hate being the focus of attention'. As a consequence of this, the item total correlations of these two items with scores on Fellowship will be positive and negative respectively.

Fellowship
Positive: 'I am the sort of person who can easily be the life of a party.'
Negative: 'I hate being the focus of attention.'

Authority
Positive: 'I don't care if some people think I am pushy so long as I get things done.'
Negative: 'People have sometimes told me I am not forceful enough.'

Conformity
Positive: 'Changing the way we do things usually makes matters worse.'
Negative: 'I am persistently on the lookout for new ideas to exploit.'

Emotion
Positive: 'It is probably true to say that I am something of a worrier.'
Negative: 'I would describe myself as being exceptionally free from stress.'

Detail
Positive: 'I have a reputation for being good at checking detail carefully.'
Negative: 'I find routine administration boring and prefer to leave it to others.'

To obtain criterion-related validity, the five Orpheus scales were validated against ten predesignated supervisors' rating scales (one positive and one negative rating for each scale). Ratings ranged from below average through average, a little above average, much above average to exceptional. The ratings were carried out by the supervisors of respondents in the standardization study. For each supervisor, their responses to the rating items were standardized within the response set, so that appraisal ratings were in comparison with their average rating rather than absolute. These results are shown in Table 10.4.

Note that the validity coefficients that appear in Table 10.4 are not adjusted for attenuation and therefore represent high values for validity coefficients of this type.

Using Orpheus

The use of Orpheus should follow the general guidelines given at the beginning of Chapter 11. It is important to emphasize to candidates that they must respond honestly, as otherwise their scores will misrepresent them. They should be informed that Orpheus contains a lie detector as well as other filters to detect accuracy of responding. Orpheus can only be scored by computer program. There is no provision for hand scoring. This is because of the complex mathematical procedures that are involved in the scoring process. These include within-subject standardization of responses, response audit, estimation of missing data, and standardization to norm groups.

Missing data

Orpheus uses its own internal procedure for dealing with missing data, although this will only operate if the amount of missing data is so small as to not risk affecting the reliability of the scores. If more than five items are missed out, the data set is rejected. If less than five items are missed out, then the missing items are replaced by the mean scores for those items from the standardization sample. An item counts as missing if

Table 10.4 Correlations of the five Orpheus major scales with supervisors' ratings (N = 214)

	F: Fellowship
Team skills	.19**
Ability to work independently	−.14*
	A: Authority
Ability to make friends with colleagues	−.13†
Ability to make tough decisions	.24**
	C: Conformity
Ability to generate new ideas	−.25**
Obedience to company policy	.23**
	E: Emotion
Level of self-confidence	−.25**
Tendency to worry	.08
	D: Detail
Attention to detail	.23**
Breadth of vision	−.22**

Notes:
* $p < .05$ (two tailed)
** $p < .01$
† $p < .05$ (one tailed)

(1) no response is made (2) more than one response is circled (e.g. both agree and disagree), or (3) the question has been changed and a response endorsed in such a manner as to suggest that the response is to the altered question.

The scored Orpheus report

The scored report gives information on a response audit, standardizes the big-five scale scores, and prints a narrative report.

The response audit searches for evidence that the respondent has completed the questionnaire correctly. This is done by scoring a set of items that constitute a lie scale, by examining patterning in the responses that represent careless answering, and by looking for contradictory responses.

The Orpheus reports include scores that have been standardized to a stanine scale. The standardization process transforms the raw score of a single respondent on the basis of its relationship to the raw scores of a representative group of respondents, referred to as the norm group. The stanine scores on a norm group have a mean of 5 and a standard deviation of 2 by definition. If any individual respondent from the norm group has a stanine score of 5, this means that he or she is at the average for that group on the scale in question. His or her score is such that 50% of the other respondents will have obtained a lower score and 50% will have obtained a higher score. If a respondent has a stanine score of 7, then he or she is scoring one standard deviation above the mean for that scale. This means that 16% of other respondents in the group will have obtained a higher score, and 84% will have obtained a lower score. (Equivalent percentages for other particular scores can be obtained from z tables in any good statistics book.)

The stanine transformation is carried out using the following equation

$$\text{stanine score} = ((A - B)*2/C) + 5$$

where A = the respondent's raw score, B = the population mean of the raw scores on the standardization sample, and C = the population standard deviation of raw scores on the standardization sample.

Stanine scores are rounded to the nearest whole number, and values less than 1 or greater than 9 are rounded up or down to 1 or 9 respectively. In interpreting a stanine score it is important to remember the effect of rounding. Thus a score of 5 represents any score in the range 4.5 to 5.5 before rounding, i.e. it represents the range of scores between −0.25 and +0.25 standard deviations around the mean. Similarly a stanine score of 6 includes the range from +0.25 to +0.75 standard deviations, and a score of 7 represents the range from +0.75 to +1.25 standard deviations, and so on.

Summary

Personality tests are now in widespread and increasing use in organizational and business psychology. Today, the five-factor model of personality is generally accepted as being the most useful and comprehensive. Orpheus is an example of a psychometric personality questionnaire utilizing this five-factor model. Its theory, development, standardization and validation are discussed.

Chapter 11

Ethical test use and integrity testing

Administrative procedures for psychometric testing

The following guidelines should be followed when administering psychometric tests in employment settings.

Before testing begins

Test administration should accord with the organization's code of practice. Care must be taken not to infringe the Data Protection Act (1984), the Sex Discrimination Act (1975), the Race Relations Act (1976) or the Disabilities Discrimination Act (1995). Candidates should receive a letter in good time before the testing session providing them with clear information about the nature of the assessment, why it is being used, and the conditions under which it will take place and the nature of any feedback. Candidates should also be assured that their test responses will be treated in confidence. They should be told who will have access to the data and for how long it will be kept. Informed consent should be obtained from the candidate before testing begins. This should be in the form of a previously prepared written statement which explains the type of test to be administered and its purpose as well as who will have access to the data. It is the responsibility of the test user to ensure that candidates understand the testing procedure.

The assessor should also ensure that all relevant background information from the candidate has been collected and verified. This information should always include full name, date of birth, sex and current employment, and will usually also include some details of employment and occupational history. Information on race may be requested in order to enable ethnic monitoring to take place.

The testing environment

The test or questionnaire should be administered in standardized conditions in order to minimize the effects of external factors on test reliability and performance. However, adherence to standard procedures does not mean that the test must be administered in a rigid and unnatural manner. Using a natural conversational tone, encouraging interest in the task and reinforcing the candidate's efforts all contribute to a cohesive and pleasant, though structured, testing situation.

Remember that the physical setting can affect the candidate's performance. To minimize any potential distractions or interference, conduct the testing in a quiet, adequately lit, well-ventilated room. As a rule, no one other than the candidate should be in the room during testing. If, however, the test is to be administered in a group setting, ensure that all candidates are far enough apart so as not to be able to interfere with each other's performance. Also when giving any further instructions to individuals take care to do this in a way that does not interfere with others in the room.

Establishing and maintaining rapport

Candidates may arrive for the testing session feeling anxious, suspicious or resentful, all of which may interfere with optimal test performance. It is particularly important, therefore, to establish rapport when the candidates arrive. This may be done by chatting to the candidate, and providing reassurances about the nature of the test and the procedures to be employed.

It is essential that the candidate be engaged in the task and be motivated to follow the instructions and complete it as accurately as possible. The administrator should explain the written instructions at the beginning of the test and ensure that the candidate understands their full import. Administrators should be aware of ways in which sabotage can take place. These are (a) leaving items out, (b) circling two responses for an item (e.g. example both 'agree' and 'disagree'), and (c) changing the question before answering. If rapport is properly established and maintained, however, sabotage is much less likely. Remember that many psychometric tests cannot be scored if more than a certain number of items have been left out or sabotaged. If this happens the administrator's, candidate's and company's time have been wasted. Always check completed questionnaires to ensure that all questions have been answered.

It is important for the administrator to maintain a positive attitude to the testing. Not all candidates are likely to be enthusiastic about psychometric testing, and if the administrator is not able to show enthusiasm any negative attitudes are likely to be reinforced.

If a candidate has a physical impairment which interferes with his or her ability to complete the test then the testing environment must be accommodated to the candidate's needs. How this was done and its likely effect should be included in the report. With visual impairment the items may be read to the candidate.

Various forms of mental impairment can also interfere with test scores. Some forms of mental illness interfere with the ability to concentrate, whereas others may necessitate the administrator reading out the items and sometimes writing down the responses. If this is necessary these facts and their likely effects should be clearly stated and written in the report.

If a candidate states that he or she does not understand an item, the administrators must use their judgement in deciding how to proceed. If due to the candidate's poor level of education then testing may have to be abandoned. If, however, it appears that the candidate is merely overcautious, then he or she should be encouraged to endorse their most likely response to the item in question. Although modifications of testing procedures may be necessary, remember that the test was not standardized with such modifications. For example, if sign language or reading of items is necessary, such alterations may have an impact on test scores. Test administrators will have to rely on their professional judgement in evaluating the impact of such modified procedures on test scores.

Administering the test or questionnaire

Candidates should be told what will happen during the testing session, how long it is likely to take, and whether or not they may leave as soon as they have completed the test. They may also wish to know whether or not they are allowed to smoke. If the test is administered in a group, however, remember that visits to the toilet, smoking and early leaving can be disruptive to other candidates. Also, it is important to be able to check completed questionnaires for missing data. It is relatively easy to point out a few missed items and encourage him or her to have another go. Once they are out of the building, however, this will normally be impossible and everyone's time may have been wasted. Remember, personality questionnaires can only be scored if candidates have answered the questions (unlike knowledge-based tests in which missed items are simply counted as 'wrong').

It is important to emphasize to candidates that they must respond honestly, as otherwise their scores will misrepresent them. They should be informed if the questionnaire contains a lie detector as well as other filters to detect accuracy of responding. The instructions should be read to the candidate clearly, and he or she should be encouraged to ask questions before the testing session begins. Candidates should not be encouraged to ask questions once testing has started. Questions about the meaning of items should be discouraged. Any comments made by the administrator may affect the candidate's response and thus bias his or her scores. At the end of the testing session, candidates should be thanked for their participation and told about any arrangements for feedback.

Administration by computer

If the test is to be administered by computer, then particular care must be taken to ensure that the candidates understand what is expected of them. An opportunity to ask questions should be given after the candidate has read the instructions and carried out the trial items. The administrator should always be available during the session to answer any questions or queries the candidate may have.

Scoring

Today, most tests and questionnaires can be scored by computer, and many can only be scored in this way. However, if you are using an older questionnaire it may need to be scored by hand. Usually you will be provided with a template, a sheet with holes that can be placed over the completed questionnaire that readily identifies which items should be totalled for each sub-scale. It is exceptionally important that your scoring procedures for a few sample questionnaires be verified by an independent person before being applied on a wholesale basis. As with the use of medical technology, simple initial mistakes in scoring could become ongoing bad practice and can put lives and jobs at risk.

Keeping records

A register should be kept of all candidates who have attended for testing. The administrator should ensure that the candidate's name or number is clearly and accurately marked on all forms and completed questionnaires. Each completed form should be checked for clerical errors.

Completed questionnaires should be kept in a locked store and should be accessed only by those with authority to do so. In no circumstances should completed questionnaires be left lying around an open office. Disposal of completed questionnaires should be by shredding and/or incineration.

Integrity testing

In many occupational settings it is the integrity of the job applicant, rather than their personality per se, that is of interest. In the USA prior to the 1990s psychophysiological lie detectors were frequently used for the assessment of integrity. Applicants would be 'wired up' to a lie detector device, and asked questions concerning their drug or alcohol use or any criminal record. However, the US government eventually ruled that such procedures were unethical for all users other than their own security services, and their use by commercial concerns has since been outlawed. They have been replaced by integrity tests based on self-report or biodata.

Most of the major integrity tests are reviewed in the Tenth Mental Measurement Yearbook (Conoley and Kramer 1989). In addition, the American Psychological Association (Goldberg *et al.* 1991) and the US Office of Technological Assessment (1990) have both reviewed the use of integrity tests, and these reports are summarized by Camara and Schneider (1994) in the *American Psychologist*. In the APA survey, fewer than half of the publishers of integrity tests supplied the information that was requested. Camara and Schneider were concerned that commercial interest has so restricted the dissemination of information concerning the effectiveness of integrity testing that the case for its use was essentially unanswered. They also pointed out that, among the various instruments available, there is little agreement on the behaviours assessed or on a precise definition of integrity. They found the concept of integrity to be overly broad and ill defined, and concluded that there was insufficient evidence to reach clear conclusions regarding the value of integrity testing. Further general criticisms of integrity testing are made by Loevinger (1994) and by Lykken (see Ones *et al.* 1996).

Sackett *et al.* (1989) classifies integrity tests into two types – (a) overt (also known as 'clear purpose tests') and (b) personality based (also known as 'disguised purpose tests'). Overt integrity tests contain direct questions and biodata items. Personality-based integrity tests, on the other hand, have not been developed solely to predict theft or theft-related behaviours. These tests are generally similar in form to any other occupationally based personality test and can be mapped on to the big-five personality factors in the same manner as other personality tests (Lilienfeld *et al.* 1995; Ones *et al.* 1995). A consequence of this is that it is not just integrity testing but the application of personality testing generally to job selection that is under attack by the critics of integrity tests.

The case in favour of integrity testing is made by Deniz Ones and her colleagues

(Ones *et al.* 1993). They report a series of meta-analytic studies which review the evidence for the validity of integrity testing and, on the basis of 650 criteria-related validity coefficients from over 500,000 subjects, conclude not only that the evidence for the validity of integrity tests is substantial but also that the broad construct of integrity is a predictor of overall job performance probably as good as or better than any one of the big-five factors either alone or in combination. In comparison with supervisors' ratings of overall job performance they find an unadjusted validity of 0.22 for integrity (0.41 adjusted for attenuation), which compares favourably with the highest validities reported by Tett *et al.* (1991) in their meta-analysis of occupational personality testing where they found a validity of 0.22 for the big-five trait of agreeableness.

The relationship between integrity testing and personality testing

How do integrity tests relate to the big five? It will be recalled that proponents of the big-five model argue that all other personality tests can in principle be reduced to the big-five factors and, if so, this should also apply to disguised-purpose integrity tests. In fact Ones *et al.* (1995) argue that many existing integrity tests are to a large extent assessing the big-five trait of conscientiousness. While there is some force in this position, it overlooks an important difference between integrity tests and most other personality tests. In the construction of most personality tests strenuous efforts are normally made to eliminate the influence of social desirability bias and with some reasonable expectation of success. In integrity tests, on the other hand, the target behaviours are generally such that some degree of social desirability bias is inevitable, and any attempt to eliminate this bias completely would result in a scale which was no longer valid in terms of its original specification. In the assessment of work-orientation, for example, it would be meaningless to require that the scale should be independent of social desirability, as work-orientation is by its very nature a desirable characteristic of employees. While the case can be made that personality tests are non-evaluative, the same claim does hold for integrity. Three important points arise from this difference.

First, as pointed out by Tellegen and his colleagues (Almagor *et al.* 1995) the five-factor model was not, as is so widely believed, based on a factor analysis of all possible natural-language personality descriptors. Rather it is based on factor analysis of the natural-language personality descriptors that remain after evaluative items have been excluded. According to Tellegen, if these evaluative terms are included in a factor analysis a better fit is obtained by a seven-factor model.

Second, while the big-five model is often believed to be non-evaluative and indeed is promoted as such, the case for this is somewhat weak. Within the big-five literature, not one positive statement appears to have been made in favour of low conscientiousness. Among employers, a similar lack of enthusiasm seems to be evident for low scorers on agreeableness, and high scorers on neuroticism also find little support. Hence the belief that the big five, or indeed any personality test, is non-evaluative is merely a convenience. While the psychological community bends over backwards to find positive things to say about disagreeable neurotics who fail to attend to detail, in practice persons with such scores are treated no more favourably than those who have been administered integrity tests.

Third, response-bias effects, such as social desirability and dishonest responding, play an important role not only in integrity testing but also in personality testing generally. The lie paradox is well known in philosophy, and is best illustrated by Bertrand Russell's example of a piece of paper that has written on both sides 'The statement on the other side of this paper is false.' This has similarities to the lie item 'I always tell the truth', or perhaps rather more tangentially 'It always pays to tell the truth', in personality or integrity tests. The impact of this paradox is also demonstrated in items designed to assess social desirability bias, such as 'I have never ever made a mistake at work'. The consequences for this latter example are worth spelling out. They are (a) a person who is deliberately lying will answer 'agree' (b) a person who especially values their honesty will reply 'disagree' (c) a person who has been encouraged to present themselves in the best possible light (say, as a result of out-placement counselling) will answer 'agree', and (d) a person who does not really care about whether he or she gets the job or not, or who is clinically depressed, will answer 'disagree'. Essentially, integrity, social desirability and lying are completely confounded in items of this type. Indeed, as Guastello and Rieke (1991) and Sackett et al. (1989) point out, if we treat social desirability and lying as synonymous then paradoxically many integrity tests have a *negative* correlation with honesty, and the same is true of the relationship between social desirability and the big-five trait of conscientiousness. Disentangling these effects takes considerable skill on the part of the test constructor.

In constructing mainstream personality tests, every effort should be made to reduce the effects of social desirability. However, this is never completely possible. The big-five trait of conscientiousness always retains some degree of social desirability bias, as does the trait of neuroticism. In fact, for all traits social desirability may have an effect under specific circumstances. Extraversion scores, for example, are likely to be affected in different ways if the job applied for involves working either in a team or independently. Generally, the more relevant the trait to the job, the more likely the scores are to be biased. With integrity tests a different approach is to be recommended. While the reduction of obvious or unnecessary sources of social desirability bias is still important, it is recognized that it would be not only impossible but also ill advised to attempt to eliminate the effects of social desirability completely. Given the nature of the traits being assessed, some degree of association with social desirability is inevitable. Instead, social desirability should be assessed in addition to the trait of interest by a specific scale designed for this purpose. Interpretation can then be based on a judgement of both of these scores taken in combination.

How can the problem of social desirability be tackled? In many ways the problem is the same as that faced by an interviewer when dealing with an accomplished liar, and there are two courses of action that can be recommended. First, the interviewer can ask indirect questions. This has the advantage that the correct answer is not so obvious and therefore lying is less likely to affect the response, but the disadvantage is that the information gained will be somewhat tangential to the main points of interest. Second, the interviewer could ask direct questions, and try to assess the extent of confidence that can realistically be placed in the answers. Where this works it will be very successful; however, where this does not work the interviewer may not only be left in the dark but may also make the wrong appointment. The first of these approaches is the one used by personality questionnaires. The second approach is recommended for integrity tests.

The current status of integrity testing

In a recent joint paper by Deniz Ones and David Lykken, an exchange of letters concerning integrity testing is reported which provides a useful summary of the debate so far (Ones *et al.* 1996). Lykken is well known for his criticism of the use of psycho-physiological lie detectors in US industry and played a part in their eventual outlawing. He now wishes to extend many of the same criticisms to the integrity tests, which he sees as having replaced the lie detector and as having many of the same characteristics. Lykken argues (1) that the database used by Ones and her colleagues for meta-analysis includes studies employing polygraph screening tests or admissions of previous dishonesty as criteria, (2) that if integrity tests are used for selection then large numbers of people may be permanently denied jobs, (3) that few procedures are less scientific or publicly accountable, (4) that validities stated are from publishers' handbooks and have not been subject to peer review by the academic community, and (5) that integrity testing is likely to do considerable harm and should be monitored and regulated.

Ones and her colleagues reply (1) that studies including polygraph admissions had been specifically excluded from their meta-analysis; they had also examined separately the studies which included admissions of previous dishonesty and those which did not, and found that the results were the same in both cases; (2) that all selection procedures had the potential for excluding a large fraction of job applicants as this was the whole point of selection; (3) that there is scientific evidence for integrity testing which is publicly available in the scientific literature; (4) that they had analysed data originating from publishers' handbooks and from academic studies separately and again found no difference; and (5) that any argument against integrity testing on the grounds of its impact would apply equally to personality and ability testing in occupational settings.

In conclusion, we can see that integrity testing, while remaining controversial, raises questions which are not different in kind from those which are already familiar from the literature on ability and personality testing. The anxieties that are generated in all these areas arise from the important role that job selection (and by default also job rejection) plays in the lives of all of us. But this is a by-product of the selection process in general, and is not a fault of the tests themselves. It should be a requirement for any selection process that it be reliable, valid and unbiased, and these psychometric criteria should be applied to the evaluation of all selection techniques, whether they be by interview, by questionnaire, by test of knowledge, by qualification, or indeed by any technique whatsoever. The value of any technique will stand or fall on the basis of publicly accountable scientific evidence. There can be no doubt that integrity tests address directly some of the major questions of interest to an employer in the selection process. There is currently an increasing interest in the utilization of personality tests, particularly those based on the big five, to assess integrity. However, the use of more focused scales to assess particular attitudes and behaviours necessarily remains of considerable interest to all involved in personnel assessment. Indeed, it is frequently the identification of those attitudes and behaviours addressed by integrity tests, such as long-term commitment, laziness and absenteeism, which is the primary argument in favour of using personality tests at all.

Theories of integrity

O'Bannon *et al.* (1989) list some of the constructs used in integrity tests. These include responsibility, long-term job commitment, consistency, proneness to violence, moral reasoning, hostility, work ethics, dependability, depression and energy level. Ones *et al.* (1993) include disciplinary problems, violence on the job, excessive absenteeism and tardiness, and theft, among target behaviours for integrity tests. Other integrity characteristics summarized by Schmidt *et al.* (1992) include violence on the job and drug abuse, as well as the more traditional personality traits of reliability, conscientiousness, adjustment, trustworthiness and sociability.

Sackett and Wanek (1996) also mention wasteful use of company time, failure to report theft by others, and waste and damage to company materials as possible candidates. They also point out the very broad range of severity of the traits covered by integrity tests, which can include not only the rather infrequent criminal activities of theft of money and major fraud but also activities such as 'time theft'. The latter may involve absenteeism, but may also amount to little more than extended visits to the toilet or cigarette breaks which in many companies may be the rule rather than the exception. In contrast to tests of personality, none of the integrity tests in either of these reviews are theoretically driven. This is odd, given that integrity is so central to ethical theory. However, we must remember that it is applied psychology, rather than ethics, that has generated these tests.

It is the received wisdom that the theories that underpin the scales of personality questionnaires are of two types – theoretical and statistical. Thus Eysenck's theory is seen as theoretical as it draws its inspiration from the four humours of Ancient Greek science, while Cattell's theory is seen as statistical as it was derived from a factor analysis of natural-language personality descriptors. However, in reality the distinction is not so clear-cut. Factor analysis is widely used in the construction of scales to assess theoretical traits, and the folk psychology implicit in the natural-language descriptors themselves has a major impact on the outcome of factor analyses of 'theoretical' data sets.

Even before Galton (1884) brought the natural-language personality descriptor to psychology, and prior to the advent of mathematical statistics, natural-language personality descriptors had already been a subject of interest to classical scholars and are considered in many works from the classical period. Probably the most influential of these was the 'Psychomachia' of Prudentius in the fourth century ad (Bergman 1926). Prudentius was a citizen of the Roman city of Caesar Augusta, today Saragossa in modern Spain. His model was later adapted by Christian theologians and became known as the seven vices and virtues. The 'Psychomachia' provided the inspiration for much of the folk psychology of the Middle Ages, including Dante Alighieri's *Divine Comedy*, and in England John Bunyan's *Pilgrim's Progress* which dates from the seventeenth century.

Prudentius saw human development as a lifelong striving for rationality. During this process the individual has to tackle various challenges. For example, greed gets you what you want, yet is irrational as a society in which personal gain was the only social motive would be untenable. Anger achieves immediate ends, yet is irrational as it allows emotion to overrule common sense. Despair enables one to cease striving, yet is irrational as it makes nonsense of human motivation. Indulgence gets one pleasure, yet is irrational as it prevents mankind from achieving its destiny.

In the 'Psychomachia' these challenges are represented by warriors in a battle. The animal Vices (the Passions) are eventually overcome by the human Virtues (the Sentiments). In comparison with psychology today, we can recognize elements of the self-actualizing tendency, multiple intelligences, cognitive therapy and psychoanalysis (Libido). The Prudentius model contrasts with that of the equally important ancient Galen of Pergamon (Turkey in the second century AD), in that certain paths of action are recognized as desirable and others as undesirable. For Galen, if we fail to attend to detail it is because of our biology, for Prudentius it is because we are slovenly.

Giotto: a psychometric test of integrity

Giotto di Bondone (c. AD 1300), the Italian renaissance artist, portrayed the virtues and vices as Prudence/Folly, Fortitude/Inconstancy, Temperance/Anger, Justice/Injustice, Faith/Idolatry, Charity/Envy and Hope/Despair. An integrity test that uses this frame-work is Giotto (Rust 1997), and it is also modelled by seven minor scales within Orpheus. The test specification for the Giotto test of integrity is a mapping of the ideas of Prudentius on to the major integrity traits provided by the integrity-testing literature, and is shown in Table 11.1.

The Giotto scales

The seven Giotto scales, then, are designed to assess a person's strengths and weak-nesses, and are based on a psychological theory of integrity originally attributed to Prudentius. In contrast to the big-five model of Orpheus, it recognizes that most assess-ments of personality in everyday life are made in terms of the consequences of particu-lar characteristics or actions for others. Because a weakness in one occupation may be neutral, or even a strength, in another, Giotto should only be used where relevant to a particular work setting. For example, entrepreneurs will often take risks in order to learn from their mistakes, whereas this approach would not be desirable for airline pilots.

Prudence is contrasted by carelessness. Many jobs require staff to work with heavy machinery or take responsibility for driving large vehicles. There are also many posts in the chemical industry where attention to hazards and safety precautions is a top priority. Preference is likely to be given to those who are naturally cautious in their temperament and who are not likely to allow their minds to wander at critical moments. A high score on Prudence provides some protection against carelessness leading to loss of life or limb, accident proneness, mindlessness, the tendency to live in a world of fantasy, not being able to see the consequences of one's actions, negligence, unreliability and irresponsible behaviour.

Fortitude refers to work orientation. Most companies prefer to employ hard work-ers, simply because they are more productive and a better investment in terms of human resources. Preference is likely to be given to those who show little absenteeism and a

Table 11.1 The test specification for Giotto is provided by a mapping of the classical theory of the 'Psychomachia' of Prudentius onto the major integrity traits

Classical virtues/vices	Integrity trait
Prudence/Folly	Competence vs. carelessness (Rust 1996e) Responsibility, consistency (O'Bannon *et al.* 1989) Reliability, conscientiousness (Schmidt *et al.* 1992)
Fortitude/Inconstancy	Work-orientation vs. absenteeism (Rust 1996e) Long-term job commitment, work ethics (O'Bannon *et al.* 1989) Excessive absenteeism and tardiness (Schmidt *et al.* 1992)
Temperance/Anger	Patience vs. hostility (Rust, 1996e) Proneness to violence, hostility (O'Bannon *et al.* 1989) Violence on the job (Schmidt *et al.* 1992)
Justice/Injustice	Fair-mindedness vs. subversion (Rust 1996e) Moral reasoning (O'Bannon *et al.* 1989) Disciplinary problems (Schmidt *et al.* 1992)
Faith/Infidelity	Loyalty vs. disloyalty (Rust 1996e) Dependability (O'Bannon *et al.* 1989)
Charity/Envy	Openness vs. disclosure (Rust 1996e) Trustworthiness (O'Bannon *et al.* 1989) Theft, drug abuse (Schmidt *et al.* 1992)
Hope/Despair	Initiative vs. inertia (Rust 1996e) Energy level and depression (O'Bannon *et al.* 1989)

good time-keeping record and do not cut corners. High scores on Fortitude provide some protection against laziness, lack of commitment, high staff turnover, absenteeism, tardiness, lack of interest in work outcomes, following the letter rather than the spirit of instructions and failure to meet required standards of dress.

Temperance is contrasted with anger. It is a desirable attribute in those whose work requires them to be part of a team, particularly when decisions need to be made under pressure. Such people will have a role in calming the situation when feelings are running high and are likely to be helpful in building a social environment at peace with itself. High scores on Temperance provide some protection against proneness to violence, violence on the job, hostility, bullying, verbal intimidation, excessive argumentation and unnecessarily raised voices.

Justice can be contrasted with intolerance. A degree of acceptance of the minor faults and foibles of others is an essential requirement for an effective line manager. Junior staff, in particular, benefit from being allowed to learn from their mistakes and from working in an environment where they can seek help from others. A high score on Justice provides some protection against disaffection, disciplinary problems, subversion, bad feelings, vexatious litigation, encouragement of formal complaints and intolerance of small mistakes by others.

Faith is contrasted with disloyalty. Faithful staff can be depended on, particularly in times of trouble, to join with their colleagues and see the company through. Without loyalty from senior staff the outlook for a troubled company is bleak. Faithful junior staff will identify with their organization and trust their management. High scores on Faith provide some protection against arrogance and disrespect to senior managers, behaviour inappropriate to the level of seniority, taking advantage, failure to report significant misdemeanours by others and putting personal interests ahead of the company. For more senior staff, high Faith scores protect against overbearing behaviour towards juniors, use of company time and property for personal affairs, poaching of staff by rival organizations, information theft and openness to bribery.

Charity is contrasted by envy in its myriad aspects. A workforce in which people are willing to help each other out without thought for themselves is essential in some organizations, particularly where demand varies from time to time. A willingness to share also encourages a positive attitude and a feeling of joint responsibility for the company's assets. Openness in communication among staff is also a considerable benefit to effective company planning. High scores on Charity provide some protection against theft of company property, feelings of being owed a living, dishonest dealing with money or timesheets, wasteful use of resources, borrowing of company property, unnecessary hoarding of internal assets, excessive privacy concerning work responsibilities and achievements, failure to share, and covering up mistakes.

Hope epitomizes a positive outlook and optimism for the future. Those with low scores on this trait tend to be backward-looking and resistant to change. Increasingly today the ability to be flexible, to consider new ideas and be willing to take some risks in putting these into practice are what enable the successful company to gain the edge in an increasingly competitive market. High scores on Hope provide protection against inertia, depression and anxiety, passive obstructiveness, lack of self-confidence, demoralizing attitudes and poor levels of self-esteem.

The psychometric properties of Giotto

The reliability of the seven Giotto scales ranged between 0.71 and 0.76. Validity was demonstrated in a number of ways. Concurrent validity was obtained by correlating the seven Giotto scales with the matching integrity traits from the Orpheus minor scales. Content validity was found from correlations with trait adjectives and an examination of the domains represented by each. Criterion-related validity was obtained from correlations between Giotto scales and relevant supervisors' ratings.

Summary

There are standard procedures for the use of psychometric tests and questionnaires, particularly in employment settings. These procedures, which address the rights and interests of job applicants, become of particular importance with integrity tests, questionnaires designed for the assessment of the candidate's own ethical functioning. Giotto is given as an example of an integrity test intended for use in occupational settings.

Chapter 12

Psychometrics in the information technology age

Computerization

Psychometric procedures have proved to be particularly amenable to computerization. However, the fact that tests usually contain information about an individual's psychological make-up, that they are normally scored by computer, and that once scored the data can easily be transferred to databases, makes this field very sensitive. Furthermore, data of this type are always of interest to personnel and credit agencies, the insurance and marketing industry, social security, and the police and intelligence services, and this does mean that special care needs to be taken, especially now that large data banks are able to extract information in 'intelligent' ways. The contribution of computers to testing for college entrance, professional licensure tests, standardized achievement batteries and scored clinical instruments is enormous, although not immediately apparent to the large number of people who are affected by it. Computerization of scoring, of test design, and of reliability and validity estimation is leading to significant improvements in the dependability of testing, and this is proceeding at an ever-increasing rate.

Computerized statistics

The impact of the computer has taken place at several levels. The first major development was of the computerized statistical package, first on mainframe computers and later on the PC. Most problems in psychometrics are extensions of matrix algebra and it has been this area of mathematics that has been most influenced. Before the 1960s, the main restrictions on the science of testing were time limitations arising from the need to carry out large numbers of calculations. In factor analysis in particular, matrix inversion is essential but time-consuming. Further, because iteration is required for the solution of multi-linear equations, each major algorithm needed to be repeated many times. In the 1960s computers became essential for these types of problem, which could be tackled in full for the first time. However, many hours of computer time were still needed. By the 1980s factor-analysis programs were available on microcomputers, and by the 1990s even complex modelling was readily available to every personal computer owner.

One difficulty with the ready availability of statistical packages is that people use them without understanding what they are doing. Thus, many inexperienced users find that the computers can produce almost endless alternative ways of analysis, different forms of significance test, and rotations of factor structure, but very little guidance on what is actually important out of all these many pages of figures. The use of knowledge-engineering techniques will certainly change this situation. Today, artificial intelligences, 'daemons' within the software, are capable of taking us through all the necessary steps in the analysis of results, from the initial assumptions to the final conclusions.

Computerized item banks

The next most important area in which computerization has had an impact is in the development and administration of item banks (see Chapter 4). The development of item response theory (IRT), and in particular of item banks containing data from which item characteristic curves can be estimated, enables a great deal of housekeeping of the bank to be done automatically. Item characteristic curve models involve complex iteration, and during the 1970s analysis of the two- and three-parameter models was too expensive in computer time, so that item banks were almost exclusively based on the Rasch one-parameter model. This was known to be inadequate in any controversial setting. However, by the 1980s the more complex models were no longer such a challenge, and were beginning to become widely available (Bock and Mislevy 1982). The IRT models allow responses from the items administered at the beginning of a testing session to be used to obtain provisional estimates of ability. This information is then used to select items of an appropriate difficulty level for the rest of the testing session (Haladyna and Roid 1983). These methods when fully developed can save up to 50 per cent on the number of items required, and can thus either save time or increase precision. The use of this technique in personality and attitude testing is discussed by Wright and Masters (1982), while Hambleton and Swaminathan (1985) have carried out an empirical study to show that sequential adaptive tests of this type can provide greater precision and reliability with fewer items than conventional achievement tests.

One important example of the use of IRT models in test construction has been the British Ability Scale. For a long time in the late 1970s, at a time when the Rasch model had fallen into disfavour, it was felt that the use of this model in the construction of the scales had been a mistake. However, the test itself proved to have been so well constructed overall, and so useful in practice, that the use of the Rasch-constructed sub-scales of numerical and other computational abilities continued to be recommended, albeit with caution. In fact, they have proved to be particularly robust in their use for the clinical assessment of children, and the generalization across ability levels from different sub-sets of items has, in spite of many misgivings, been found to be informative. Elliot (1983) argues that many of the doubts about the Rasch model have arisen from situations where it has been applied to pre-existing data, or to test data that had not been specifically designed to fit the model. If the Rasch model is used carefully and with a full knowledge of its limitations, as in the development of the British Ability Scale, then it is possible to make use of its subject-free and item-free characteristics.

Computerized item generation

Computer programs have been written that can create new items, or tailor and alter existing items during test administration. The use of computers in the construction of test items goes back to the work of Atkinson and Wilson (1969). They designed a series of small computer program sections (macros) that allowed for individual test-like events in instruction, such as checking whether recently presented material had been learned, to be varied at will. These were incorporated within a computer-assisted learning (CAL) program, and this pattern of instructional material, leading to a test and then the presentation of more material, forms the backbone of many CAL programs in use today. The utility of the computer in designing test items is based largely on the existence of a series of standard formats in items. Thus many items have a frame, which is held constant, and elements, which can vary. Take the object relations format, a is to b as x is to y. Possible insertions here are, for example, glove is to hand as sock is to ? (foot), but there are many millions of possible sets of semantic relations which could participate in an item of this type. The same is true for most item types. In fact, the number of basic item types is severely limited, it is the enormous number of possible elements they can contain that provides for variation. There are many circumstances where sets of possible elements can be held in store and inserted by computer at random into a fixed format to generate a large series of new items. This applies particularly in memory tests but also in perceptual and numeric tests. Indeed, the possibility for a degree of computerization exists in almost every type of test item. The advantages of this are several, but particularly lie in the ability to create novel items in circumstances where respondents need to be tested several times. This form of item generation is used by the British Army Recruitment Battery (BARB).

Interactive administration

The overlap between psychometrics and curriculum implementation is in many ways at its most explicit within computer-assisted learning (CAL), and this usefully illustrates both the limitations and strengths of the psychometric model. The CAL model normally involves the sitting of the pupil in front of a computer screen, following which a program will be initiated that presents information on the screen and asks the pupil questions about the material. A CAL program needs to be able to utilize the responses of the pupil to identify his or her learning needs, to present material that will stimulate learning, and to form some assessment of its (and the pupil's) success or failure. Within CAL the main aim is towards the learning of the subject, and the test items within a CAL program are subsidiary; they exist to identify very specific, and hopefully temporary, blocks in understanding, and to diagnose the best way forward. They mirror the type of dialogue that might occur between a teacher and a student, and can be considered as teacher-expert systems.

Computerized questioning

The common characteristics of CAL and computerized psychometrics might seem to imply that they are really the same process and only differ as a matter of degree. However, this is probably misleading. Psychometric computerized test administration differs from CAL in that the questions are intended to identify long-term characteristics of the respondent. The test items thus need to be more carefully constructed and piloted. This is in fact true even within educational settings involving continuous assessment. While there is no clear dividing line between the immediate demands of CAL-based questioning and the longer-term psychometric items, it could be said that psychometrics as such only begins once written reports are made. Thus the difference between the CAL question item and the psychometric question item is that between the immediate response that goes towards initiating the next step in a CAL program, and the stored response that makes a concrete contribution to a more permanent record. With the latter there is clearly the expectation that what has happened during the session has implications for the future, and can be relied on to some extent in the prediction of later behaviour. The subsequent use of test scores for judging the child, teacher or school is normally justified in terms of psychological or educational theory. Within education, it will be defined around steps in the curriculum process, in psychology around theoretical constructs.

Narrative reports

A further way in which the use of the computer is being extended is in the generation of reports. Many computerized testing or scoring programs no longer report mere numbers, to be interpreted by experts, but are able to produce narrative reports in a form suitable for the respondent or other end user. Where the test is a profile battery, the computer is able to identify extremes, to interpret these in the light of other sub-scale scores, and to make recommendations. This extension of use also implies an extension of the validation process from end score to end interpretation. However, it does mean that a much more rigid series of justification rules are required. Consider the similar case of computerized medical diagnosis. If, within this procedure, an error is made the wrong medication prescribed and the patient dies as a result, who is accountable for this mistake? Is it the computer, the clinician, or the person who wrote the diagnostic program? When diagnosis was carried out by the clinical expert alone there was at least a clear knowledge of who was accountable in the event of error. As computers obviously cannot be held accountable in law, the use of computer recommendations might appear to pass the responsibility to the test constructor; however, it is more likely the end user who will be left with de facto responsibility. The publishers of such computer programs should also publish material that clearly sets out the decision rules followed by the program. Thus, the professional user should be in a position to understand the full implications of the program's recommendations. It should never be the case that a person is in the position where he or she can say, 'This is the computer's decision.' This meaningless statement can only be eradicated if the advisors are taken by the computer through the steps required to back up the decision, so that the computer can fulfil its proper role as an aid to decision making.

The ethical issues associated with computerized advice of this type are reviewed by Zachary and Pope (1983). Roid (1986) points out that there are four major concerns which arise from the use of computers in test interpretation: (1) that it is questionable whether computers are any better than human experts, (2) that the computerized reports may reach the hands of inexperienced or unqualified people, (3) that the decision rules may not be public, and (4) that computerized reports may not be sufficiently validated. Many of these arguments are directed towards 'expert' computer systems in general, and although they all include an element of truth, it is already too late to argue for abolition. As with expert systems in general, the problems both ethical and social which they present to society will have to be tackled one way or another, for better or worse. A code of conduct is required for each application, which specifies where records are kept, who shall have access, the purposes for which they shall be used, the validation techniques, and the procedures for making public the decision rules. The problems are similar to those encountered in the use of computerized expert systems for any decision-making process involving human beings, where thought has to be given to the consequences of a wrong decision that may have to be justified in a court of law.

Automated recommendations and issues of responsibility

These ethical issues also apply wherever psychometric tests are combined with actuarial prediction procedures. McDermott (1980) developed a program which was able to identify students in a variety of special education categories based on scores on the Wechsler Intelligence Scale for Children (revised edition) (WISC-R), the revised version of the Wide Range Achievement Test (WRAT-R), the Adaptive Behaviour Scales and several other tests. On the basis of these scores the program would print out probability estimates for each category. This technique could be carried out by hand, and therefore has no new pitfalls that are not already covered by legislation on the use of these tests individually. However, a program by Barclay (1983), the Barclay Classroom Assessment System, provides an example of a computerized battery which was so extensive in scope and complexity that the procedures, involving sociometric choices by each member of each classroom among all other members, could not be realistically replicated without the program. The value of the computer in these circumstances is that it makes possible an analysis that would be otherwise impossible, but this is at the expense of a diminution in clarity about the lines of responsibility. Actuarial programs have also been developed for use with the Minnesota Multiphasic Personality Inventory (MMPI), and studies comparing these programs with human experts have generally given them a good success rate (Lachar 1974). Today, neural network programs developed by artificial intelligence epitomize the problems of the computerized actuary. While they can learn from experience to make excellent predictions, the internal procedures they follow are often much too complicated for any human to understand.

Computerized test administration

Computerized administration of tests has been used for some time, with several advantages over paper-and-pencil testing. Individual test administration in particular is a time-consuming yet fairly automatic process for many tests, so that computerization offers potential savings in professional time. Klinger *et al.* (1976) have shown that when used in clinical settings there is also an increased acceptance by patients. It seems that often people are happier to answer questions for a computer than they are for their fellow human beings! However, the mere placing of a test on a computer for easier administration is only the first step in the utilization of computers for test administration. Because of their speed and infallible memory computer programs can easily be written which allow the computer to adapt its questioning to the initial responses of the respondent. In a paper-and-pencil test we have no way of knowing how a respondent will respond, so that all eventualities have to be covered. With a computerized adaptive test, on the other hand, any questions that turn out to be irrelevant after some initial information is known can be eliminated. It is also possible to tailor the difficulty level of a test to the ability level of an applicant. If the respondent encounters difficulty, the test can be made progressively easier, and if the respondent finds the test too easy it can be made more difficult. This procedure tends to increase the motivation of the respondent in either case. It is further possible to target special areas of the blueprint and allow the program to select questions that focus in on a particular area. Thus if we are interested in whether a person scores above a particular cut-off on a test it is possible to use a Bayesian approach which always chooses as the next item one which will maximize information towards making a decision, and to stop as soon as a specified probability level of acceptance or rejection is reached. Adaptive testing seems such an obvious way forward that it is surprising that it has not become more widely used. There are several studies that have shown it to be more successful than classical techniques for both criterion-referenced (Haladyna and Roid 1983) and norm-referenced tests (Hambleton and Swaminathan 1985). Reasons for the technique not becoming universally popular may include the lack of software, the sophistication needed to interpret the item response theory models involved, and the lack of faith of educational and psychological professionals in models they cannot understand.

Artificial intelligence

The psychometric test as an expert system

Expert systems are computer programs that have been developed to emulate the decision-making procedures of experts. Thus, an expert system can be used in medicine to make a diagnosis. Instead of the patient being questioned by a doctor, he or she will answer questions suggested by a computer that has been programmed to emulate the ideal and fully informed consultant. The expertise will be based on rules (e.g. if the patient complains of a pain in the big toe, then check the level of uric acid in the blood), and on data (e.g. all the possible causes of pain in the big toe). Because the memory of a computer is enormous and easily accessible, such a computerized expert system should in principle be able to outperform any consultant, so long as it has had a good role model. While the use of computerized diagnosis is in its infancy, there are many areas in which artificial expert systems have already supplanted their human analogues, e.g. the role of bank managers in allowing credit to customers.

For psychometrics, the relevant expert is the professional interviewer. Indeed, it is possible to consider even the classical psychometric test as a rudimentary expert system. Most of the questions in the type of questionnaires used in personnel offices are, after all, similar in many ways to the sort of questions a job interviewer might ask. However, until the advent of artificial intelligence, the human interviewer has always had the ultimate edge in that they are able to explore different pathways to the same end point. They can recognize that the same skill can be obtained through many different routes. In particular, a human can use conditionals when making decisions. The questions asked will depend on how the respondent has replied to previous questions. Classical psychometric tests do not have this ability. They can only be scored by asking exactly the same questions of all applicants, and by weighting each question in the same way, regardless of the level of its application to a particular individual. While this type of data is ideal for the statistical analysis, it lacks the flexibility of the true expert. Statistical models that combine weighted scores in this way are called linear. If the decision depends on conditionals, e.g. only utilize the response to item x if there is a certain response to item y, then the model is non-linear. While statisticians do have some models for simple forms of non-linearity, the true complexity of these models is beyond its scope.

An expert system is a form of artificial intelligence. However, it is not the only form. Today increasing interest is being expressed in what are called artificial neural networks. These are computer programs that are able to learn from experience. The inner workings of the artificial neural network are a set of nodes held within the software, each of which behaves in many ways like an individual neuron in the human brain. By increasing the number of nodes, allowing signals to flow freely between them, and by making the size of these signals depend on the node's history, it is possible to emulate the forms of learning of which living organisms are capable. One area in which such models have been particularly successful is that of pattern recognition. Thus, an artificial neural network can be trained to recognize car number plates seen from different angles in a murky environment under different lighting conditions. In many circumstances such artificial neural networks consistently outperform recognition programs based on the models of classical linear statistics. The ability of the artificial neural network to recognize patterns makes it of particular interest to psychometricians in that it provides an alternative model of the interviewer as expert. Perhaps the good interview is best emulated not as a person who identifies and follows sets of rules of the type found in expert systems, but rather is a person adept at pattern recognition. The interviewer is required to recognize true potential amidst the complexity of behaviours, moods and motives that make up the person applying for the job.

Neural networks in psychometrics

Artificial intelligence today can be broadly divided into two major fields, expert systems and neural networks. Expert systems offer a procedure whereby the decision rules of an assessment can be explicated and incorporated into a software routine. Recent expert systems can be very sophisticated, and offer the advantage of being able to make decisions quickly and consistently. In the early years, psychologists were often at the forefront of expert system development, and indeed many computer adaptive testing programs and narrative report generators are simple expert systems.

Neural networks also began in psychology with D.O. Hebb in the 1940s, but today are more at home in cognitive science and mathematics under the guise of neural programming or machine learning. The tables have been reversed and today's artificial intelligence networks are more often the inspiration for new theories in psychology rather than the other way round. Can these models be used in the development of psychometric assessments? In principal, yes. For example there is a great deal of similarity between psychometrics and econometrics in which neural networks have found wide application (e.g. stockmarket prediction or credit risk assessment). Indeed a credit rating is de facto scored biodata. Similarly, there are links between predictive validity and the actuarial estimation of insurance risk carried out by underwriters.

There are differences, however. Classical psychometrics has evolved alongside mathematical statistics and has established almost all of its performance standards within that framework. This has consistently been a problem for computer adaptive testing and other expert systems in psychometrics, in that new paradigms have demanded new and untried approaches to reliability, validity, standardization and bias. These have generally lacked the simplicity and clarity of the old formula and have not always met with widespread acceptance, particularly where legal case law has been established on the basis of tradition. This is exemplified by the difficulties encountered in the introduction of Rasch scaling techniques in the 1970s. This having been said, there can be no doubt that the new techniques do in principle offer many advantages over traditional method. However, any new system does need to address two important questions. First, is the gain in benefit sufficiently substantial to justify the implementation of a relatively untried process? and second, can we obtain a set of standards for its use which will meet the stringent requirements of the human resource professional?

Advances in our mathematical understanding of machine learning force us to reconceptualize the first of these questions. It is now recognized that traditional statistics and neural networks are not in theoretical conflict as approaches to data analysis, rather one can be seen as a sub-set of the other. It can be demonstrated that all classical statistical procedures can be formulated as special cases of simple neural networks (in most instances a single-layered perceptron). In these cases the neural network solution is not simply similar to the solution of classical statistics, it is an algebraic identity with it. Thus, their relationship is rather like that between Newtonian and Einsteinian mechanics. One can be reduced to the other when certain simple principles hold. The simple principle in this case is that of linearity. One consequence of this is that if we use neural programming to carry out a psychometric item analysis we can, if we use a single-layered network, at the very least duplicate the classical item-analytic procedures. Furthermore, if we add hidden layers to the network we may increase our predictive power by including true non-linear relationships within the model. If no increase in predictive power is obtained we can rest comfortably in the knowledge that our linear solution, with its easily understood explanatory statistics, is adequate and probably the best available. When non-linearity adds significant power to the prediction we have the option of promulgating a new design for the test, and often the inspiration for a new theory. If we choose this route, however, we are still left with the second question – can we justify our procedures at a sufficiently precise level to be understood and accepted by our community of fellow professionals? In fact, machine learning is today so ubiquitous in industry and commerce that there are already standards for their use available from the Department of Trade and Industry (DTI 1994). How these will integrate into our pre-existing traditions within psychometrics has yet to be seen.

The availability of a predictive technology that addresses non-linearity has important implications for several long-standing problems in psychometrics. For example, it has often been noted that a limitation of psychometric test use is its tendency to produce 'clone workers'. If a particular personality profile is identified as that of, for example, the ideal salesperson, then the use of the test will tend to select a team of individuals all of whom have this profile. Not only is this somewhat creepy, but also probably undesirable as any effective team depends not on sameness but on a balanced diversity among its members. However, we know that there are many different combinations of traits that may be equally effective in producing any ideal salesperson. Different individuals arrive at their particular set of marketing skills through diverse and myriad pathways. A neural network trained to recognize the possibility of diverse pathways to the same standards of excellence could potentially outperform any paradigm from classical psychometrics that was by its nature restricted to linear prediction.

An example of a possible application for neural networks in psychometrics is in the analysis of item-analytic data from an ipsative test. Here the potential of the neural

189

network to deal with true non-linearity is of particular interest. While the issue of ipsativity has been conceptualized in many ways the only real difficulty for the statistician has been that ipsative items are not statistically independent of one another and cannot therefore be treated additively – that is, they are non-linear. It is this aspect of ipsative testing that presents so many problems for factor analysis, as indeed it must to any of the analytic procedures of classical statistics. Neural networks, however, offer the potential for modelling this non-linearity, and consequently may provide an item-analytic methodology for ipsative tests. It is worth mentioning here that the non-linearity inherent in a neural network is of a completely different order than that of so called non-linear statistics, the latter being merely conventions whereby certain aspects of non-linearity can be approximated linearly, for example with Tchebycheff's polynomials. Classical non-linear statistics never did offer the possibility for true non-linear item analysis that neural programming has now made available.

An example of a psychometric test that has been developed using neural networks is the integrity test Giotto. The test specification of Giotto involved seven bipolar traits. The Giotto items consist of pairs of adjectives (e.g. generous–enthusiastic), and the respondent is asked to choose which of the the two applies most strongly to them. An item from each trait was paired ipsatively with an item from each of the other six traits, thus filling out all the possible combinations of seven fields (if a, b, c, d, e, f, g are the fields; then ab, ac, ad, . . . fg are the combinations). There are 21 of these. There were four instances of each in the pilot, and the item analysis was carried out to reduce this number while maximizing trait reliability. Phase 1 of the item analysis involved the construction of a simulated data set based on the underlying ipsative structure. This generated all possible hierarchical orderings of seven traits (over 7,000 pseudo-subjects in all), and a network was trained using these data to establish the interrelatedness of the underlying ipsative model. The intrinsic correlation between the seven predicted pseudo-traits is 0.16667 in every case. Data from an 800-subject pilot study of Giotto was then randomly interspersed within this dataset and the network retrained. The resultant beta weights provided the item analysis for each trait. Furthermore, after exploring several network configurations, it was found that the linear (single-layered) model in fact provided a good fit to the data. Clearly any factor analysis of such data would produce widely spurious results and would not be at all suitable for item analysis and scale construction.

The use of neural network techniques in Giotto is in fact very conservative. The procedure allowed an analysis of ipsative data that was able to cope with the intrinsic non-linearity such a model implies. At the same time it was possible to demonstrate that a linear model was more than adequate in this case, which has enabled a falling back on the classical criteria of psychometric reliability and validity that are so widely understood and respected. This is in many ways a best-case scenario, but what would have been the consequences if it had been discovered that a non-linear model fitted the data more accurately? Current programming practice within artificial intelligence would be to encapsulate the network of best fit into a software package that could be distributed as the scoring program. The ability to incorporate non-linearity into prediction is the major strength of neural programming and there are many cases of successful and widely used machine-learning software packages that utilize this important property. There are also DTI standards for the reliability and generalizability of the networks incorporated into such packages. These standards, however, do not readily map on to those used in psychometrics to date, and lack the benefits of comprehensibility and the considerable case law that has developed over the past century.

One major characteristic of the traditional psychometric concepts of reliability and validity is that, functional psychometrics apart, they are based on the theory of latent traits that postulate an abstract entity being measured. The solutions offered by neural networks, by contrast, have no latent traits and are purely actuarial in their predictions. The advantage of a good neural network is that its predictive power is second to none, the downside is that hardly ever do we have a clear understanding of how this is achieved within the inner workings of the computer program. Unlike expert systems, neural networks include no explicit rules and have no justification other than their success in prediction. We can only speculate at this time on how predictions based on such networks will ultimately be received in courts of law. However, it should not be forgotten that there are already well established legal precedents for such actuarial predictions, namely those used by the insurance industry to underwrite risk. Certainly, if market forces were to decide the issue, the advantages of improved prediction within the human resource marketplace would outweigh any initial trepidation, and neural programming techniques would have an assured future.

Summary

Information technology is having a revolutionary impact on psychometrics. The first stage was the application of the number-crunching power of mainframe computers to the necessary statistical calculations of item analysis, reliability estimation and more general experimental design. More recently the computer has been able to take over the role of test administration, and here, because the machine is able to make decisions so quickly, a new stage of development has been reached where results obtained at the beginning of a testing session can be analysed in time to modify the progress of the session. Artificial intelligence using both expert systems and neural technology can also be applied to psychometrics, and offer exciting prospects in terms of their ability to deal with non-linear data and to recognize complex patterns. In the future, the potential for computers to model decision processes at a linguistic as well as an information-processing level promises to be one of the most productive and controversial areas of development not just in psychometrics but in social decision making generally.

Part two

Constructing your own questionnaire

Questionnaires are often no more than a series of items that are not necessarily related to each other and which are scored and interpreted individually. This is a guide to the construction of psychometric questionnaires, i.e. where items can be combined to produce an overall scale.

Questionnaires are used to measure a wide variety of attributes and characteristics. The most common examples are knowledge-based questionnaires, i.e. questionnaires of ability, aptitude and achievement; and person-based questionnaires, i.e. questionnaires of personality, clinical symptoms, mood and attitudes. Whatever type of questionnaire you wish to develop, this guide will take you through the main stages of construction and will also show you how to tailor your questionnaire to its particular purpose. Throughout the guide the construction of the Golombok Rust Inventory of Marital State (GRIMS) (Rust *et al.* 1988) will be described (between ruled lines) as a practical example.

The purpose of the questionnaire

The first step in developing a questionnaire is to ask yourself 'What is it for?' Unless you have a clear and precise answer to this question your questionnaire will not tell you what you want to know.

With the GRIMS we wanted to develop a questionnaire *to assess the quality of the relationship in heterosexual couples who are married or living together*. We intended that the GRIMS would be of use in research, either to help therapists or counsellors to evaluate the effectiveness of therapy for couples with relationship problems, or to investigate the impact of social, psychological, medical or other factors on a relationship. In addition, we hoped that it would be used clinically as a quick and easy-to-administer technique for identifying the severity of a problem, for finding out which partner perceives a problem in the relationship, and for identifying any improvement or lack of improvement in either or both partners over time.

Write down clearly and precisely the purpose of your questionnaire.

Making a blueprint

A blueprint, sometimes known as the test specification, is a framework for developing the questionnaire. A grid structure is generally used with (1) CONTENT AREAS along the horizontal axis and (2) MANIFESTATIONS (ways in which the content areas may become manifest) along the vertical axis. For practical reasons, between four and seven categories are usually employed along each axis. Fewer often results in too narrow a questionnaire, and more can be too cumbersome to deal with.

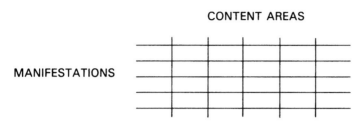

CONTENT AREAS

MANIFESTATIONS

(1) Content areas   A clear purpose will enable you to specify the content of your questionnaire. The content areas should cover everything that is relevant to the purpose of the questionnaire.

The many different ideas about what constitutes a good or bad marriage posed a problem when trying to specify the content areas of the GRIMS. For this reason we used the expertise of marital therapists/counsellors and their clients. The therapists/counsellors were asked to identify areas that they believed to be important in marital harmony as well as the areas they would assess during initial interviews. Information from clients was obtained by asking them to identify their targets for change. The views of these experts were collated to provide the following content areas that were generally considered to be important for assessing the state of a relationship: (a) interests shared (work, politics, friends, etc.) and degree of dependence and independence, (b) communication (verbal and non-verbal), (c) sex, (d) warmth, love and hostility, (e) trust and respect, (f) roles, expectations and goals, (g) decision making, (h) coping with problems and crises.

Write down the content areas to be covered by your questionnaire. If these are not clear-cut, consult experts in the field.

(2) Manifestations   The ways in which the content areas may manifest themselves will vary according to the type of questionnaire under construction. For example, questionnaires designed to measure educational attainment may use Bloom's taxonomy of educational objectives to tap different forms of knowledge. For questionnaires that are more psychological in nature, behavioural, cognitive and affective manifestations of the content areas may be more appropriate. For personality questionnaires you will need to balance socially desirable and socially undesirable aspects of the trait, and also to

balance acquiescence. The latter is achieved by allowing half of the items to manifest positively (e.g. 'I am outgoing' in an extraversion scale), and half to manifest negatively (e.g. 'I am shy' in an extraversion scale). In specifying manifestations it is important to ensure that different aspects of the content areas will be elicited.

In constructing the GRIMS we again took account of the experts' information to obtain the following manifestations: (a) beliefs about, insight into and understanding of the nature of dyadic relationships, (b) behaviour within the actual relationship, (c) attitudes and feelings about relationships, (d) motivation for change, understanding the possibility of change, and commitment to a future together, (e) extent of agreement within the couple.

As you can see from the GRIMS blueprint, what is described as a content area and what is described as a manifestation may not always be clear-cut.

> Write down ways in which the content areas of your questionnaire may become manifest.

You will now be able to construct your blueprint. The number of cells will be the number of content areas × the number of manifestations. Between 16 and 25 cells (i.e. 4×4, 4×5, 5×4 or 5×5) are generally considered ideal for sufficient breadth while maintaining manageability.

> Draw your blueprint, labelling each content area (columns) and each manifestation (rows).

Each cell in the blueprint represents the interaction of a content area with a manifestation of that content area. By writing items for your questionnaire that correspond to each cell of the blueprint, you will ensure that all aspects which are relevant to the purpose of your questionnaire will be covered.

A decision that has to be made when designing the blueprint is whether to give different weightings to each of the cells, i.e. whether to write more items for some cells than for others. This will depend on whether or not you feel that some content areas or some manifestations are more important than others. In the blueprint below it has been decided that content area A should receive a weighting of 40%, content area B a weighting of 40%, content area C a weighting of 10% and content area D a weighting of 10%. For the manifestations, a weighting of 25% has been allocated to each.

Content areas

	A 40%	B 40%	C 10%	D 10%
A 25%				
B 25%				
C 25%				
D 25%				

Manifestations

For the GRIMS, equal weightings were assigned to each cell as we had no reason to believe that any of the content areas or manifestations were more important than the others.

Assign percentages to each content area of your blueprint so that the total of the percentages across the content areas adds up to 100%.
　　Assign percentages to each manifestation in your blueprint so that the total of the percentages across the manifestations adds up to 100%.
　　Insert these percentages into your blueprint.

Assigning weightings will tell you what proportion of all items in the questionnaire should be written for each cell. The next step is to decide upon the total number of items to include. You must consider factors such as the size of your blueprint (a large blueprint with many content areas and manifestations will need a greater number of items than a small one) and the amount of time available for administering the questionnaire. There is no point in asking people with little time to spare to complete a lengthy inventory, as the quality of their response will be poor and items may be omitted. Characteristics of the respondents are also important. Children, the elderly and the physically or mentally ill may be slow and unable to maintain concentration. Although it is important to include a sufficient number of items to ensure high reliability, compliance among respondents is crucial and a balance must be struck between the two. A minimum of 12 items per scale is usually required to achieve adequate reliability. In the plan, however, a minimum of 20 items should be aimed for, and a fairly straightforward questionnaire of this length should take the average respondent no longer than 6 minutes to complete. As it is necessary to construct a pilot version of your questionnaire in the first instance, you must remember to allow for at least 50% more items in the blueprint than you intend to include in the final version.

The GRIMS was intended as a short questionnaire for use with both distressed and non-distressed couples. As we hoped to achieve a final scale of about 30 items, we planned a pilot version with 100 items.

Decide how many items to include in the pilot version of your questionnaire by taking into account the desired number of items in the final version, the size of your blueprint, the time available for testing and the characteristics of the respondents.

Once you have assigned weightings to the cells and decided upon the total number of items you require for your pilot questionnaire, you will be able to work out how many items to write for each cell. The blueprint below, with given weightings, shows the number of items that have to be written for each cell to obtain a pilot questionnaire with 80 items. The first step is to work out the total number of items for each content area and for each manifestation. The blueprint specifies that 40% of the items (32 items) should be on content area A, 40% on content area B (32 items), 10% (8 items) on content area C and 10% (8 items) on content area D. These numbers are entered in the bottom row of the blueprint. Similarly, the blueprint specifies that 25% of the items (20 items) should concern each of the manifestations and this is entered into the right-hand column of the blueprint. To calculate the number of items in each cell of the blueprint, multiply the total number of items in a content area by the percentage assigned to the manifestation in each row. For example, the number of items for the top left-hand cell (content area A/manifestation A) is 25% of 32 items, which is 8 items. The number of items to be written for each cell is calculated in the same way. If you do not obtain an exact number of items for a cell, approximate to the number above or below while trying to maintain the same total number of items as you had originally planned.

| | | Content areas | | | | |
		A 40%	B 40%	C 10%	D 10%	No. of items
	A 25%	8	8	2	2	20
	B 25%	8	8	2	2	20
Manifestations	C 25%	8	8	2	2	20
	D 25%	8	8	2	2	20
	No. of items	32	32	8	8	80

The 100 items in the equally weighted 40-cell GRIMS blueprint allowed between 2 and 3 items per cell.

Enter the number of items to be written for each cell into your blueprint.

Writing items

There are several types of item that are used in questionnaires, the most common of which are **alternate choice** items, **multiple choice** items and **rating scale** items. Different item types are suitable for different purposes and consideration of the attribute or characteristic that you wish your questionnaire to measure will guide you towards an appropriate choice.

Alternate choice item

An item for which the respondent is given two choices from which to select a response, for example 'true' or 'false', 'yes' or 'no'.

Use   Most commonly used in knowledge-based questionnaires, e.g. Bogota is the capital of Colombia – true or false?

Sometimes used in personality questionnaires, e.g. I never use a lucky charm – yes or no?

Generally considered inappropriate for clinical symptoms, mood or attitude questionnaires but used occasionally.

Advantages   Good for assessing knowledge of facts and comprehension of material presented in the question. Fast and easy to use.

Disadvantages   For ability, aptitude and achievement items, the correct response is often not clear cut, i.e. completely true or completely false. Another problem is that the respondent has a 50% chance of obtaining the correct response by guessing. For personality, clinical symptoms, mood and attitude questionnaires, there are no right or wrong answers. However, respondents often consider the narrow range of possible responses to be too restricting.

Multiple choice item

An item for which the respondent is given more than two choices from which to select a response. It consists of two parts: (a) the stem – a statement or question which contains the problem, and (b) the options – a list of possible responses of which one is correct or best and the others are distractors. Often 4 or 5 possible responses are used to reduce the probability of guessing the answer.

Use   Most widely used item type in knowledge-based questionnaires, e.g.:

What is the capital of Colombia?
A La Paz
B Bogota
C Lima
D Santiago

Not used in person-based questionnaires.

Advantages   Well suited to the wide variety of material that may be presented in ability, aptitude and achievement questionnaires. Challenging items can be constructed that are easy to administer and score. The effects of guessing are also reduced with multiple-choice items. For example, an item with 5 options gives a 20% chance of guessing the correct answer compared with 50% in alternate response items.

Disadvantages   Time and skill are needed for writing good multiple-choice items. A common problem is that not all of the options are effective, i.e. that they are so unlikely to be correct that they do not function as possible options. This can reduce what is intended as a 5-choice item to a 3- or 4-choice item or even to an alternate choice item.

Rating-scale item

An item for which the possible responses lie along a continuum, for example 'yes', 'don't know', 'no'; 'true', 'uncertain', 'false'; 'strongly disagree', 'disagree', 'agree', 'strongly agree'; 'always', 'sometimes', 'occasionally', 'hardly ever', 'never'. Up to 7 options are generally used as it is difficult for respondents to differentiate meaningfully among more than that number. Although rating-scale items are similar to multiple-choice items in giving several response options, the options in rating scales are ranked while multiple-choice item options are independent of each other.

Use   Not used in knowledge-based questionnaires. It is the most widely used item type in person-based questionnaires, e.g.:

I am not a superstitious person

    A strongly disagree

    B disagree

    C agree

    D strongly agree

Advantages   Respondents feel able to express themselves more precisely with rating-scale items than with alternate-choice items.

Disadvantages   Respondents differ in their interpretations of the response options, e.g. 'frequently' has a different meaning to different individuals. Some respondents tend always to choose the most extreme options. When an uneven number of response options is used, many respondents tend to choose the middle one, e.g. 'don't know', or 'occasionally'.

The *type of option* should be chosen to suit the material to be presented in the questionnaire. There are no fixed rules about which type of option is best. A personality or mood questionnaire might require responses in terms of the options 'not at all', 'somewhat' and 'very much'. Attitude questionnaires generally consist of statements about an attitude object followed by the options 'strongly agree', 'agree', 'uncertain', 'disagree' or 'strongly disagree'. For clinical symptoms questionnaires, you might find that options relating to the frequency of occurrence, such as 'always', 'sometimes', 'occasionally', 'hardly ever' or 'never', are the most suitable.

    The most appropriate *number of options* to choose will also depend on the nature of the questionnaire. It is important to provide a sufficient number for respondents to feel able to express themselves adequately while ensuring that there are not so many that they have to make meaningless discriminations. In questionnaires using rating-scale items where strength of response should be reflected in the respondent's score, it is usual for at least 4 options to be used.

    It is sometimes necessary to use different types of item in a questionnaire because of the nature of the material to be included. However, it is preferable to use only one item type wherever possible to produce a neatly presented questionnaire.

Rating-scale items are the most appropriate for a scale of marital state. The items are presented as statements to which the respondents are asked to 'strongly agree', 'agree', 'disagree' or 'strongly disagree'. This spread of options allows strength of feeling to affect scores. The items are forced choice; i.e. there is no 'don't know' category.

Decide which item type is most appropriate for your questionnaire. In general, multiple-choice items are best for knowledge-based questionnaires, and rating-

> scale items are best for person-based questionnaires unless you have good reason, such as speed or simplicity, for choosing alternate-choice items. A good method for deciding which to choose is to try to construct items of each type using different options. The most appropriate choice for your questionnaire will soon become clear.

Before beginning to write items for your questionnaire, read the following summary of important points to remember. For a more detailed discussion of how to write good items see Thorndike and Hagen (1977) and Guilford (1959).

All questionnaires

Make sure that your items match your blueprint. The allocation of items to specific cells may become a bit fuzzy as some items may be appropriate for more than one cell. If you find that some cells are inappropriate and you decide to omit them, do not do so without proper consideration. Remember, however, that the blueprint is a guide and not a strait-jacket.

Write each item clearly and simply. Avoid irrelevant material and keep the options as short as possible. Each item should ask only one question or make only one statement. Where possible, avoid subjective words such as 'frequently', as these may be interpreted differently by different respondents. It is also important that all options are functioning as feasible responses, i.e. that none is clearly wrong or irrelevant and, therefore, unlikely to be chosen.

After writing your items, read them again a few days later. Also ask a colleague to look at them to ensure that they are easily understood and unambiguous.

Knowledge-based questionnaires

Make sure that alternate-choice items can be classified without doubt as true or false, otherwise some respondents will think of exceptions to the rule.

For multiple-choice items, ensure that each item has only one correct or best response. Ideally, each distractor option should be used equally by respondents who do not choose the correct response. Remember that the more similar the options, the more difficult the item.

Person-based questionnaires

Sometimes respondents will complete a questionnaire in a certain way irrespective of the content of the items:

Acquiescence is the tendency to agree with items regardless of their content. This can be reduced by ensuring that an equal or almost equal number of items is scored in each direction. To do this, it is usually necessary to reverse some of the items. For example, the item 'I am satisfied with our relationship' can be reversed to 'I am dissatisfied with our relationship'. When reversing items it is important to check that the reversed item really does have the opposite meaning to the original item. It is best to avoid double negative statements as these cause confusion. Acquiescence is less likely to occur with items that are clear, unambiguous and specific.

Social desirability is the tendency to respond to an item in a socially acceptable manner. This can be reduced by excluding items that are clearly socially desirable or undesirable. If this is unavoidable due to the nature of your questionnaire, try to ask the question indirectly to evoke a response that is not simply a reflection of how the respondent wishes to present him or herself. For example, an item to measure paranoia may be subtly phrased as 'There are some people whom I trust completely' rather than 'People are plotting against me'. Social desirability can also be reduced by asking respondents to give an immediate response rather than a careful consideration of each item.

Indecisiveness is the tendency to use the 'don't know' or 'uncertain' option. This is a common problem that can easily be eliminated by omitting the middle category. It is advisable to do so unless respondents are likely to become irritated by items that they feel are unanswerable.

Extreme response is the tendency to choose an extreme option regardless of direction. Some respondents will use one direction for a series of items and then switch to the other direction and so on. Again, this can be reduced by the use of clear, unambiguous and specific items.

It is important to bear in mind these habitual ways of responding when writing items. However, a careful item analysis will eliminate items that are biased towards a particular response.

Examples of GRIMS items:
   'We both seem to like the same things' was written for the blueprint cell representing content area (A) and manifestation (B).
   'I wish there was more warmth and affection between us' was written for the blueprint cell representing content area (D) and manifestation (D).

Write each of your items on a small card so that you can easily make changes in wording and ordering. To order the items for your questionnaire pick an interesting and unthreatening item to start with and then shuffle the cards to randomize the rest. Make adjustments if too many similar-looking items occur together. For knowledge-based questionnaires that have items of increasing difficulty order the items from easy to hard.

Designing the questionnaire

Good design is crucial for producing a reliable and valid questionnaire. Respondents feel less intimidated by a questionnaire that has a clear layout and is easy to understand, and take their task of completing the questionnaire more seriously.

Background information   Include headings and sufficient space for the respondent to fill in his or her name, age, sex or whatever other background information you require. It is often useful to obtain the date on which the questionnaire is completed, especially if it is to be administered again.

Instructions   The instructions must be clear and unambiguous. They should tell the respondent how to choose a response and how to indicate the chosen response on the questionnaire. Other relevant instructions should be given, e.g. Respond as quickly as possible, Respond to every item, or Respond as honestly as possible. Information that is likely to increase compliance, for example regarding confidentiality, should be stressed.

Sample instructions for a knowledge-based multiple-choice questionnaire:

> *Instructions.* Each item is followed by a choice of possible responses: A, B, C, D or E. Read each item carefully and decide which choice best answers the question. Indicate your answer by circling the letter responding to your choice. Your score will be the number of correct answers so respond to each question even if you are not sure of the correct answer.

Sample instructions for a person-based rating-scale questionnaire:

> *Instructions.* Each statement is followed by a series of possible responses: strongly disagree, disagree, agree or strongly agree. Read each statement carefully and decide which response best describes how you feel. Then put a tick over the corresponding response. Please respond to every statement. If you are not completely sure which response is more accurate, put the response which you feel is most appropriate. Do not spend too long on each statement. It is important that you answer each question as honestly as possible.

> *All information will be treated with the strictest confidence.*

Layout   The following tips will help you to arrange items on the page so that they are easy to read:

(a)   Number each item.
(b)   Keep each line short with no more than 10 or 12 words on a line.
(c)   Ensure that the items produce a straight vertical margin down the left-hand side of the page.

1. — — — — — — — — — — — — — — — —
2. — — — — — — — — — — — — — — —
3. — — — — — — — — — — — — — — —— — — —
   — — — — — — —
4. — — — — — — — — — — — — —
5. — — — — — — — — — — — — — — — —

(d)   Arrange the response options to produce a straight vertical margin down the right-hand side of the page. Insert headings at the top and symbols next to each item. There should be a clear visual relationship between each item and its response options. This can be done by inserting a dotted line from the item stem to its response option.

	STRONGLY DISAGREE	DISAGREE	AGREE	STRONGLY AGREE
1. — — — — — — — — — — — — —	SD	D	A	SA
2. — — — — — —	SD	D	A	SA
3. — — — — — — — — — — —— — — — —				
— — — — — —	SD	D	A	SA
4. — — — — — — — — —	SD	D	A	SA

(e)   Separate each item with a space rather than a horizontal line. If your items, instructions and background information all fit on one page, then good. However, it is better to produce a neat 2- or 3-page questionnaire than one page that looks cramped.

(f)   If using more than one type of item, group similar items together. Each type will need different instructions and response options.

(g)   Have the questionnaire printed using a top quality printer. Ensure that the type is large enough to be read easily. Capitals are difficult to read and should not be used for the item stems. However, capitals can be used for headings to make them stand out. Use your word processor creatively to plan the layout. Experiment with different fonts, colours, sizes of type and different spacings to see which look best.

(h)   You can use design as a tool to portray or disguise the purpose of your questionnaire. For example, small closely set type can make a questionnaire look very formal while larger type with items spaced well apart on coloured paper is friendlier. Design can set an atmosphere – use it!

THE GRIMS was designed with simplicity of administration in mind. The respondent has to answer 28 questions on one side of paper with the same response options for each question. This makes it quick and uncomplicated to complete.

> Try different layouts of your questionnaire using a word processor and printer until the arrangement looks logical. then experiment with font, colour, size of type, spacing and number of pages to see what looks best.

To score your questionnaire, allocate a score to each response option and then add up the score for each item to give a total score for the questionnaire.

For *knowledge-based questionnaires*, it is usual to give the correct or best option for each item a score of 1 and the distractor options a score of 0. The higher the total score, the better the performance.

For *person-based questionnaires*, scores should be allocated to response options according to a continuous scale, for example always = 5, usually = 4, occasionally = 3, hardly ever = 2, never = 1; yes = 2, uncertain = 1, no = 0; true = 1, false 0. For reversed items, it is necessary to reverse the scoring (e.g. always = 1, usually = 2, occasionally = 3, hardly ever = 4, never = 5) so that each item is scored in the same direction. After reversing the scores, add up the score for each item to obtain the total score for the questionnaire. Depending on the way in which you have allocated scores to response options, the higher the total score, the greater or lesser the presence of the characteristic being measured.

A scoring key that fits over the questionnaire to identify which option the respondent has chosen for each item and its score can be useful for quick and easy scoring. In the example below, the respondent has obtained a total score of 10 (3 + 3 + 1 + 3).

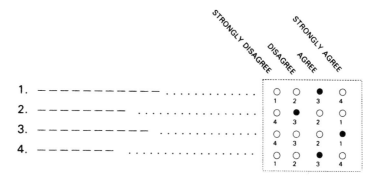

Simple computer programs can also be written for scoring questionnaires. This method is particularly useful for scoring large numbers of questionnaires.

Piloting the questionnaire

The next stage in constructing your questionnaire is the pilot study. This involves having the questionnaire completed by people who are similar to those for whom the questionnaire is intended. Analysis of these data will help you to select the best items for the final version of your questionnaire.

If, for example, your questionnaire is intended for married women with pre-school children you might carry out the pilot study at a baby clinic or a mothers and toddlers club. If it is for use with the general population, you would need to find a group of people who are representative of the population at large. This is often more difficult than finding a more specific group. You could make use of the electoral register, which is available from libraries, but this is usually too time-consuming to be worthwhile for a pilot study. When a truly representative group is impossible to find, an approximation is usually good enough. A common strategy is to hand out questionnaires in public places such as shopping centres, train and bus stations, airport lounges, doctors' waiting rooms, or canteens of large organisations. The respondents who take part in the pilot study should vary in terms of demographic characteristics such as age, sex and social class. There is little point in piloting a questionnaire intended for both sexes only with men, or a questionnaire to be used throughout an industry only with managers and not manual workers. It is important to obtain relevant demographic information from the respondents in the pilot study to help with the validation of your questionnaire at a later stage.

The pilot version of your questionnaire should be administered to as many people as possible. The minimum number of respondents required is one more than the number of items. If it is not possible to obtain this many, it is better to use fewer people than to omit the piloting stage altogether.

The pilot version of the GRIMS was administered to both partners in 60 client couples from marital therapy and marriage guidance clinics throughout the country.

Administer your questionnaire and obtain relevant demographic information from a group of people who are similar to those for whom the final questionnaire is intended.

Item analysis

Item analysis of the data collected in the pilot study to select the best items for the final version of your questionnaire involves an examination of the **facility** and the **discrimination** of each item. For knowledge-based multiple-choice items it is also important to look at **distractors**

The first step is to draw an item analysis table with each column (a, b, c, d, e, etc.) representing an item and each row (1, 2, 3, 4, 5, etc.) representing a respondent. For knowledge-based items, insert '1' in each cell for which the respondent gave the correct answer, and '0' for an incorrect answer. For person-based items, insert the actual score for each item remembering to ensure that reversed items are scored in the opposite direction to non-reversed items. Add up the score for each cell to give a total score for each row (i.e. each respondent) and a total score for each column (i.e. each item).

The following is a sample item-analysis table for a knowledge-based questionnaire:

		a	b	c	d	e	Sum
	1	1	1	0	1	1	4
	2	0	1	0	0	1	2
Respondents	3	1	0	0	1	1	3
	4	1	0	0	0	1	2
	5	0	0	0	1	1	2
Sum		3	2	0	3	5	13

Items

Facility

Most questionnaires are designed to differentiate respondents according to whatever knowledge or characteristic is being measured (see discussion of norm- and criterion-referenced testing in Chapter 3). A good item, therefore, is one for which different respondents give different responses. The facility index gives an indication of the extent to which all respondents answer an item in the same way. These items are redundant and it is important to get rid of them. For example, if every respondent gives the correct response to a particular item, this simply has the effect of adding one point to the total score for each respondent and does not discriminate among them.

For knowledge-based questionnaires, the facility index is calculated by dividing the number of respondents who obtain the correct response for an item by the total number of respondents. Ideally, the facility index for each item should lie between 0.25 and 0.75, averaging 0.5 for the entire questionnaire. A facility index of less than 0.25 indicates that the item is too difficult as very few respondents obtain the correct response; and a facility index of more than 0.75 shows that the item is too easy as most respondents obtain the correct response. For the sample item analysis table above, the facility index for each item is as follows: (a) 3/5 = 0.6, (b) 2/5 = 0.4, (c) 0/5 = 0, (d) 3/5 = 0.6, and (e) 5/5 = 1. Here we would probably wish to eliminate items (c) and (e) from the final questionnaire as everyone has responded to these items in the same way.

Similarly, the facility index for person-based items is calculated by summing the score for the item for each respondent, and then dividing this total by the total number of respondents. An item with a facility index that is equal to or approaching either of the extreme scores for the item should not be included in the final version of the questionnaire. It is also important to ensure by looking at the scores in the item analysis table that a good facility index, i.e. lying somewhere between the extreme scores, does not simply mean that everyone has chosen the middle option.

Discrimination

This is the ability of each item to discriminate respondents according to whatever the questionnaire is measuring, i.e. respondents who perform well on a knowledge-based questionnaire or who exhibit the characteristic being measured by a person-based questionnaire should respond to each item in a particular way. Items should only be selected for the final version of the questionnaire if they measure the same knowledge or characteristic as the other items in the questionnaire.

Discrimination is measured by correlating each item with the total score for the questionnaire. The higher the correlation coefficient, the more discriminating the item. There are no hard-and-fast rules about inclusion criteria for items in the final questionnaire. It is usual to choose 70–80% of the original items. The higher the correlation between the item and the overall questionnaire the better, and a minimum correlation of 0.2 is generally required. Items with negative or zero correlations are almost always excluded.

The Pearson product-moment formula is generally used to calculate the correlation coefficient between each item and the total score for the questionnaire. The score for each respondent for an item is correlated with the total score for each respondent for the questionnaire. This can be calculated easily by computer. If a computer is not available the formula below can be used to calculate the Pearson product-moment correlation coefficient by hand. Remember that correlation coefficients always lie between 1 and –1. If you obtain a coefficient outside this range then you have made a mistake in your calculation.

The Pearson product-moment formula:

$$r = \frac{N\Sigma XY - (\Sigma X)(\Sigma Y)}{\sqrt{[N\Sigma X^2 - (\Sigma X)^2][N\Sigma Y^2 - (\Sigma Y)^2]}}$$

where

r is the product-moment correlation coefficient
X is each of the scores on the item
Y is each of the scores on the questionnaire
N is the number of pairs of scores
Σ is 'the sum of'

In order to compute the Pearson product-moment correlation coefficient, you will need the sum of the respondents' scores on the item (ΣX), the sum of the respondents' scores on the total questionnaire (ΣY), the sum of the squares of the respondents' scores on the item (ΣX^2), the sum of the squares of the respondents' scores on the total questionnaire (ΣY^2), and the sum of the products of the scores on the item and the total questionnaire (ΣXY). Putting these figures into the formula will enable you to calculate the correlation coefficient. The following example shows an easy way of doing this. Remember to repeat the calculation for each item.

Respondents	Score on item	Score on item squared	Score on questionnaire	Score on questionnaire squared	Score on item × score on questionnaire
N	(X)	(X^2)	(Y)	(Y^2)	(XY)
1	1	1	30	900	30
2	3	9	57	3,249	171
3	5	25	94	8,836	470
4	4	16	76	5,776	304
5	3	9	80	6,400	240
6	1	1	33	1,089	33
7	2	4	54	2,916	108
8	2	4	58	3,364	116
9	5	25	83	6,889	415
10	4	6	76	5,776	304
	$\Sigma X = 30$	$\Sigma X^2 = 110$	$\Sigma Y = 641$	$\Sigma Y^2 = 45,195$	$\Sigma XY = 2,191$

$$r = \frac{10\,(2,191) - (30)\,(641)}{\sqrt{[10\,(110) - (30)^2]\,[10\,(45,195) - (641)^2]}}$$

$$= \frac{21,910 - 19,230}{\sqrt{(1,100 - 900)\,(451,950 - 410,881)}}$$

$$= \frac{2,680}{\sqrt{(200)\,(41,069)}}$$

$$= \frac{2,680}{\sqrt{8,213,800}}$$

$$= \frac{2,680}{2,866}$$

$$= 0.935$$

Distractors

An examination of the use of distractor options by respondents who do not choose the correct or best option should be carried out for each item to ensure that each distractor is endorsed by a similar proportion of respondents. This can be done for each item counting the number of times that each of its distractors has been endorsed. The number of endorsements should be similar for all these distractors. Items for which distractor options are not functioning properly should be considered for exclusion from the final questionnaire.

When deciding which items to include in the final version of your questionnaire you will have to take many factors into account and balance one against another. In addition to facility, discrimination and distractors, you will need to consider the number of items you require for the final version (at least 12 and more usually 20 are necessary for a reliable questionnaire), and how well the items fit the blueprint. For example, you might include an item with fairly poor discrimination if you have very few items from that area of the blueprint, or you might include an item with poor facility if it has reasonable discrimination. In a personality questionnaire it is also important to ensure that there are approximately equal numbers of reversed and non-reversed items. Ways of improving items may become clear at this stage. For example, changing the wording of an item from 'sometimes' to 'always' may improve facility, or a distractor may be made more realistic. However, it is not a good idea to change very many items as you will not know how these changes affect the reliability and validity of the questionnaire. The procedures of item analysis will inform you about the characteristics of each item. It is then up to you to decide which criteria are most important for the purpose of your particular questionnaire.

> Decide which items from the pilot version of your questionnaire to include in the final version, taking account of facility, discrimination and, if appropriate, distractors. Order the items and design the questionnaire as before.

Reliability

Reliability is an estimate of the accuracy of a questionnaire. For example, a questionnaire is reliable if a respondent obtains a similar score on different occasions, providing the respondent has not changed in a way that affects his or her response to the questionnaire. There are several ways of measuring reliability: **test–retest**, **parallel forms** and **split half**.

Test–retest This involves administering the same questionnaire to the same respondents under the same circumstances on two occasions and correlating the scores. A problem with this method is that respondents may remember their responses on the second occasion, so it is a good idea to have as long a time interval as possible between the two administrations of the questionnaire.

Parallel forms In this case it is necessary to construct two equivalent forms of the questionnaire and to administer both to the same respondents in order to correlate the scores. The main difficulty is in selecting two equivalent sets of items.

Split half Here the questionnaire is divided into two halves (usually odd items and even items) and the correlation between the halves is used to produce an estimate of reliability for the whole questionnaire. This method does not give reliability over a period of time.

For test–retest reliability and parallel forms, the correlation coefficient is calculated with the Pearson product-moment formula. This procedure is described in the section on item analysis. For split-half reliability, the Pearson product-moment coefficient between the two halves of the questionnaire is used in the Spearman–Brown formula (below) to give an estimate of reliability for the whole questionnaire.

$$r_{11} = \frac{2r_{\frac{1}{2}\frac{1}{2}}}{1 + r_{\frac{1}{2}\frac{1}{2}}}$$

where

r_{11} is the estimated reliability for the whole questionnaire
$r_{\frac{1}{2}\frac{1}{2}}$ is the correlation between two halves of the questionnaire

For example, if the Pearson product-moment correlation coefficient between two halves of a questionnaire is 0.80:

$$r_{11} = \frac{2\,(0.80)}{1 + 0.80} = 0.88$$

It has been argued that the best procedure for obtaining a measure of reliability is to administer parallel forms several weeks or months apart. However, this can be extremely time-consuming and split-half reliability is more commonly used. This provides an estimate of reliability from one administration of the same test, and can be carried out with data collected in the pilot study. The greater the number of respondents, the better the estimate of reliability. If fewer than 50 respondents were included in the pilot study, it is necessary to have the final version of the questionnaire completed by more people, ensuring once again that they are similar to those for whom the questionnaire is intended. The dual use of the pilot study data for item selection and reliability estimation will mean that reliabilities are overestimated. Ideally, data from at least 200 respondents who were not part of the pilot study should be used in calculating reliability. Where the questionnaire is intended for different types of respondents, it is usual to show that it is reliable for each type. In this case, a total of 200 respondents would be needed altogether. Whatever measure of reliability is used, a coefficient of at least 0.7 is generally required for person-based questionnaires and at least 0.8 for knowledge-based questionnaires.

For the GRIMS, split-half reliabilities were obtained for men and women separately for the respondents in the pilot study, marital therapy clients and a general population group. Reliabilities ranged from 0.81 to 0.94. Test–retest reliability was also calculated for marital therapy clients before and after therapy. Not surprisingly, these were much lower as the clients showed considerable change as a result of therapy.

Calculate the split-half reliability for the final version of your questionnaire using data from the relevant items from all of the respondents in the pilot study plus additional respondents if necessary. For each respondent, calculate the total score for the even items in the final version of your questionnaire and the total score for the odd items. Correlate the odd items with the even items using the Pearson product-moment formula. Use this correlation coefficient in the Spearman–Brown formula to obtain an estimate of reliability for the whole questionnaire.

Validity

The validity of a questionnaire is the extent to which it measures what it is intended to measure. Validity must be determined, therefore, in relation to the purpose of the questionnaire. There are several types of validity of which the most straightforward are: **face validity**, **content validity**, **criterion-related validity** and **predictive validity**.

Face validity describes the appearance of the questionnaire to respondents, i.e. whether or not it looks as if it is measuring what it claims to measure. If not, respondents may not take the questionnaire seriously.

Content validity is the relationship between the content and the purpose of the questionnaire, i.e. whether or not there is a good match between the test specification and the task specification. For example, the blueprint for a questionnaire used in job selection should match the job description.

Criterion-related validity is the relationship between scores on the questionnaire and a criterion measure. For example, with a marital-problems questionnaire we would expect couples on the verge of separation to obtain a score which is indicative of marital distress. It is important to select a criterion measure that is relevant, reliable and available.

Predictive validity is similar to criterion-related validity but relates scores on a questionnaire to a future criterion measure. For example, the predictive validity of a job-selection questionnaire can be calculated by correlating questionnaire scores with future achievement at work, and the predictive validity of a marital-problems questionnaire can be calculated by correlating questionnaire scores with future separation or divorce.

For your questionnaire to have face validity, you must ensure that it looks reasonable to the respondents for whom it is intended. Content validity is generally taken care of in constructing the blueprint and in the item analysis. However, it is important to check that the balance of items in the final version of your questionnaire matches the original blueprint. Criterion-related validity and predictive validity are obtained by correlating the questionnaire score with a criterion measure for a group of at least 50 respondents. The higher the correlation coefficient, the better the validity. The Pearson product-moment correlation formula is generally used to calculate the correlation coefficient.

Content validity of the GRIMS is high with respect to its specification, and good face validity has been incorporated into the item selection. It is also important for the GRIMS to have good diagnostic validity. This was established by determining that couples who presented at marriage guidance clinics had significantly higher scores than a matched sample from the general population. Moreover, couples presenting for marital therapy had significantly higher scores than couples presenting for sex therapy. Because the GRIMS was intended as a measure of improvement after therapy, it was important to obtain a rating of the validity of the GRIMS as an estimator of change. Couples were asked to complete the GRIMS before and after therapy, and the therapists, who were blind to their clients' GRIMS scores, were asked to rate the couple on a 5-point scale ranging from '0 – improved a great deal' to '4 – got worse'. The GRIMS scores for the male and female partners were averaged for each couple. The average score before therapy was subtracted from the average score following therapy to give a change score representing change during therapy. The change scores were correlated with the therapists' ratings of change giving a correlation coefficient of 0.77. This is firm evidence for the validity of change in the GRIMS score as an estimate of change in the quality of the relationship, or in the effectiveness of therapy.

Ensure that your questionnaire has good face validity, content validity, criterion-related validity and/or predictive validity as well as any other relevant types of validity such as diagnostic validity or validity of change scores.

Standardization

Standardization involves obtaining scores on the final version of your questionnaire from appropriate groups of respondents. These scores are called norms. Large numbers of respondents must be carefully selected according to clearly specified criteria in order for norms to be meaningful.

With good norms it is possible to interpret the score of an individual respondent, i.e. whether or not his or her score on the questionnaire is typical. This is useful if, for example, you wish to know how an individual child performs on an ability test compared with other children of the same age, or if you wish to determine how a person with a suspected clinical disorder compares with patients who have been diagnosed as having that disorder.

It is not always necessary to produce norms. If your questionnaire has been developed for research which involves comparing groups of respondents, norms can be useful in interpreting the performance of a group as a whole, but they are not crucial. If, however, you wish to interpret the score of an individual, it is necessary to have good norms against which to compare the individual score.

It is important to include as many respondents as possible in the standardization group, and to ensure that the respondents are truly representative. A minimum of several hundred is generally required but this depends to a large extent on the nature of the respondents. Some are easier to find than others, and it is often better to obtain a smaller group of very appropriate respondents than a larger but less appropriate one. In some cases it is necessary to obtain several standardization groups, or to stratify the standardization group according to relevant variables such as age, sex or social class. Ideally, there should be several hundred respondents in each group or stratification. Norms should be presented in terms of the mean and standard deviation for each group or stratification.

Mean:

$$\bar{X} = \frac{\Sigma X}{N}$$

where

$\bar{X}$ is the mean score
X is each of the scores on the total questionnaire
N is the number of respondents
Σ is 'the sum of'

Standard deviation:

$$SD = \sqrt{\frac{N\Sigma X^2 - (\Sigma X)^2}{N(N-1)}}$$

where

SD is the standard deviation
X is each of the scores on the total questionnaire
N is the number of respondents
Σ is 'the sum of'

The following example shows an easy way of doing this

X	X^2
3	9
4	16
7	49
8	64
8	64
9	81
10	100
$\Sigma X = 49$	$\Sigma X^2 = 383$
$N = 7$	

$$\text{mean} = \frac{49}{7}$$

$$= 7$$

$$\text{standard deviation} = \sqrt{\frac{7\,(383) - (49)^2}{7\,(7-1)}}$$

$$= \sqrt{\frac{2681 - 2401}{42}}$$

$$= \sqrt{\frac{280}{42}}$$

$$= \sqrt{6.67}$$

$$= 2.58$$

The GRIMS was standardized using two groups: (a) a random sample of people attending their family doctor with the usual variety of medical problems (a general population group), and (b) clients attending marriage guidance clinics and marital and sexual therapy clinics (a marital problems group).

Standardize your questionnaire using a relevant group or groups of as many respondents as possible. Present the norms in terms of the mean and standard deviation for each group or stratification.

Bibliography

Adorno, T.W., Frenkel-Brunswick, R., Levinson, D.J. and Sanford, R.N. (1950) *The Authoritarian Personality*, New York: Harper & Row

Allport, G.W. (1961) *Patterns and Growth in Personality*, New York: Holt, Rinehart & Winston

Allport, G.W. and Odbert, H.S. (1936) 'Trait-names: a psycho-lexical study', *Psychological Monographs* 47, (1, Whole No. 211)

Almagor, M., Tellegen, A. and Waller, N.G. (1995) 'The Big Seven model: a cross-cultural replication and further exploration of the basic dimensions of natural language trait descriptors', *Journal of Personality and Social Psychology* 69, 300–7

Anastasi, A. (1982) *Psychological Testing*, 5th edn, New York: Macmillan

Angoff, W.H. and Ford, S.F. (1973) 'Item–race interaction on a test of scholastic aptitude', *Journal of Educational Measurement* 10, 95–106

Atkinson, R.C. and Wilson, H.A. (1969) *Computer Assisted Instruction: A Book of Readings*, New York: Academic Press

Bandura, A. (1977) *Social Learning Theory*, Englewood Cliffs, NJ: Prentice Hall

Barclay, J.R. (1983) *Barclay Classroom Assessment System Manual*, Los Angeles: Western Psychological Services

Barrett, G.V. and Depinet, R.L. (1991) 'A reconsideration of testing for competence rather than for intelligence', *American Psychologist* 46, 1012–24

Barrick, M.R. and Mount, M.K. (1991) 'The Big Five personality dimensions and job performance: a meta-analysis', *Personnel Psychology* 44(1), 1–26

Beck, A.T., Ward, C.H., Mendelson, M., Mock, J., and Erbaugh, J. (1961) 'An inventory for measuring depression', *Archives of General Psychiatry* 4, 53–63

Bennun, I., Rust, J., and Golombok, S. (1985) 'The effects of marital therapy on sexual satisfaction', *Scandinavian Journal of Behaviour Therapy* 14(2), 65–72

Bergman, J. (1926) *Aurelii Prudentii Clementis*, Corpus Scriptorum Ecclesiasticorum Latinorum, 61, Vienna: Hoelder-Pichler-Tempsky A.G

Berk, R.A. (1984a) *A Guide to Criterion-Referenced Test Construction*, Baltimore, MD: Johns Hopkins University Press

Berk, R.A. (1984b) *Screening and Diagnosis of Children with Learning Disabilities*, Springfield, IL: Charles C. Thomas

Berk, R.A. (1986) 'Minimum competency testing: status and potential', in B.S. Plake and J.C. Witt (eds), *The Future of Testing*, Hillsdale, NJ: Erlbaum, 89–144

Birnbaum, A. (1968) 'Some latent trait models and their use in inferring an examinee's ability', in F.M. Lord and M.R. Novick (eds), *Statistical Theories of Mental Test Scores*, Reading, MA: Addison-Wesley

Bloom, B. (1956) *Taxonomy of Educational Objectives, Handbook I: Cognitive Domain*, New York: Longmans, Green & Co

Bock, R.D. and Mislevy, R.J. (1982) 'Adaptive EAP estimation of ability in a microcomputer environment', *Applied Psychological Measurement* 6, 431–44

Braden, J.P. and Weiss, L. (1988) 'Effects of simple difference versus regression discrepancy methods: an empirical study', *Journal of School Psychology* 26, 133–42

Broadfoot, P. (1986) *Profiles and Records of Achievement*, Eastbourne: Holt, Rinehart & Winston

Buros, O.K. (1978) *The Mental Measurement Yearbooks*, vols I–VIII, Highland Park, NJ: Gryphon Press

Buss, D. and Cantor, N. (1989) *Personality Psychology: Recent Trends and Emerging Directions*, New York: Springer-Verlag

Camara, W.J. and Schneider, D.L. (1994) 'Integrity tests: facts and unresolved issues', *American Psychologist* 49, 112–19

Campbell, D.T. and Fiske, D.W. (1959) 'Convergent and discriminant validation by the multitrait-multimethod matrix', *Psychological Bulletin* 56, 81–105

Carnap, R. (1962) *Logical Foundations of Probability*, 2nd edn, Chicago: University of Chicago Press

Cattell, R.B. (1943) 'The description of personality: basic traits resolved into clusters', *Journal of Abnormal and Social Psychology* 38, 476–506

Cattell, R.B. (1957) *Personality and Motivation Structure and Measurement*, Yonkers-on-Hudson, NY: World Publishers

Cattell, R.B. (1965) *The Scientific Analysis of Personality*, London: Penguin

Cattell, R.B. (1986) *The Handbook for the 16 Personality Factor Questionnaire*, Champaign, IL: Institute for Personality and Ability Testing

Cattell, R.B. (1995) 'The fallacy of the five factors in personality', *The Psychologist* (May), 207–8

Chambers, W. and Chambers, R. (1972) *Chambers Twentieth Century Dictionary*, Edinburgh: Chambers

Claridge, G.S. and Birchall, P.M. (1978) 'Bishop, Eysenck, Block and psychoticism', *Journal of Abnormal Psychology* 87, 604–68

Cleary, T.A. (1968) 'Test bias: prediction of grades of Negro and white students in integrated colleges', *Journal of Educational Measurement* 5, 115–24

Cleary, T.A. and Hilton, T.G. (1968) 'An investigation of item bias', *Educational and Psychological Measurement* 28, 61–75

Cohen, R., Montague, P., Nathanson, L. and Swerdlik, M. (1988) *Psychological Testing: An Introduction to Tests and Measurement*, Mountain View, CA: Mayfield Publishing

Cole, N. (1973) 'Bias in selection', *Journal of Educational Measurement* 10, 237–55

Conoley, J.J. and Kramer, J.C. (eds) (1989) *Tenth Mental Measurement Yearbook*, Buros Institute of Mental Measurement, Lincoln, NB: University of Nebraska Press

Costa Jr, P.T., McCrae, R.R. and Dembroski, T.M. (1989) 'Agreeableness vs. antagonism: explication of a potential risk factor for CHD', in A. Siegman and T.M. Dembroski (eds), *In Search of Coronary-Prone Behavior: Beyond Type A*, Hillsdale, NJ: Erlbaum

Costa, P.T. and McCrae, R.R. (1992) 'Four ways five factors are basic', *Personality and Individual Differences* 13, 653–65

Couch, A. and Keniston, K. (1960) 'Yeasayers and naysayers: agreeing response set as a personality variable', *Journal of Abnormal and Social Psychology* 60, 151–74

Cronbach, L.J., Gleser, G.C., Nanda, H. and Rajaratnan, N. (1972) *The Dependability of Behavioral Measurements: Theory of Generalizability for Scores and Profiles*, New York: Wiley

Darlington, C. (1971) 'Another look at "cultural fairness" ', *Journal of Educational and Psychological Measurement* 8, 71–82

Darwin, C. (1888) *The Descent of Man*, 2nd edn, London: John Murray

Debra P. v. Turlington, 644 F.2.d 397, 404 (5th Cir 1981)

Dembroski, T.M., McDougall, J.M., Costa Jr, P.T. and Grandits, G. (1988) 'Components of hostility as predictors of sudden death and myocardial infarction in the multiple risk intervention trial', *Psychosomatic Medicine* 51, 514–22

Department of Trade and Industry (1994) *Neural Computing: Best Practice Guidelines*, Crown copyright

Digman, J.M. (1990) 'Personality structure: emergence of the five factor model', *Annual Review of Psychology* 41, 417–40

Digman, J.M. and Takemoto-Chock, N.K. (1981) 'Factors in the natural language of personality: re-analyses, comparison and interpretation of six major studies', *Multivariate Behavioral Research* 16, 149–70

Einhorn, H. and Bass, A. (1971) 'Methodological considerations relevant to discrimination in employment testing', *Psychological Bulletin* 75, 261–9

Elliot, C.D. (1983) *British Ability Scales Technical Handbook*, Windsor: NFER-Nelson

Erikson, E.H. (1950) *Childhood and Society*, New York: Norton

Eysenck, H.J. (1947) *Dimensions of Personality*, London: Routledge & Kegan Paul

Eysenck, H.J. (1967a) *The Biological Basis of Personality*, Springfield, IL: Thomas Books

Eysenck, H.J. (1967b) 'Intelligence assessment: a theoretical and experimental approach', *British Journal of Educational Psychology* 37, 81–98

Eysenck, H.J. (1970) *The Structure of Human Personality*, 3rd edn, London: Methuen

Eysenck, H.J. (1973) *The Inequality of Man*, London: Maurice Temple-Smith

Eysenck, H.J. (1986) 'The theory of intelligence and the psychophysiology of cognition', in R.J. Sternberg (ed.), *Advances in the Psychology of Human Intelligence*, vol. III, Hillsdale, NJ: Erlbaum, 1–34

Eysenck, H.J. and Eysenck, M.W. (1975) *Manual of the Eysenck Personality Questionnaire*, San Diego: Educational and Industrial Testing Service

Eysenck, H.J. and Eysenck, M.W. (1985) *Personality and Individual Differences: A Natural Science Approach*, New York: Plenum

Eysenck, S.B.G., Rust, J., and Eysenck, H.J. (1977) 'Personality and the classification of adult offenders', *British Journal of Criminology* 17(2), 169–79

Ferguson, G.A. (1981) *Statistical Analysis in Psychology and Education*, 4th edn, New York: McGraw-Hill

Fiske, D.W. (1949) 'Consistency of the factorial structures of personality ratings from different sources', *Journal of Abnormal and Social Psychology* 44, 329–44

Freud, S. (1957) 'On narcissism: an introduction', in J. Strachey (ed.), *The Standard Edition of the Complete Psychological Works of Sigmund Freud*, London: Hogarth Press

Furnham, A. (1986) 'Response bias, social desirability and dissimulation', *Personality and Individual Differences* 7, 385–406

Galton, F. (1869) *Hereditary Genius*, London: Macmillan

Galton, F. (1884) 'Measurement of character', *Fortnightly Review* 42

Gardner, H. (1983) *Frames of Mind: The Theory of Multiple Intelligences*, New York: Basic Books

Gipps, C. (1986) 'A critique of the APU', in D.L. Nuttall (ed.), *Assessing Educational Achievement*, Lewes: Falmer Press

Goldberg, L.R. (1982) 'From ace to zombie: some explorations in the language of personality', in C.D. Spielberger and J.N. Butcher (eds), *Advances in Personality Assessment*, Hillsdale NJ: Erlbaum

Goldberg, L.R. (1990) 'An alternative "Description of Personality": the big five structure', *Journal of Personality and Social Psychology* 59, 1216–29

Goldberg, L.R. (1992) 'The development of markers of the big five structure,' *Psychological Assessment* 4, 26–42

Goldberg, L.R., Grenier, J.R., Guion, R.M., Sechrest, L.B. and Wing, H. (1991) *Questionnaires Used in the Prediction of Trustworthiness in Pre-employment Selection Decisions*, Washington DC: American Psychological Association

Golden, C.J., Hammeke, T.A. and Purisch, A.D. (1978) 'Diagnostic validity of a standardized neuropsychological battery derived from Luria's neuropsychological tests', *Journal of Consulting and Clinical Psychology* 46, 1258–65

Goleman, D. (1996) *Emotional Intelligence: Why It Can Matter More Than IQ*, London: Bloomsbury

Golombok, S. and Rust, J. (1992) 'The UK revision', in D. Wechsler (ed.), *The Manual of the Wechsler Intelligence Scale for Children – 3rd Revision UK (WISC-III (UK))*, London: The Psychological Corporation

Golombok, S. and Rust, J. (1993a) 'The measurement of gender role behaviour in pre-school children', *Journal of Child Psychology and Psychiatry* 34, 805–11

Golombok, S. and Rust, J. (1993b) 'The pre-school activities inventory', *Psychological Assessment* 5, 131–6

Golombok, S., Rust, J. and Pickard, C. (1984) 'Sexual problems encountered in general practice', *British Journal of Sexual Medicine* 11, 171–5

Gough, H.G. (1971) 'The assessment of wayward impulse by means of the Personal Reaction Blank', *Personnel Psychology* 24, 669–77

Graziano, W.G. and Eisenberg, N.H. (1993) 'Agreeableness: a dimension of personality', in S.R. Briggs, R. Hogan and W.H. Jones (eds), *Handbook of Personality Psychology*, New York: Academic Press

Greg, W.R. (1868) 'On the failure of natural selection in the case of man', *Fraser's Magazine* 78 (September), 353–62

Griggs v. *Duke Power Co.*, 401 US. 424 (1971)

Gross, A.L. and Su, W. (1975) 'Defining a "fair" or "unbiased" selection model: a question of utilities', *Journal of Applied Psychology* 60, 345–51

Guastello, S.J. and Rieke, M.L. (1991) 'A review and critique of honesty test research', *Behavioral Sciences and the Law* 9, 501–23

Guilford, J.P. (1959) *Personality*, New York: McGraw-Hill

Guilford, J.P. and Zimmerman, W.S. (1949) *The Guilford-Zimmerman Temperament Survey*, Beverley Hills, CA: Sheridan Supply

Haladyna, T.M. and Roid, G.H. (1983) 'A comparison of two approaches to criterion referenced test construction', *Journal of Educational Measurement* 20, 271–82

Haier, R.J., Siegel, B., Tang, C., Abel, L. and Buchsbaum, M.S. (1992) 'Intelligence and changes in regional cerebral glucose metabolic rate following learning', *Intelligence* 16, 415–26

Hambleton, R.K. and Swaminathan, H. (1985) *Item Response Theory: Principles and Applications*, Boston: Kluwer-Nijhoff

Harmon, L.W., Hansen, J.C., Borgen, F.H. and Hammer, A.L. (1994) *Strong Interest Inventory: Applications and Technical Guide*, Palo Alto, CA: Consulting Psychologists Press

Hartshorn, H., May, M.A. and Maller, J.B. (1929) *Studies in the Nature of Character*, New York: Macmillan

Hathaway, S.R. and McKinley, J.C. (1965) *Minnesota Multiphasic Personality Inventory: Manual for Administration and Scoring*, New York: The Psychological Corporation

Hendrickson, A.E. (1982a) 'The biological basis of intelligence. Part 1: Theory', in H.J. Eysenck (ed.), *A Model for Intelligence*, New York: Springer Verlag

Hendrickson, A.E. (1982b) 'The biological basis of intelligence. Part 2: Measurement', in H.J. Eysenck (ed.), *A Model for Intelligence*, New York: Springer Verlag

Herrnstein, R. and Murray, C. (1994) *The Bell Curve: Intelligence and Class Structure in American Life*, New York: Free Press

Holland, J.L. (1985) *Making Vocational Choices: A Theory of Vocational Personalities and Work Environments*, Englewood Cliffs, NJ: Prentice-Hall

Horney, K. (1945) *Our Inner Conflicts*, New York: Norton

Hunter, J.E., Schmidt, F.L. and Hunter, R. (1979) 'Differential validity of employment tests by race: a comprehensive review and analysis', *Psychological Bulletin* 86, 721–35

Jackson, D.N. (1977) *Jackson Vocational Interest Survey Manual*, Ontario: Research Psychologists Press

James, W. (1907) *Pragmatism: A New Name for some Old Ways of Thinking*, London: Longmans Green

Jensen, A.R. (1973) *Educability and Group Differences*, London: Methuen

Jensen, A.R. (1980) *Bias in Mental Testing*, New York: Macmillan

John, O.P. (1990) 'The big five factor taxonomy: dimensions of personality in natural language and in questionnaires', in L.A. Pervin (ed.), *Handbook of Personality Theory and Research*, New York: Guilford

Kamin, L.J. (1974) *The Science and Politics of IQ*, New York: Wiley

Kelly, G.A. (1955) *The Psychology of Personal Constructs*, New York: Norton

Kitcher, P. (1985) *Vaulting Ambition: Sociobiology and the Quest for Human Nature*, Cambridge, MA: MIT Press

Klinger, D.E., Johnson, J.H. and Williams, T.A. (1976) 'Strategies in the evaluation of an on-line computer-assisted unit for intake assessment of mental health patients', *Behavior Research Methods and Instrumentation* 8, 95–100

Lachar, D. (1974) 'Accuracy and generalizability of an automated MMPI interpretation system, *Journal of Consulting and Clinical Psychology* 42, 267–73

Lilienfeld, S.O., Alliger, G. and Michell, K. (1995) 'Why integrity testing remains controversial', *American Psychologist* 50, 457–8

Linn, R.L. and Gronlund, N.E. (1995) *Measurement and Assessment in Teaching*, 7th edn, Upper Saddle River, NJ: Prentice Hall

Loehlin, J. (1992) *Latent Variable Models*, Hillsdale, NJ: Erlbaum

Loevinger, J. (1957) 'Objective tests as instruments of psychological theory', *Psychological Reports* 3, 635–94

Loevinger, J. (1994) 'Has psychology lost its conscience?', *Journal of Personality Assessment* 62, 2–8

Lord, F.M. (1977) 'A study of item bias using item characteristic curve theory', in Y.H. Poortinga (ed.), *Basic Problems in Cross-Cultural Psychology*, Amsterdam: Swets & Zeitlinger

Lord, F.M. and Novick, M.R. (1968) *Statistical Theories of Mental Test Scores*, Reading, MA: Addison-Wesley

Lorenz, K. (1940) 'Systematik und Entwicklungsgedanke im Unterricht', *Der Biologe* 9, 29

Luria, A.R. (1973) *The Working Brain*, London: Penguin

McClelland, D. (1973) 'Testing for competency rather than intelligence', *American Psychologist* 28, 1–14

McClelland, D.C., Atkinson, J.W., Clark, R.A. and Lowell, E.L. (1953) *The Achievement Motive*, New York: Appleton-Century-Crofts

McClelland, J.L. and Rumelhart, D.E. (1987) *Parallel Distributed Processing: Explorations in the Microstructure of Cognition*, vol. II: *Psychological and Biological Models*, London: MIT Press

McCrae, R.R. (1987) 'Creativity, divergent thinking and openness-to-experience', *Journal of Personality and Social Psychology* 52, 1258–65

McCrae, R.R. and Costa Jr, P.T. (1987) 'Validation of the five factor model of personality across instruments and observers', *Journal of Personality and Social Psychology* 52, 81–90

McCrae, R.R. and John, O.P. (1992) 'An introduction to the Five-Factor model and its applications', *Journal of Personality* 60, 175–215

McDermott, P.A. (1980) 'A systems-actuarial method for differential diagnosis of handicapped children', *Journal of Special Education* 50, 223–8

Maslow, A.H. (1967) 'Self-actualization and beyond', in J.F.T Bugenthal (ed.), *Challenges of Humanistic Psychology*, New York: McGraw-Hill

Maslow, A.H. (1970) *Motivation and Personality*, New York: Harper & Row

Menninger, K.A. (1953) *The Human Mind*, New York: Knopf

Mershon, B. and Gorsuch, R.L. (1988) 'Number of factors in the personality sphere: does increase in factors increase predictability of real-life criteria?', *Journal of Personality and Social Psychology* 55, 675–80

Mischel, W. (1973) 'Toward a cognitive social learning reconceptualization of personality', *Psychological Review* 80, 272–83

Mischel, W (1986) *Introduction to Personality*, 5th edn, New York: CBS Publishing Japan

Mischel, W. (1993) *Introduction to Personality*, Fort Worth: Harcourt Brace Jovanovich

Murray, H.A. (1938) *Explorations in Personality*. Cambridge, MA: Harvard University Press

Myers, I.B. and McCauley, M.H. (1985) *Manual: A Guide to the Development and Use of the Myers-Briggs Type Indicator*, Palo Alto, CA: Consulting Psychologists Press

Nie, N.H. and SPSS Inc. (1983) *SPSSX User Guide*, Chicago: SPSS Inc

Norman, W.T. (1963) 'Towards an adequate taxonomy of personality attributes: replicated factor structure in peer nomination personality ratings', *Journal of Abnormal and Social Psychology* 66, 574–83

O'Bannon, R.M., Goldinger, L.A. and Appleby, G.S. (1989) *Honesty and Integrity Testing*, Atlanta, GA: Applied Information Resources

Ones, D.S., Schmidt, F.L., Viswesvaran, C. and Lykken, D.T. (1996) 'Controversies over integrity testing: two viewpoints', *Journal of Business and Psychology* 10, 487–501

Ones, D.S., Viswesvaran, C. and Schmidt, F.L. (1993) 'Comprehensive meta-analysis of integrity test validities: findings and implications for personnel selection and theories of job performance' (Monograph), *Journal of Applied Psychology* 78, 679–703

Ones, D.S., Viswesvaran, C. and Schmidt, F.L. (1995) 'Integrity tests: overlooked facts, resolved issues, and remaining questions about predictive validity, construct validity, and in-house research', *American Psychologist* 50, 456–7

Passini, F.T. and Norman, W.T. (1966) 'A universal conception of personality structure?', *Journal of Personality and Social Psychology* 4, 44–9

Paulhus, D.L. (1984) 'Two-component model of socially desirable responding', *Journal of Personality and Social Psychology* 46, 598–609

Paulhus, D.L. (1991) 'Measurement and control of response bias', in P.J. Robinson (ed.), *Measures of Personality and Social Psychological Attitudes*, New York: Academic Press

Pervin, L.A. (1970) *Personality: Theory, Assessment and Research*, New York: Wiley

Peterson, N. (1980) 'Bias in the selection rule – bias in the test', in L.J.T. van der Kamp, W.F. Langerak and D.N.M. de Gruijter (eds), *Psychometrics for Educational Debates*, Chichester: Wiley, 103–22

Plomin, R., Reiss, D., Hetherington, E.M. and Howe, G.W. (1994) 'Nature and nurture: genetic contributions to measures of the family environment', *Developmental Psychology* 30, 32–43

Popham, W.J. (1978) *Criterion-Referenced Measurement*, Englewood Cliffs, NJ: Prentice Hall

Popper, K.R. (1972) *The Logic of Scientific Discovery*, Tiptree: Anchor Press

Psychological Corporation (1992) *The Manual of the Differential Aptitude Test*, 5th revision, San Antonio, TX: The Psychological Corporation

Rasch, G. (1980) *Probabilistic Models for Intelligence and Attainment Testing*, Chicago: University of Chicago Press

Raven, J.C., Court, J.H. and Raven, J., (1995) *Manual for Raven's Progressive Matrices and Vocabulary Scales – Section 1: General Overviews*, 1995 edn, Oxford: Oxford Psychologists Press

Reitan, R.M. (1955) 'An investigation of the validity of Halstead's measures of biological intelligence', *Archives of Neurology and Psychiatry* 73, 28–35

Reynolds, C.R. (1985) 'Critical measuring issues in learning disabilities', *Journal of Special Education* 18, 451–76

Reynolds, C.R. (1990) 'Conceptual and technical problems in learning disability diagnosis', in C.R. Reynolds and R.W. Kamphaus (eds), *Handbook of Psychological and Educational Assessment of Children: Intelligence and Achievement*, New York: Guilford Press, 571–92

Rogers, C.R. (1951) *Client-Centred Therapy*, Boston: Houghton Mifflin

Rogers, C.R. (1970) *On Becoming a Person: A Therapist's View of Psychotherapy*, Boston: Houghton Mifflin

Rogers, C.R. (1980) *A Way of Being*, Boston: Houghton Mifflin

Roid, G.H. (1986) 'Computer technology in testing', in B.S. Plake and J.C. Witt (eds), *The Future of Testing*, Hillsdale, NJ: Erlbaum, 29–69

Rokeach, M. (1954) 'The nature and meaning of dogmatism', *Psychological Review* 61, 194–204

Rorschach, H. (1942) *Psychodiagnostics: A Diagnostic Test Based on Perception*, transl. P. Lemkau and B. Kroenburg, Berne: Huber (1st German edn, 1921; USA distributor, Grune & Stratton)

Rotter, J.B. (1966) 'Generalized expectancies for internal versus external locus of control or reinforcement', *Psychological Monographs* 80(1)

Rumelhart, D.E. and McClelland, J.L. (1986) *Parallel Distributed Processing: Explorations in the Microstructure of Cognition*, vol I: *Foundations*, London: MIT Press

Rust, J. (1974) 'Interactions of reliabilities in personality measurement', *Social Behaviour and Personality* 2(l), 108–10

Rust, J. (1975a), 'Genetic effects in the auditory cortical evoked potential: a twin study', *Electroencephalography and Clinical Neurophysiology* 39(4), 321–7

Rust. J. (1975b) 'Cortical evoked potential, personality and intelligence', *Journal of Comparative and Physiological Psychology* 89(10), 1220–6

Rust, J. (1984) 'Genetic sources of variation in electrodermal measures: a twin study,' *Indian Journal of Psychophysiology* 2, 12–20

Rust, J. (1987) 'The Rust Inventory of Schizoid Cognitions (RISC): a psychometric measure of psychoticism in the general population', *British Journal of Clinical Psychology* 26(2), 151–2

Rust, J. (1988) 'The Rust Inventory of Schizotypal Cognitions', *Schizophrenia Bulletin* 14(2), 317–22

Rust, J. (1989) *Manual of the Rust Inventory of Schizotypal Cognitions*, London: The Psychological Corporation

Rust, J. (1996a) *The Manual of the Wechsler Individual Achievement Test, UK Edition (WIAT-UK)*, London: The Psychological Corporation

Rust, J. (1996b) *The Manual of the Wechsler Objective Language Dimensions (WOLD)*, London: The Psychological Corporation

Rust, J. (1996c) *The Manual of the Wechsler Objective Numerical Dimensions (WOND)*, London: The Psychological Corporation

Rust, J. (1996d) *The Manual of the Wechsler Quick Test*, London: The Psychological Corporation

Rust, J. (1996e) *Orpheus Handbook*, London: The Psychological Corporation

Rust, J. (1997), *Giotto Handbook*, London: The Psychological Corporation

Rust, J., Bermun, I., Crowe, M. and Golombok, S. (1988) *Handbook of the Golombok Rust Inventory of Marital State (GRIMS)*, Windsor: NFER-Nelson

Rust, J. and Golombok, S. (1985) 'The Golombok Rust Inventory of Sexual Satisfaction (GRISS)', *British Journal of Clinical Psychology* 24(l), 63–4

Rust, J. and Golombok, S. (1986a) *The Golombok Rust Inventory of Sexual Satisfaction (GRISS)*, Windsor: NFER-Nelson

Rust, J. and Golombok, S. (1986b) 'The GRISS: a psychometric instrument for the assessment of sexual dysfunction', *Archives of Sexual Behaviour* 15(2), 153–61

Rust, J., Golombok, S. and Trickey, G. (1993) *Manual of the Wechsler Objective Reading Dimensions*, London: The Psychological Corporation

Sackett, P.R., Burris, L.R. and Callahan, C. (1989) 'Integrity testing for personnel selection: an update', *Personnel Psychology* 37, 491–529

Sackett, P.R. and Wanek, J.E. (1996) 'New developments in the use of measures of honesty, integrity, conscientiousness, dependability, trustworthiness and reliability for personnel selection', *Personnel Psychology* 49(4), 787–830

Scheuneman, J. (1975) 'A new method of assessing bias in test items', paper presented at the meeting of the American Educational Research Association, Washington, April 1975, ERIC Document Reproduction Service No. ED 106–359

Scheuneman, J. (1980) 'Latent-trait theory and item bias', in L.J.T. van der Kamp, W.F. Langerak and D.N.M. de Gruijter (eds), *Psychometrics for Educational Debates*, Chichester: Wiley, 139–51

Schmidt, F.L., Ones, D.S. and Hunter, J.E. (1992) 'Personnel selection', *Annual Review of Psychology* 43, 627–70

Schmit, J.M. and Ryan, A. (1993) 'The big five in personnel selection: factor structure in applicant and non-applicant populations', *Journal of Applied Psychology* 78, 966–74

Shepard, L.A. (1980) 'An evaluation of the regression discrepancy method for identifying children with learning disabilities', *Journal of Special Education* 14, 79–91

Snyder, M. (1974) 'Self-monitoring of expressive behavior', *Journal of Personality and Social Psychology* 30, 526–37

Spearman, C. (1904) 'General intelligence: objectively determined and measured', *American Journal of Psychology* 115, 201–92

Spearman, C. and Wynn-Jones, L. (1950) *Human Ability*, London: Macmillan

Sternberg, R.J. (1977) *Intelligence, Information Processing, and Analogical Reasoning: The Componential Analysis of Human Abilities*, Hillsdale, NJ: Erlbaum

Sternberg, R.J. (1990) *Wisdom: Its Nature, Origins, and Development*, Cambridge, MA: MIT Press

Strelau, J., Angleinter, A., Bantelman, J. and Ruch, W. (1990) 'The Strelau Temperament Inventory – Revised (STI-R): theoretical considerations and scale development', *European Journal of Personality* 4, 209–35

Sutcliffe, J.P. (1965) 'A probability model for errors of classification, I: General considerations', *Psychometrika* 30, 73–96

Taylor, J.A. (1953) 'A personality scale of manifest anxiety', *Journal of Abnormal and Social Psychology* 48, 285–90

Terman, L.M. (1919) *Measurement of Intelligence*, London: Harrap

Tett, R.P., Jackson, D.N. and Rothstein, M. (1991) 'Personality measures as predictors of job performance: a meta-analytic review', *Personnel Psychology* 44(4), 703–42

Thorndike, R.L. (1947) *Research Problems and Techniques*, Report No. 3 AAF, Aviation Psychology Program Research Reports, Washington DC: US Government Printing Office

Thorndike, R.L. (1963) *The Concepts of Over- and Under-Achievement*, New York: Bureau of Publication, Teachers College, Columbia University

Thorndike, R.L. (1964) 'Reliability', in *Proceedings of the 1963 Invitational Conference on Testing Problems*, Princeton, NJ: Educational Testing Service, 23–32

Thorndike, R.L. (1971) 'Concepts of culture-fairness', *Journal of Educational Measurement* 8, 63–70

Thorndike, R.L. and Hagen, E.P. (1977) *Measurement and Evaluation in Psychology and Education*, 4th edn, New York: Wiley

Thurstone, L.L. (1934) 'The vectors of the mind', *Psychological Review* 41, 1–32

Thurstone, L.L. (1947) *Multiple Factor Analysis: A Development and Expansion of Vectors of the Mind*, Chicago: Chicago University Press

Trevelyan, C. (1848) *The Irish Crisis*

Tupes, E.C. and Christal, R.E. (1961) 'Stability of personality factors based on trait ratings', USAF ASD Technical Report No. 61–97, Lackland Air Force Base, TX: US Air Force

Tversky, A. and Kahneman, D. (1983) 'Extensional versus intuitive reasoning: the conjunction fallacy in probability judgement', *Psychological Review* 90, 293–315

US Congress, Office of Technology Assessment (1990) *The Use of Integrity Tests for Pre-employment Screening (OTA-SET-442)*, Washington DC: US Government Printing Office

van der Kamp, L.J., Langerak, W.F. and de Gruijter, D.N.M. (eds) (1980) *Psychometrics for Educational Debates*, Chichester: Wiley

Vassend, O. and Skrondal, A. (1995) 'Factor analytic studies of the NEO personality inventory and the five factor model: the problem of high structural complexity and conceptual indeterminacy', *Personality and Individual Differences* 19, 135–47

Wallace, A.R. (1865) 'How to civilize savages', *Reader* 5, 670–2

Wallace, A.R. (1870) *Contributions to the Theory of Natural Selection*, London: Macmillan

Wason, P.C. and Johnson-Laird, P.N. (1972) *The Psychology of Reasoning: Structure in Content*, Cambridge, MA: Harvard University Press

Wechsler, D.W. (1958) *The Measurement and Appraisal of Adult Intelligence*, 4th edn, Baltimore: Williams & Wilkins

Wechsler, D. (1991) *The Manual of the Wechsler Intelligence Scale for Children*, – 3rd revision, San Antonio: The Psychological Corporation

White, R.W. (1959) 'Motivation reconsidered: the concept of competence', *Psychological Review* 66, 297–333

Wilson, E.O. (1975) *Sociobiology: The New Synthesis*, Cambridge, MA: Harvard University Press

Wilson, G.D., Rust, J. and Kasriel, J. (1977) 'Genetic and family origins of humour preferences: a twin study', *Psychological Reports* 41(2), 659–60

Windel, M. and Lerner, R.M. (1986) 'Reassessing the dimensions of temperamental individuality across the life span: the Revised Dimensions of Temperament Survey (DOTS-R)', *Journal of Adolescent Research* 1, 213–30

Wissler, C. (1901) 'The correlation of mental and physical tests', *Psychological Monographs* 3(16), 1–62

Wittgenstein, L. (1958) *Philosophical Investigations*, 2nd edn, London: Blackwell

Wright, B.D. and Masters, G.N. (1982) *Rating Scale Analysis: Rasch Measurement*, Chicago: MESA Press

Zachary, R.A. and Gorsuch, R.L. (1985) 'Continuous norming: implications for the WAIS-R', *Journal of Clinical Psychology* 41, 86–94

Zachary, R.A. and Pope, K.S. (1983) 'Legal and ethical issues in the clinical use of computerized testing', in M.D. Schartz (ed.), *Using Computers in Clinical Practice*, New York: Haworth Press

Zuckerman, M., Kuhlman, D.M., Joireman, J., Teta, P. and Craft, M. (1993) 'A comparison of three structural models for personality: the big three, the big five, the alternative five', *Journal of Personality and Social Psychology* 65, 757–68

Index

231